MIRCEA ELIADE

GARLAND REFERENCE LIBRARY
OF THE HUMANITIES
(VOL. 128)

MIRCEA ELIADE
An Annotated Bibliography

Douglas Allen
Dennis Doeing

GARLAND PUBLISHING, INC. • NEW YORK & LONDON
1980

Library of Congress Cataloging in Publication Data

Allen, Douglas, 1941–
Mircea Eliade : an annotated bibliography.

(Garland reference library of the humanities ; v. 128)
Includes indexes.
1. Eliade, Mircea, 1907– —Bibliography.
I. Doeing, Dennis, joint author.
Z8258.67.A43 [BL43.E4] 016.291 78-68240
ISBN 0-8240-9817-X

Printed on acid-free, 250-year-life paper
Manufactured in the United States of America

CONTENTS

PREFACE

Mircea Eliade has established himself as a major twentieth-century figure both as a historian of religions and as an important Romanian novelist. With his very general, interdisciplinary concerns, Eliade has considerable significance for anthropology, sociology, literature, hermeneutics, philosophy of language, phenomenology, philosophy of religion, philosophical anthropology, and other disciplines. He is often referred to as the world's foremost interpreter of myth and symbolism.

Over the years, the compilers of this book, like numerous other scholars interested in Eliade, have encountered many problems and frustrations in attempting to track down specific items or to assemble the relevant publications on a particular topic. Some of the difficulties lie in the diversity of Eliade's writings. Not only has he been a prolific writer, producing many books and articles in Romanian, French, and English, but also most of his works have been reprinted or translated. After devoting considerable time to searching for some rather obscure article, one often finds that he or she has already read it either in a different language or as a chapter in one of Eliade's books.

Other difficulties arise from the unavailability or inadequacy of previous bibliographies. Mention may be made of a bibliography prepared by Serv. Informarea ştiinţifică, Biblioteca Centrală de Stat, in Bucharest (date unknown). This unpublished list, sixty-seven typed pages in length, covers the period 1927 to 1942 and was circulated privately. The first published bibliography was J.A. Vázquez, "Para una biobibliografia de Mircea Eliade," *Universidad*, in 1964 (see F302). This short work is very incomplete and contains many errors. The University of California at Santa Barbara published a bibliography in 1968 (see F239), which was revised and updated in 1974 (F121). Both of these editions had limited circulation and contain many omissions and technical inaccuracies.

"Bibliography of Mircea Eliade" in *Myths and Symbols. Studies in Honor of Mircea Eliade* (D8), published in 1969, was the first "comprehensive" bibliography to appear in print. It is the bibliography with the widest circulation and the one most often cited by other scholars. Unfortunately, users have frequently repeated the numerous errors, repetitions, and typographical mistakes it contains. The section on articles by Eliade omits a vast number of literary and critical items published to a large extent in Romanian. This section also is misleading since it simply lists articles chronologically without indicating which are revisions or translations of other articles, and which have been reproduced in books by Eliade. Nevertheless, this bibliography represented a tremendous improvement over previous checklists.

A more comprehensive bibliography of Eliade's writings is included in Dennis Doeing's Ph.D. dissertation (E6) of 1975. This bibliography is very strong on the Romanian entries; also, many cross-references are integrated into the biographical text itself. It has served as a major source for us in compiling the present work.

The most comprehensive previous bibliography to be published appeared in the 1978 French edition of *Mircea Eliade* (D11). This represents an improvement over the bibliography in *Myths and Symbols* (D8), but shares its weaknesses. This work was also one of our major sources.

Mircea Eliade: An Annotated Bibliography is intended to overcome the difficulties caused by the nature and diversity of Eliade's writings and by the unavailability and weaknesses of earlier bibliographies. It will make publications by and about Eliade much more accessible both to the specialized scholar and to the general reader. At least 2,000 items are cited here for the first time. Most of these new items are book reviews and Romanian publications, but they also include a large number of books and articles by Eliade. This volume is also the first comprehensive listing of publications *about* Eliade. The most inclusive previous secondary bibliography (D11) listed seventy-five articles about Eliade; this book contains more than three hundred such articles. We have also been able to correct the many errors that appeared in previous bibliographies.

Although this bibliography is extremely comprehensive, it is not absolutely exhaustive. We were able to track down almost all of our obscure references, but there were a few leads or hints, mostly to pieces about Eliade, that we were never able to confirm. Such publications, if they exist, seem to be listed in no library in the United States or Europe nor in any catalogue or bibliography, and other attempts to establish their existence have proved unsuccessful. In addition, our bibliography was completed in late 1978, and we were still uncovering recent publications up to the time of our deadline. Undoubtedly some recent works have been omitted.

In general, our access to publications and our confidence in the reliability of our information varies for the different sections of the bibliography. We have had access to almost all of Eliade's books (Section A) and newspaper articles (Section H) and to the vast majority of his articles (Section B). At the other extreme, we have had to depend heavily on national bibliographies and catalogues for the international translations of Eliade's works (Section I).

Cross-references throughout this bibliography provide the reader with information about translations and instances in which a publication appeared under different titles or as a chapter in a book.

In addition to the annotations of books and articles by Eliade (Sections A, B, and H) and books and articles about Eliade (Sections D and F), there are major annotations of about thirty of Eliade's books (Section A), of some of his most significant articles (Section B), and of books written about him (Section D). These lengthy annotations discuss the purpose, summarize the contents, and sometimes evaluate the strengths and weaknesses of various works. Longer reviews and review articles by Eliade are included in Section B with Eliade's articles; shorter reviews by him are listed in Section C.

We have taken the liberty in Section A of including unpublished manuscripts together with published works. While this may seem unusual, it was done for the sake of completeness, with the intention of enabling the reader to better follow Eliade's development as a writer. It also provides identification of works lost and of those works partially published as articles.

Many volumes listed in Section A are collections of articles or of works of fiction which had been independently published. Within such listings, cross-references are given to the independent, usually original, publications. Annotations can be found either under the collected volume or under each cross-referenced item, depending on the nature of the volume itself.

For the sake of clarity and ease of use, Eliade's articles are organized into two sections: B and H. Those in Section B, which are all accessible, are generally considered to be more important than those in Section H, which are more obscure and many of which are practically inaccessible to the reader. If the articles had been listed together, those currently in Section B would have become "lost" in the maze of over 1,000 entries currently in Section H.

Asterisks are used to indicate items falling within two or more sections. An asterisked item is followed by a cross-reference to the primary citation.

In compiling this bibliography, we have employed many resources. In addition to the previously mentioned bibliographies of Eliade, especially D11 and E6, we made extensive use of all the national and other bibliographies and catalogues to which we had access. Several years ago Dennis Doeing was able to investigate library resources in Romania, and recently Douglas Allen spent three months working at the British Library. Eliade's autobiography and journal (see A85 and A104) have been valuable resources, since in them he refers to various obscure writings and gives important background information. Also very valuable were Eliade's personal files and collection of items; they contained numerous works that had never been listed in any catalogue or bibliography.

We would especially like to thank Mircea Eliade for his generosity, kindness, and assistance, which we have enjoyed over a period of many years. During 1978, he met with us on several occasions, gave us access to his personal files, answered our many questions, and offered valuable suggestions concerning the organization of this bibliography. He gave us permission to use the biographical chronology he had prepared for *Mircea Eliade* (D11); this appears in revised and expanded form in the present volume. We hope that we have partially returned his kindness by compiling a definitive annotated bibliography that will make his writings more accessible and will assist others in their research.

CHRONOLOGY

1907 *March 9, Bucharest.* Born Mircea Eliade, second son of captain Gheorghe Eliade and Joana Stoenesco.

1913 *October.* Enters primary school, 10 Mântuleasa Street.

1917–25 Secondary studies at lycée Spiru-Haret in Bucharest. Has a passion for reading, but reads only what is stimulating to him. Handicapped by myopia.

1919 Writes first short stories.

1921 *January.* Publishes his first written article: "How I Found the Philosopher's Stone" in *Ziarul ştiinţelor populare.* Also begins his diary, *Jurnalul.*

1921–25 Contributes to a number of periodicals: *Ziarul ştiinţelor populare*; *Orizontul*; *Vlăstarul*; *Curentul Studenţesc*; *Foaïa Tinerimii*; *Lumea*; *Ştiu-tot.* The contributions concern his youthful interests in entomology, alchemy, orientalism, as well as his impressions of trips to the Carpathians and the Danube, short stories, essays, and literary criticism.

1923–25 Learns Italian in order to read G. Papini and V. Macchioro, and English to read Max Müller and Frazer. Also studies Hebrew and Persian. Writes most of his autobiographical novel, *Romanul adolescentului miop.*

1925 *October.* Passes his baccalaureate exam and enrolls in the Faculty of Letters and Philosophy at the University of Bucharest. Favorite professor: Nae Ionescu.

1926 *January.* Founds *Revista Universitară,* but it is suppressed after only three issues because of his excessively critical review of N. Iorga's work *Essai d'histoire universelle.*

November. Begins to contribute regularly to the daily newspaper *Cuvântul.* For many years thereafter, Eliade publishes on the average two small articles a week, which include portraits of artists and scholars, reviews of works on orientalism and the philosophy of religion, impressions of journeys, etc.

1927 Publishes over a hundred short articles, most notably the series "Itinerariu spiritual."

March-April. Takes first trip to Italy, where he visits G. Papini in Florence; E. Buonaiuti, A. Panzini, and G. Gentile in Rome; and V. Macchioro in Naples.

July-August. Journeys through Austria and Switzerland.

1928 *January.* Preoccupied with writing *Gaudeamus*, the sequel to *Romanul adolescentului miop*, both of which are unpublished and lost, except for fragments.

April-June. Travels to Rome where he works on his master's thesis on Italian Renaissance Philosophy from Marsilio Ficino to Giordano Bruno.

After reading Surendranath Dasgupta's *A History of Indian Philosophy*, Eliade writes to the professor, communicating his desire to study under him at the University of Calcutta. He writes at the same time to Maharajah Manindra Chandra Nandy of Kassimbazar, who was a patron of scientific studies.

June. He returns to Bucharest by way of Naples, Athens, and Constantinople.

September. Receives encouraging responses from Dasgupta and the Maharajah. The latter promises him a bursary for his sojourn in India.

October. He obtains his master's degree in Philosophy.

November 20. Departs for India.

November 25–December 5. Voyages in Egypt.

December 17–20. Disembarks at Colombo and visits Ceylon.

December 21. Arrives in Madras where he meets Professor Dasgupta.

December 26. Arrives in Calcutta and takes up residence in an Anglo-Indian boarding house, 82 Ripon Street.

1929 *January-June.* Eliade attends Dasgupta's courses and studies Sanskrit.

March. Travels to Benares, Allahabad, Agra, and Jaipur.

July. Sojourns at Darjeeling and Sikkim.

August. Completes the novel *Isabel şi apele Diavolului*, which is published in Bucharest the following year.

September-December. Dasgupta suggests that he work with a pandit in order to accustom himself to conversing in Sanskrit with religious Hindus.

1930 *January-September.* Resides at the home of Dasgupta, 120 Bakulbagan Street, in Bhowanipore quarter. Each morning, under the direction of Dasgupta, he works for an hour on textual analysis (the commentary of Patañjali).

February. He decides on the subject of his doctoral thesis: a comparative history of techniques of Yoga.

June-July. Dasgupta dictates to him his book on the philosophy of the Upanishads.

Publication of his first studies on Indian philosophies and religions in *Revista de Filosofie*, Bucharest, and *Ricerche Religiose*, Rome.

September. Has disagreement with Dasgupta. Leaves Bhowanipore and departs for Hardvar in the Himalaya.

October. Takes up residence in a *kutiar* at Rishikesh where, for a period of six months, he practices Yoga under the direction of Swami Shivananda.

December. Visits a number of yogins at Lakshmanjula and joins pilgrims returning from Badrinath.

1931 *January-March.* Practices Yoga and meditates.

April. Returns to Calcutta.

April-November. Researches in the library of the Asiatic Society of Bengal and becomes friends with the librarian, the Tibetanist Johan van Manen. Eliade begins the redaction of his thesis.

December. Called to military service, he departs for Bucharest.

1932 *January-November.* Serves in the first regiment of anti-aircraft artillery, Bucharest.

Begins to translate into Romanian the English text of his thesis on Yoga.

1933 *January-May.* Wins a competition for unpublished works with his manuscript *Maitreyi.* When it is then published in May, the work is recognized as a great success by critics and the public alike.

June. Obtains a Doctorate in Philosophy. The University of Bucharest encourages him to publish his thesis in French and to begin looking for a translator who is also familiar with English, Romanian, and Sanskrit.

November. Appointed assistant to Nae Ionescu, Professor of Logic and Metaphysics, Eliade presents a course on "The Problem of Evil in Indian Philosophy."

1934 *January.* Marries Nina Mareş; they take an apartment on Dinicu Golescu Boulevard.

Confronted with financial difficulties, he contributes to many periodicals and publishes four volumes: two novels, *Intoarcerea din rai* and *Lumina ce se stinge*; a collection of articles, *Oceanografie*; and his travel journal, *India.*

August. Travels to Berlin where he engages mostly in research.

November. Gives a course on "Salvation in Oriental Religions" in Bucharest.

1935 Publications: *Alchimia Asiatică,* his first scientific book; *Şantier,* an autobiographical novel of his sojourn in India; and a two-volume novel, *Huliganii.*

Winter. Gives seminar on the *Docta ignorantia* of Nicholas da Cusa.

August. Travels again to Berlin where he researches Babylonian cosmology and alchemy.

November. Begins a course on "The Upanishads and Buddhism."

1936 *Domnişoara Christina* is published and becomes the center of public attention over the issue of pornography.

Winter. Gives a seminar on Book X of Aristotle's *Metaphysics.*

June. Works on a critical edition of selected writings of B.P. Hasdeu. His doctoral thesis is published as *Yoga. Essai sur les origines de la mystique indienne.*

July-August. Travels to London, Oxford, and Berlin.

1937 Offers course on "Religious Symbolism."

Publication of *Scrieri literare, morale şi politice* of Hasdeu in two volumes, and *Cosmologie şi alchimie babiloniană*.

Summer. Voyages to Switzerland and Italy.

1938 Offers course on "History of Buddhism."

Prepares the first volume of *Zalmoxis. Revue des Études Religieuses*, with the collaboration of R. Pettazzoni, J. Przyluski, Ananda Coomaraswamy, Carl Clemen, C. Hentze, B. Rowland, and others.

November. Publication of novel, *Nuntă în Cer*.

1939 *Spring.* Publication of first volume of *Zalmoxis*.

Summer. Prepares second volume of *Zalmoxis*, which appears in 1940.

Fall. Publication of *Fragmentarium*, a collection of fragments of essays.

1940 *March.* Appointed cultural attaché with the Royal Legation of Romania in London. Mourns death of Nae Ionescu.

April. Departs for London.

September. Leaves London for Oxford.

1941 *January.* Named cultural adviser to the Royal Legation of Romania in Lisbon.

February. Arrives in Lisbon where he remains through September, 1945.

1942–44 Publication, in Bucharest, of the third volume of *Zalmoxis* and four Romanian works: *Salazar şi revoluţia în Portugalia*, a historical sketch; *Insula lui Euthanasius*, a collection of essays; and *Mitul Reintegrării* and *Comentarii la legenda Meşterului Manole*, both small scientific works.

1942 *August.* Returns briefly to Bucharest, where he is watched by the Gestapo and Romanian secret service agents.

1943 Publication in Lisbon of *Os Romenos, Latinos do Oriente*.

1944 *November.* Death of his spouse, Nina.

December. Resides in Cascaes, a fishing village near Lisbon.

1945 Edits in Romanian *Prolégomènes à l'histoire des religions*, a work begun in Oxford in 1940–41, and which appeared in 1949 under the title *Traité d'histoire des religions*.

September. Arrives in Paris with Adalgiza, the daughter of Nina.

November. Invited by Professor G. Dumézil, Eliade gives a course at l'École des Hautes Études of the Sorbonne (the course constitutes the first three chapters of *Traité*).

December. Elected member of the Asiatic Society.

1946–49 Resides at l'Hôtel de Suède, rue Vaneau.

Encounters his Bucharest friends E.M. Cioran, Eugène Ionescu, Nicolas Herescu. Contributes to the periodicals *Critique*; *Revue de l'Histoire des Religions*; *Comprendre*; *Paru*; etc.

1947 *Spring.* Offers course at l'École des Hautes Études on "The Myth of the Eternal Return."

1948 *Spring.* Publication of *Techniques du Yoga* by Gallimard.

June. Participates in the International Congress of Orientalists, Paris.

Fall. Founds *Luceafărul*, a periodical of Romanian writers in exile.

1949 *Winter. Traité d'histoire des religions.*

Spring. Le Mythe de l'éternel retour.

1950 *January 9.* Marries Christinel Cottesco.

Spring. Travels to Italy with his wife.

March. Participates in conferences at the University of Rome, invited by Professors R. Pettazzoni and G. Tucci.

August. Participates in first *Eranos* conference at Ascona, where he meets C.G. Jung, G. van der Leeuw, Louis Massignon, and others.

September. Participates in the International Congress for the History of Religions, Amsterdam.

1951–56 Recipient of research grant from the Bollingen Foundation of New York.

Dr. and Mrs. René Laforgue, as well as Dr. and Mrs. Roger

Godel, invite the Eliades to stay at their apartments in Paris and at Val d'Or.

Becomes friends with Henry Corbin, Father Jean Daniélou, Luc Badesco, and others.

Participates in conferences at the University of Rome, Padua, Strasbourg, Munich, Freiburg am Main, Lund, Uppsala.

Principal publications: *Le Chamanisme*; *Images et symboles*; *Le Yoga. Immortalité et liberté*; *Forgerons et alchimistes*; and *Forêt interdite*, a novel translated from the Romanian manuscript. First published play: *Iphigenia*.

Participates in the International Congress of Orientalists at Munich, and in the International Congress for the History of Religions at Rome.

1956 *September.* Departs for the United States.

October. Appointed Visiting Professor of History of Religions at the University of Chicago.

October-November. Gives the "Haskell Lectures" at the University of Chicago, later published as *Birth and Rebirth*.

1957 *March.* Accepts the position of Professor and Chairman of the History of Religions Department, University of Chicago.

Publication: *Das Heilige und das Profane*.

1958 *January.* Presents a course at the University.

June. Returns to Paris.

August-September. Participates, with his wife, in the International Congress for the History of Religions in Tokyo and visits Japan in the company of his colleague and friend Professor J. M. Kitagawa and his wife.

October. Returns to Chicago via Hawaii and San Francisco.

Publication of three books in English translation: *Patterns in Comparative Religion*; *Yoga. Immortality and Freedom*; *Birth and Rebirth*.

1959 Teaches two trimesters at the University of Chicago, directs doctoral theses the third trimester, and spends the summer vacationing in Europe.

Founds, with Ernst Jünger, the periodical *Antaios*.

Publishes *The Sacred and the Profane*.

1960 *September.* Participates in the International Congress for the History of Religions at Marburg.

1961 Collaborates in founding of journal *History of Religions*.

1963 First major book on Eliade: *Mircea Eliade and the Dialectic of the Sacred* by T. J. J. Altizer.

Publications: *Myth and Reality*; *Nuvele*.

1964 University of Chicago confers on Eliade the title "Sewell L. Avery Distinguished Service Professor."

Publication: *Shamanism*.

1965 *February-March.* Travels to Mexico; gives a course on Indian religions at the Colegio de México.

1966 Publishes *Aminitiri*, autobiography from 1907 to 1928.

May. Elected member of the American Academy of Arts and Sciences.

June. Receives Doctor Honoris Causa in Humane Letters, Yale University.

1967 Publication of source book *From Primitives to Zen*.

1968 Receives "Christian Culture Award Gold Medal for 1968," University of Windsor, Canada.

1969 Publication: *The Quest*, concerning methodological issues in History of Religions.

Also published: *Myths and Symbols. Studies in Honor of Mircea Eliade*.

April-May. Journeys to Argentina; participates in conferences at the Universidad de la Plata.

Receives Doctor Honoris Causa in Philosophy of Religions, Universidad de la Plata.

Other honors: Profesor Extraordinario de la Escuela de Estudios Orientales, Universidad de San Salvador; Doctor Honoris Causa in Sacred Theology, Ripon College.

1970 Publication: *De Zalmoxis à Gengis-Khan*.

January. Receives Doctor Honoris Causa of Humane Letters, Loyola University, Chicago.

July. Named "Corresponding Fellow, British Academy."

August-September. Journeys to Sweden and Norway. Participates in the International Congress for the History of Religions, Stockholm.

1971 Publication in Romanian of his literary masterpiece: *Noaptea de Sânziene*.

June. Receives Doctor Honoris Causa in Science of Religion, Boston College.

1972 Publication: *Religions australiennes*.

May. Receives Doctor Honoris Causa of Law, La Salle College, Philadelphia; Doctor of Humane Letters, Oberlin College.

1973 *May*. Elected corresponding member of the Austrian Academy of Sciences (Philosophisch-historische Klasse).

August. Travels to Finland. Participates in the International Congress for the History of Religions, Turku.

Fall. Publication of *Fragments d'un journal*, covering period from 1945 to 1969.

1974 Completes writing the first volume of *Histoire des croyances et des idées religieuses*, published by Payot in 1976.

1975 *August*. Receives Doctor Honoris Causa of Letters, University of Lancaster.

September. Elected member of the Royal Academy of Belgium.

1976 *February*. Receives Doctor Honoris Causa, l'Université de Paris-Sorbonne.

Publications: *Histoire des croyances et des idées religieuses. 1*; and *Occultism, Witchcraft, and Cultural Fashions*.

1977 Publications: *No Souvenirs* and *In curte la Dionis*, a collection of short stories.

1978 Publications: *A History of Religious Ideas. 1*; *Histoire des croyances et des idées religieuses. 2*; *The Forbidden Forest*; *Mircea Eliade*, L'Herne edition; and *L'Epreuve du Labyrinthe*.

Part 1
Major Works of Mircea Eliade

A

BOOKS

Note: Several unpublished works are cited in this section because of their memorable significance for the author. References to most of these are found in his autobiography, *Amintiri* A85.

Pre-1930

A1 *Nuvele şi povestiri* (Tales and Narrations). Unpublished series of short stories written in 1919.

A2 *Călătoria celor cinci cărăbuşi în ţara furnicilor roşii* (Voyage of Five Cockchafers in the Land of the Red Ants). Unpublished fantasy written in 1921-22. Mixture of entomology and humor.

A3 *Jurnalul*. Unpublished record of events at school, 1921-22. **Parts contained in *Romanul adolescentului miop* A5.**

A4 *Memoriile unui soldat de plumb* (Memories of a Lead Soldier). Unpublished, unfinished novel of the author's vision of what he called "Universal History."

In the moment of a train wreck, a boy's talisman (lead soldier) describes to him its presence through great events of the past: from the formation of the cosmos to the appearance of man, the creation and destruction of civilizations, the crucifixion of Christ, the Crusades, and so on.

A5 *Romanul adolescentului miop* (Novel of a Nearsighted Adolescent). Autobiographical novel of exemplar youth, written from 1922 to 1925. Parts published as articles from 1925 to 1927: see H87, H113, H228, H243-45, H247, H250.

A6 *Istorie a descifrării hieroglifelor* (History of Hieroglyphic Decipherings). Unpublished, written in 1923.

A7 *Gaudeamus*. Autobiographical novel about college life, written in 1927-28. Part published as article in 1928: see H321.

A8 *Jurnalul*. Autobiographical journal written from 1928 to present. Parts published as articles from 1953 on: see H932, H934, H953, H972, H982, H1001-2, H1006-7, H1009, H1011, H1015, H1019. Parts from 1945 to 1969 translated into French as *Fragments d'un journal* A104. The latter is translated into German as *Im Mittelpunkt* A116; and the parts from 1957 to 1969 into English as *No Souvenirs* A117. See A117 for annotation.

1930

A9 *Isabel şi apele Diavolului* (Isabel and the Devil's Waters). Bucharest: Naţională Ciornei, 1930, 237 pp. Author's first published novel, written in Calcutta, 1929.

Told in the first person, it is full of action but poorly written and confusing. A fictional work with many autobiographical references. Deals with the ambiguity of sin and the problem of evil. See especially chapter 7, "Dream of a Summer's Night," which recounts an actual experience of the author.

1932

A10 *Soliloquii*. Bucharest: Carte cu Semne, 1932, 83 pp. A collection of youthful aphorisms written from 1928 to 1932.

A small but significant book containing some of Eliade's first philosophical musings. Reveals an unusual mixture of Western and Eastern influences. It reads like a journal of abstract ideas stressing such notions as "truth," "mystery," the "fantastic," and "cosmic consciousness."

1933

A11 *Intr'o mânăstire din Himalaya* (In a Monastery in Himalaya). Bucharest: Cartea Românească, 1933, 32 pp. Contains autobiographical articles published in 1931-32: see H367-70, H374, H449. Revised in *India* A13 pp. 165-98, 214-19. French translation of parts: A122.

A12 *Maitreyi*. Bucharest: Cultura Naţională, 1933, 266 pp. Numerous editions published since 1938 by Editura Cugetarea. Novel of Indian love, written in 1932-33. Parts published as articles in 1933: see H547, H562. Reprinted in *Maitreyi. Nuntă în Cer* A91. German translation: *Das Mädchen Maitreyi* A40. French translation: *La Nuit Bengali* A45.

Aesthetically and financially, one of Eliade's most successful works. It gained him recognition in Romania as a significant literary writer. Based upon actual experiences of 1930 in Calcutta, it is actually a journal of his own discovery of love of one named Maitreyi. The main characters, Allan and Maitreyi, exchange several expressions of love to an "interchange of their beings" and an "integration into the Cosmos." Maitreyi at first appears commonplace to Allan, but eventually he is both charmed and puzzled by her actions, which are startling and upsetting to the reader. A discovery of the Indian spirit, of an exotic world of Indian values.

1934

A13 *India*. Bucharest: Cugetarea, 1934, 280 pp. 2nd ed. with new pref. Cugetarea, 1935. Contains autobiographical articles published from 1929 to 1933: see H332-34, H352-58, H361, H363, H365, H367-71, H373-75, H398, H447-54, H536, H552. Part is a revision of A11. This part is translated into French in *Mircea Eliade* A122 pp. 47-60.

A technical journal of author's three years in India, 1929 to 1931. Reads like a reporter's notebook giving both a detailed account of and a running commentary on his impressions of India. Some parts simply relate events; other parts describe the author's excitement from adventures and encounters. Of particular interest is his six-month stay in the monasteries of Hardwar, Rishikesh, and Svargashram in the Himalaya during 1930 and 1931. This work also contains transcriptions of radio talks about India given a year or so after his return to Romania.

A14 *Întoarcerea din rai* (The Return from Paradise). Bucharest: Naţională Ciornei, 1934, 419 pp. 2nd rev. ed. Bucharest:

Cugetarea, 1943, 392 pp. See H383, H393, H596.

A complicated work in which the characters convey many different ideologies, anecdotes, and subjective experiences. At the time Eliade was considered a leading writer of his generation, and this work reveals his concern for that "young generation" with its own anxieties and with its frustrations over the older generation of World War I. The main character, Pavel Anicet, is a young modern who is very ambitious, yet he fears failure. He also loves two women at the same time. He finally commits suicide as his only answer to success. Death is valorized as a reintegration into Cosmic vitality. Though appearing "epical," the novel is too lengthy, has too many characters.

A15 *Lumina ce se stinge* (The Light that Fails). Bucharest: Cartea Românească, 1934, 415 pp. Novel written in Calcutta, 1930-31. Part published as a serial in the newspaper *Cuvântul*, 1931: see H372.

Not one of Eliade's more popular novels. Concerns a mysterious fire that breaks out in a library. Cesare, blinded by the fire, cannot forget the events of that night, such as an orgiastic ritual and his encounter with the demonic character Manoil. Based on elements of magic and tantrism. The technique of inner monologue highlights Cesare's intellectual confusion. For instance, Manoil invokes Nietzsche, Gide, Zarathustra, and Śiva to overcome the bonds of sensuality.

A16 *Oceanografie*. Bucharest: Cultura Poporului, 1934, 304 pp. Contains articles published from 1932 to 1934: see H414-15, H437-38, H443, H465-66, H468, H476-80, H482, H488, H491, H502, H540, H543, H546, H550, H553-59, H561, H563, H568, H570-73, H575-77, H580, H585, H598-99, H604-5, H612.

A collection of heterogeneous essays intended to be "open and authentic" accounts of author's "deeper explorations" (hence title) into a variety of topics. By this kaleidoscopic approach to what he calls "impersonal themes," Eliade attempts to stimulate "active valences" for everything around him, including the most commonplace. Reflects his philosophy at the time: take on all possibilities, yet renounce any one limited possibility. See especially the Introduction, which distinguishes "thinking" from "understanding." The work also contains five "Letters to a Provincial." These letters criticize the restrictive attitude of those Romanians who were concerned mainly with their own internal affairs or who read French literature to the exclusion of other, more ecumenical works.

1935

A17 *Alchimia Asiatică* (Asiatic Alchemy). Bucharest: Cultura Poporului, 1935, 76 pp. Eliade's first scientific book to be published; it was researched from 1925 to 1932. Parts published as articles from 1933 to 1935: see H493, H641. Part in French in *Yoga. Essai sur les origines* A21 chap. 8 [which has rev. French and Eng. pub.]. Material also in *Forgerons et alchimistes* A55 [which has Eng. and Ger. trans.]. Intended to be the first of several works on Oriental physical and natural sciences.

A18 *Huliganii* (The Hooligans). Bucharest: Naţională Ciornei, 1935, 2 vols. 3rd ed. Bucharest: Cugetarea, 1943, 457 pp. Novel continuing A14.

Through irresponsible acts and supreme self-confidence, Petru Anicet and his companions try to overcome their fear of the "terror of history." A violent book with multiple amoral and erotic episodes.

A19 *Şantier* (lit. Construction Site; fig. Work in Progress). Bucharest: Cugetarea, 1935, 277 pp. Autobiographical journal or "indirect novel" of Eliade's stay in India, written from 1928 to 1931. Parts published as articles from 1932 to 1934: see H382, H484, H583, H621.

A companion to A13 but portraying much more personal and intimate events: the author's experiences living in a boarding house, walking the streets of Calcutta, visiting opium parlors, etc. Eliade called this an "indirect novel" and considered it not so much fiction as a confession or unfolding of lived experiences. Told in the first person, it is an attempt to be "authentic"--that is, to render unmediated self-expression without recourse to conventional standards.

1936

A20 *Domnişoara Christina* (Mistress Christina). Bucharest: Cultura Naţională, 1936, 236 pp. 1943 ed. Editura

Contemporana, 240 pp. French translation: *Mademoiselle Christina* A121.

Fantastic horror novel containing Romanian folkloric motifs. Vampire-like ghost, Christina, possesses her prepubescent niece, Simina, who subsequently matures rapidly and in three nights time nearly seduces the hero, Egor. Just short of the consummation of their passion, Egor senses death and flees. Later he finds the grave of Christina and ponders his own tragic condition of living, now having lost the presence of the fantastic. This work was accused by authorities of being pornographic.

A21 *Yoga. Essai sur les origines de la mystique indienne.* Paris: Librairie Orientaliste Paul Geuthner; and Bucharest: Fundaţia pentru Literatură şi Artă "Regele Carol II," 1936, ix + 346 pp. Originally written in English in 1931 and then translated into Romanian and enlarged by Eliade in 1932, from which it was retranslated into French by M.S. Rivain. Based on doctoral research at the University of Calcutta, 1929 to 1931. Material contained in articles published from 1930 to 1937: see B3-5, B7, B13, B23. Contains translated parts of A17. Parts revised and rewritten as *Techniques du Yoga* A41 and *Patañjali et le Yoga* A76 [which has Eng. trans.]. Fully revised and rewritten as *Le Yoga. Immortalité et liberté* A53 [which has Ger. trans. and Eng. trans. and revision].

Poorly translated, it was Eliade's first major scientific work, and was so recognized at the time by leading scholars. Compares forms of Yoga in the Vedic and popular traditions. Discerns a popular pre-Aryan resistance, or "autochthonous substratum," to Brahmanical juridical structures. Consequently views India's history as the result of two contrary processes: the assimilation of dominant Indo-Aryan influences and a reaction to this by popular pre-Aryan elements, particularly by the ways of mysticism. Identifying the roots of this mysticism, or the causes of this reactionary tendency, constitutes a problem of the philosophy of culture. The author's thesis: techniques of Yoga attempt to homologize and unify contrary biological, psychological, spiritual (and consequently historical) states such that Chaos is transformed into Cosmos. See also annotation of A63.

A22 Ionescu, N. *Roza Vânturilor* (Wind Rose). Edited with afterword by M. Eliade. Bucharest: Cultura Naţională,

1936, 450 pp. Reprinted in Munich: Colecţia "Omul Nou," 1973. Collected writings of Ionescu. Part of Eliade's afterword published as articles in 1936 and 1963.

A tribute to Ionescu, who was Eliade's professor and later his colleague at the University of Bucharest; and who was editor in chief when Eliade was a writer for the newspaper *Cuvântul*. In the afterword, Ionescu's philosophy of "sympathy-soteriology" is outlined as a method of achieving the New Man.

1937

A23 *Cosmologie şi alchimie babiloniană* (Babylonian Cosmology and Alchemy). Bucharest: Vremea, 1937, 135 pp. Part published as articles in 1937: see H732, H734. Another part revised, enlarged, and published in English as *Metallurgy, Magic and Alchemy* A27. Material also contained in *Forgerons et alchimistes* A55 [which has Eng. and Ger. trans.].

A24 *Şarpele* (The Snake). Bucharest: Naţională Ciornei, 1937, 252 pp. 1943 ed. Cugetarea, 273 pp. Novel written in 1935. Book includes two short stories: "Intâlnire" and "Aventură." Reprinted in *La Ţigănci* A92 pp. 145-247. German translation: *Andronic und die Schlange* A42. "Aventură" translated into French H929.

Eliade terms this a "fantastic novel." It is purely imaginary. He composed it without a plan and wrote it in only two weeks time, yet it has stylistic unity. It is a story with banal characters who meet a stranger, Andronic, on their way to a picnic at a monastery, and who eventually become entwined involuntarily in strange happenings with a snake. Dorina, the heroine, finally unites with Andronic on an island in the middle of a lake. A major theme: the "Fantastic" emerges from ordinary profane events.

A25 Hasdeu, B.P. *Scrieri literare, morale şi politice* (Literary, Moral and Political Writings). Edited with Introduction and notes by M. Eliade. Bucharest: Fundaţia Regală pentru Literatură şi Artă, 1937, 2 vols.

In the eighty-page Introduction to his collection of the writings of a nineteenth-century Romanian "encyclopedist," Eliade acclaims Hasdeu's "romantic" and "magical" insight into reality: the ability to perceive in everyday life harmonies on all levels of existence, including the "beginnings" in which were generated "mythical" as well as "historical" consciousness. Myths preserve primordial values of universal stature.

A26 *Viaţă Nouă* (New Life). Unfinished, unpublished novel written from 1937 to 1941. Continues A18.

1938

A27 *Metallurgy, Magic and Alchemy*. Cahiers de Zalmoxis, 1. Paris: Librairie Orientaliste Paul Geuthner, 1938, 49 pp. Published also as article in periodical *Zalmoxis* B49. Revised and enlarged English publication of part of A23.

Scientific treatise dealing with extraordinary functions of metallurgical knowledge. For many cultures of the past, stones and metals were not "profane data" because they came from "sacred zones" and contributed to "creative processes." Inorganic objects were animated with sexuality and cosmic significance; they were in fact "archetypes" with magical valences. Alchemy united the sacred theory with the profane experiment such that it was both a cosmological science and a soteriological technique.

A28 *Mitologiile Morţii* (Mythologies of Death). Unfinished, unpublished, begun in 1938.

1939

A29 *Fragmentarium*. Bucharest: Vremea, 1939, 160 pp. Contains fragments of articles published from 1932 to 1939: see H385, H388, H625, H659, H662, H674, H680, H689, H697, H716, H722, H726, H728, H738-39, H741, H747-52, H754, H761-62, H803-4, H806, H815. Selections translated into French in *Mircea Eliade* A122 pp. 61-78.

A small, heterogeneous, though highly significant book. It illustrates points of union between Eliade's literary creations and his more theoretical, scientific works. In addition to discussing Rudolf Otto, Pascal, Gioacchino da Fiore, Dostoevsky, and others, it issues terse commentaries on the following subjects: symbols, fear of the unknown, values of the Middle Ages and the Renaissance, anthropology, primitive mentality, folklore, nostalgia, authenticity, the fantastic, literature, the sacred and the profane, superstitions, the age of history, the Center, liberty, orgy, suffering, melancholy.

A30 *Nuntă în Cer* (Marriage in Heaven). Bucharest: Cugetarea, 1939, 280 pp. Part published as articles in 1938: see H825-26. Reprinted in *Maitreyi. Nuntă în Cer* A91 pp. 159-313.

Composed of a dialogue between Hasnaş and Mavrodin who, having met by chance, relate to each other their great romances. The reader discovers that, without their ever realizing it, they were in love with and loved by the same woman. The woman left the older Hasnaş because he wanted her to bear him a child; she left the younger Mavrodin because he refused to let her bear a child. Themes: predestined love, the paradoxical but transcendent quality of love, the "unrecognizability" of the miracle of love, the "infertility" of time.

1940

A31 *Secretul Doctorului Honigberger* (Doctor Honigberger's Secret). Bucharest: Socec, 1940, 189 pp. Contains *Nopţi la Serampore*. Two short stories, the former published also as "Tărâmul nevăzut" in periodical *Revista Fundaţiilor Regale* B68. Both reprinted in *La Ţigănci* A92. German translation: *Nächte in Serampore* A50 [which is trans. into French as *Minuit à Serampore* A56]. English translation: *Two Tales of the Occult* A96.

1941

A31a *Le Labyrinthe*. Begun in 1941. Unfinished and probably lost. Deals with symbolism of labyrinths.

1942

A32 *Apocalips*. Unfinished, unpublished novel written from 1942 to 1944.

A33 *Mitul Reintegrării* (Myth of Reintegration). Bucharest: Vremea, 1942, 109 pp. Contains articles published in

1939-40: see H827-34, H845, H849, H857.

A scientific book little known outside Romania. Centers on the notions of polarity and *coincidentia oppositorum* in such topics as Goethe's Mephistopheles; Great Mother goddesses; gods of fertility and war; time and destiny; sacred and profane; Indian conception of life; snakes; good and evil brothers; androgynies, particularly in Balzac's *Séraphita*; Adam and Eve; Logos-Anthropos drama. The importance of the book rests upon the theoretical concepts the author applies: the metaphysical and multivalent nature of symbols; the systematics of mythical thought; archetypes; planes of reality; homologization and totalization of forms; return to the primordial reintegration of the human being into the Cosmos; degradation of symbols; the human fall into history.

A34 *Salazar şi revoluţia în Portugalia* (Salazar and the Revolution in Portugal). Bucharest: Gorjan, 1942, 247 pp.

A historical sketch of the political and cultural climate of Portugal in the nineteenth century through events leading up to civil war and the establishment of the Salazarian State. Salazar is seen as leading Portugal from anarchy and chaos through a spiritual revolution consisting of Latin, Christian, and European values which results in a reintegration of Portugal into organic and cosmic unity.

1943

A35 *Comentarii la legenda Meşterului Manole* (Commentaries on the Legend of Master Manole). Bucharest: Publicom, 1943, 144 pp. Based on lectures given at the University of Bucharest, 1936-37.

Another small but very important scientific book little known outside Romania. The object of study: sacrificial death. The author draws parallels and variations on the theme of Master Manole, the mason in Romanian legend who walled up his wife in the foundation of the monastery of the Curte de Argeş in order to stabilize and animate the structure. Author's interpretation: Each folkloric creation is a completely unique "mental universe," yet from a structural and functional point of view different folkloric creations are "homologable." Stories such as Master Manole portend anthropocosmic significance where micro- and macrocosmic universes become interrelated. Archetypes, in the past as well as in the present, are the key to understanding such universes, since they are impersonal universal models that each popular memory imitates in its own quest for metaphysical truth. Eliade employs "commentary" as a scientific method because myths, since they contain archetypes or models, need only be demonstrated and elaborated; that is, they need to be reconstituted and not to be broken down by personal analysis or argument.

A36 *Insula lui Euthanasius* (The Island of Euthanasius). Bucharest: Fundaţia Regală pentru Literatură şi Artă, 1943, 381 pp. Contains articles published from 1932 to 1939: see B12, B16-19, B21-22, B25, B27-28, B31, B33-36, B38, B40-41, B45, B47-48, B54, B57-60, H392, H399-401, H411, H417, H431-32, H434, H475, H499, H510, H513, H584, H613, H702, H705, H718, H724. The first four articles below are translated from Romanian into French in *Mircea Eliade* A122 pp. 168-81, 233-40, 246-49.

Some of the more noteworthy articles collected in this volume (titles translated): "Folklore as an Instrument of Knowledge"; "Barabudur, Symbolic Temple"; "The Conception of Liberty in Indian Thought"; "About a Philosophy of the Moon"; "Island of Euthanasius"; "Before the Greek Miracle"; "Symbolism of the Sacred Tree"; "A New Mode of Revolutionary Literature"; "Concerning an Ethics of Power"; "Lucian Blaga and the Meaning of Culture"; "Ananda Coomaraswamy"; "Papini, Historian of Italian Literature"; "Notes on Indian Art and Iconography"; "Gioacchino da Fiore"; "Folkloric Themes and Artistic Creation."

A36a *Oameni şi pietre*. Unpublished play, written in 1943. Manuscript probably lost.

A37 *Os Romenos, Latinos do Oriente* (The Romanians, Latins of the East). Translated from the original French manuscript by E. Navarro. Collecção Gládio, 12. Lisbon: Livraria Clássica Editora, 1943, 95 pp. Published also as *Los Rumanos, Breviario Historico*. Madrid: Instituto Rumano de Cultura, 1943. Note: Included in section A because originally published in these languages.

Focuses on the leadership qualities of outstanding persons in Romanian history. From the invasion of the Romans to the crisis of World War II, Romanians have preserved their culture intact while they have assimilated the qualities of their would-be conquerors. Focuses on the Christian orthodoxy as well as the folkloric and popular traditions which are unique to Romania, including the myths of "Master Manole" and the "Mioritza."

1944

A38 Hasdeu, B.P. *Răzvan şi Vidra: Poezii, Magnum Etymologicum.* Edited by M. Eliade. Bucharest: Cugetarea, 1944, 253 pp. Note: Eliade has never seen a copy of this book.

1946

A39 *Aventura spirituală* (Spiritual Adventure). Unpublished play, written in 1946.

1948

A40 *Das Mädchen Maitreyi*. Translation of A12 by G. Spaltmann. Munich: Nymphenbürger Verlagsbuchhandlung, 1948, 238 pp. New translation by E. Silbermann. Frankfurt: Suhrkamp Verlag, 1975, 220 pp.

A41 *Techniques du Yoga*. Collection la Montagne Sainte-Geneviève. Paris: Gallimard, 1948, 266 pp. Rev. and enl. ed. Collection Idées, 328. Paris: Gallimard, 1975, 313 pp. Revised part of A21. Extract republished as *Patañjali et le Yoga* A76. Fully revised and enlarged as *Le Yoga. Immortalité et liberté* A53 [which has Ger. trans. and Eng. trans. and revision].

1949

A42 *Andronic und die Schlange*. Translation of A24 by G. Spaltmann. Munich: Nymphenbürger Verlagsbuchhandlung, 1949, 152 pp.

A43 *Le Mythe de l'éternel retour: Archétypes et répétition*. Les Essais, 34. Paris: Gallimard, 1949, 254 pp. Rev. and enl. ed. Collection Idées, 191. Paris: Gallimard,

1969, 187 pp. Written from 1945 to 1949. German translation: *Der Mythos der ewigen Wiederkehr* A49. Revised English translation: *The Myth of the Eternal Return* A51.

A44 *Traité d'histoire des religions*. Preface by G. Dumézil. Paris: Payot, 1949, 405 pp. Rev. ed. Bibliothèque Scientifique. Paris: Payot, 1964, 393 pp. Based upon lectures given at the University of Bucharest, pre-1940, and on lectures at the École des Hautes Études of the Sorbonne, 1946 to 1948. German translation: *Die Religionen und das Heilige* A52. Revised English translation: *Patterns in Comparative Religion* A62.

1950

A45 *La Nuit Bengali*. Translation of A12 by A. Guillermou. Collection la Méridienne. Paris: Gallimard, 1950, 260 pp.

1951

A46 *Le Chamanisme et les techniques archaïques de l'extase*. Paris: Payot, 1951, 447 pp. Rev. and enl. ed. Bibliothèque Scientifique. Paris: Payot, 1968, 405 pp. Based on lectures and articles from 1946 to 1951: see B71, B85, B94, B105, B243. German translation: *Schamanismus und archaische Ekstasetechnik* A59. Revised and enlarged English translation: *Shamanism. Archaic Techniques of Ecstasy* A81.

A47 *Iphigenia*. Valle Hermoso, Argentina: Cartea Pribegiei, 1951, 172 pp. Also published in periodical *Manuscriptum* H1012. A play in three acts, written in 1939. Performed in Bucharest in the winter of 1940-41.

Iphigenia, who must face a sacrificial death, accepts her destiny by rejecting Achilles who would save her and by ascending to the altar as a gift and encouragement to the "sons of war."

1952

A48 *Images et symboles. Essais sur le symbolisme magico-religieux*. Les Essais, 60. Paris: Gallimard, 1952, 238 pp. Contains articles published from 1939 to 1951: see B65, B73, B91, B93, B102. German translation: *Ewige Bilder und Sinnbilder* A61. English translation: *Images and Symbols* A71.

1953

A49 *Der Mythos der ewigen Wiederkehr*. Translation of A43 by G. Spaltmann. Düsseldorf: Eugen Diederichs Verlag, 1953, 252 pp. Reprinted as *Kosmos und Geschichte* A86.

A50 *Nächte in Serampore*. Translation of A31 by G. Spaltmann. Munich and Planegg: Otto-Wilhelm-Barth Verlag, 1953, 178 pp. Reproduced in P. Dumitriu, ed. *Rumanien erzahlt*. Fischer Bucherei, 1967, pp. 105-45.

1954

A51 *The Myth of the Eternal Return*. Revised and enlarged translation of A43 by W.R. Trask. Bollingen Series, 46. New York: Pantheon Books, 1954; and London: Routledge and Kegan Paul, 1955, xi + 195 pp. Reprinted with new pref. as *Cosmos and History* A64. Published as *The Myth of the Eternal Return, or, Cosmos and History* by Princeton: Princeton University Press and Princeton/ Bollingen Paperback ed., 1971, xv + 195 pp.

Eliade's first major work to appear in English. He identifies a fundamental characteristic of archaic societies: "their revolt against concrete, historical time, their nostalgia for a periodical return to the mythical time of the beginnings of things." This theme is examined through four chapters: Archetypes and Repetition, the Regeneration of Time, Misfortune and History, and the Terror of History. Eliade formulates the fundamental primitive ontological conception: "an object or an act becomes real only insofar as it imitates or repeats an archetype." Everything which lacks exemplary models and does not allow for repetition and participation is "meaningless" and lacks reality. In the last chapter, Eliade confronts the modern historical person with the archaic ontological conception. He concludes that none of the historicistic philosophies succeeds in defending a person from "the terror of history"; that all modern secular "solutions" result in nihilism and despair.

A52 *Die Religionen und das Heilige. Elemente der Religionsgeschichte*. Translation of A44 by M. Rassem and I. Köck. Salzburg and Munich: Otto Müller Verlag, 1954, 601 pp. Reprinted as Darmstadt: Wissenschaftliche Buchgesellschaft, 1966.

A53 *Le Yoga. Immortalité et liberté*. Bibliothèque Scientifique. Paris: Payot, 1954, 427 pp. Rev. ed. Petite Bibliothèque, 120. Paris: Payot, 1968, 434 pp. Full revision of A21. Contains parts of A17. Also contains revisions of A41. English translation: *Yoga. Immortality and Freedom* A63. German translation: *Yoga. Unsterblichkeit und Freiheit* A70.

1955

A54 *Forêt interdite*. Translation of Romanian manuscript by A. Guillermou. Du Monde Entier, 160. Paris: Gallimard, 1955, 640 pp. Manuscript published as *Noaptea de Sânziene* A98. The latter is translated into English as *The Forbidden Forest* A119.

1956

A55 *Forgerons et alchimistes*. Collection Homo Sapiens. Paris: Flammarion, 1956, 212 pp. Rev. and enl. ed. Idées et recherches, 12. Paris: Flammarion, 1977, 188 pp. Based on parts of A17, A23, and A27. Contains articles published in 1955 and 1956: see B127, B132, B137, B139, B146. German translation: *Schmiede und Alchemisten* A69. English translation: *The Forge and the Crucible* A74.

A56 *Minuit à Serampore*. Translation of A50 by A.M. Schmidt. Paris: Librairie Stock, 1956, 244 pp.

1957

A57 *Das Heilige und das Profane. Vom Wesen des Religiösen*. Translation of original French manuscript by E. Grassi. Rowohlt Deutsche Enzyklopädie, 31. Hamburg: Rowohlt Taschenbuchverlag, 1957, 154 pp. English translation of original manuscript: *The Sacred and the Profane* A67. French publication: *Le Sacré et le profane* A84.

A58 *Mythes, rêves et mystères*. Les Essais, 84. Paris: Gallimard, 1957, 312 pp. 2nd ed. Collection Idées, 271. Paris: Gallimard, 1972, 279 pp. Contains articles published from 1948 to 1956: see B78, B107-8, B111, B113, B118, B124, B135-36, B143. English translation: *Myths, Dreams and Mysteries* A68. German translation: *Mythen, Träume und Mysterien* A73.

A59 *Schamanismus und archaische Ekstasetechnik*. Translation of A46 by I. Köck. Zürich and Stuttgart: Rascher Verlag, 1957, viii + 472 pp.

1958

A60 *Birth and Rebirth. The Religious Meaning of Initiation in Human Culture*. Translation of *Naissances mystique* A66 by W.R. Trask. New York: Harper and Brothers; and London: Harvill Press, 1958, 190 pp. Reprinted as *Rites and Symbols of Initiation* A83. Based on the Haskell Lectures delivered at the University of Chicago in 1956 under the title "Patterns of Initiation."

Analyzing initiation in primitive cultures, Eliade argues that these societies understand puberty rites and various specialized initiations in terms of supernatural or transcendent models revealed to them by their mythical ancestors or by supernatural beings. The basic initiatory symbolism is one of death and rebirth or resurrection, the necessity of dying to the old in order to be born to the new. In the various initiations, traditional religious societies believe that they are recapturing their sacred history and are being spiritually regenerated. Eliade states that "initiation lies at the core of any genuine human life" and that "in the modern Western world significant initiation is practically nonexistent." The author suggests that "modern" human beings, without the traditional rites and symbols of initiation, cannot deal adequately with their existential crises.

A61 *Ewige Bilder und Sinnbilder. Von unvergänglichen menschlichen Seelenraum*. Translation of A48 by T. Sapper. Olten and Freiburg: Walter Verlag, 1958, 264 pp.

A62 *Patterns in Comparative Religion*. Revised translation of A44 by R. Sheed. New York and London: Sheed and Ward,

1958, xv + 484 pp. Meridian ed. Cleveland: World Publishing Co., 1963. New York: New American Library, 1974.

Rather than presenting a historical interpretation of the development of religious phenomena, Eliade examines the nature of religion through a morphological analysis of "sacred manifestations." The focus of his synchronic analysis is "system," especially the structural systems of religious symbols. The brief but important Foreword establishes the author's view of "the irreducibility of the sacred," a controversial principle to which he returns throughout his writings. The first chapter, "Approximations: The Structure and Morphology of the Sacred," introduces Eliade's interpretation of the structure and nature of religious experience in terms of the sacred and the profane and the "dialectic of hierophanies." Following this chapter are the various morphological studies of the sacred: the sky and sky gods; the sun and sun worship; the moon and lunar symbolism; water symbolism; sacred stones; the earth, woman, and fertility; vegetation and regeneration; agriculture and fertility. The final chapters on sacred space, sacred time, myths, and symbols constitute good introductions to topics discussed in greater detail in other works. This is Eliade's most important publication for gaining an overall understanding of the theoretical framework of symbolic systems that serve as the basis for most of his interpretations of religious meaning.

A63 *Yoga. Immortality and Freedom*. Translation of A53 by W.R. Trask. Bollingen Series, 56. New York: Pantheon Books; and London: Routledge and Kegan Paul, 1958, xxii + 529 pp. 2nd rev. and enl. ed. Princeton: Princeton University Press, 1969, xxii + 536 pp. New York: Pantheon Books ed., 1970. Princeton/Bollingen Paperback ed., 1970. Contains full English revision of A17, A21, and A41.

In an important Foreword, the author argues the relevance of studying Yoga and Indian philosophy for recent Western philosophy. The "problem of the human condition--that is, the temporality and historicity of the human being"--that is at the center of Western philosophy has always preoccupied Indian philosophy. The first two chapters, "The Doctrines of Yoga" and "Techniques for Autonomy," present a formulation of Patañjali's *Yoga-sūtras* and the Yoga commentaries. Among the goals of Yoga are "emancipation from temporality," "freedom from psychophysiological structures," and the realization of a transcendent and unconditioned mode of being of absolute freedom.

The remaining seven chapters show the diverse forms taken by the doctrines and techniques of Patañjali's Yoga in Indian history: Yoga and Brahmanism; the Triumph of Yoga (mainly the *Mahābhārata* and *Bhagavad Gītā*; Buddhism; Tantrism; Alchemy; Aboriginal India; Conclusions. The book ends with a lengthy section of informative "additional notes" and a very comprehensive bibliography. By devoting so much time to tantrism, alchemy, folklore, and aboriginal cults, Eliade interprets profound meanings in phenomena that other investigators have often dismissed as aberrant and superstitious. Eliade believes that all of the Yoga manifestations--from the most spiritual to the lowest and most "infantile"--are organically interrelated and can be "homologized" and integrated as part of a coherent structural system. Refer to annotation of A21.

1959

A64 *Cosmos and History. The Myth of the Eternal Return.* Reprint with new pref. of A51 [which is a trans. of A43]. New York: Harper Torchbooks, 1959, xvi + 176 pp.

In the Preface added to this paperback edition, Eliade defines "archetype" as "exemplary model" or "paradigm" ("in the last analysis, in the Augustinian sense") and explicitly distinguishes this from the Jungian sense of archetypes as structures of the collective unconscious. This is Eliade's primary meaning for archetype, although he is sometimes ambiguous, and passages in several books (A60, A67, A68, A71, A82) occasionally resemble Jungian accounts. See A51 for annotation.

A65 Eliade, M., and J.M. Kitagawa, eds. *The History of Religions. Essays in Methodology.* Chicago: University of Chicago Press, 1959, xi + 164 pp. Paperback ed., University of Chicago Press, Phoenix Books, 1973. German translation: *Grundfragen der Religionswissenschaft* A78.

This collection of eight essays emphasizing methodological questions includes Eliade's "Methodological Remarks on the Study of Religious Symbolism," which is the best introduction to his view of symbolism and is reproduced as the final chapter in A82. The sacred "speaks" or "reveals" itself through symbols. In his description of the nature and function of religious symbolism in general,

Eliade asserts that religious symbols can reveal structures of the world not evident on the level of immediate experience; are multivalent; can unify diverse meanings into wholes or systems; can express paradoxical situations; and always have an "existential value." This essay is extremely important for understanding Eliade's methodology and hermeneutics not only because he believes that "all religious facts have a symbolic character," but also because his view of symbolism provides the methodological framework in terms of which he most often interprets the meaning of religious phenomena.

A66 *Naissances mystiques. Essai sur quelques types d'initiation.* Les Essais, 92. Paris: Gallimard, 1959, 276 pp. Reprinted as *Initiation, rites, sociétés secrètes* A111. Based on the Haskell Lectures at the University of Chicago, 1956. English translation: A60. German translation: *Das Mysterium der Wiedergeburt* A72.

A67 *The Sacred and the Profane. The Nature of Religion.* Translation of original French manuscript by W.R. Trask. New York: Harcourt, Brace and Co., 1959, 256 pp. Harper and Row, Harper Torchbook ed., 1961. Harcourt Brace Jovanovich, Harvest/HBJ paperback ed., 1968. German publication: A57. French publication: *Le Sacré et le profane* A84.

A popular introduction to Eliade's view of the nature of religion intended for the general reader. The sacred and the profane are "two modes of being in the world, two existential situations assumed by man in the course of his history." Religious persons base their existence on the experience of the sacred: the recognition of a transhistorical and transcendent ultimate reality, which manifests itself in the world and provides exemplary models allowing religious persons to know all that is meaningful and real. By contrast, the modern nonreligious person "assumes a new existential situation; he regards himself solely as the subject and agent of history, and he refuses all appeal to transcendence." In his discussion of the sacred and the profane, Eliade offers interpretations of sacred space, sacred time, myth, ritual, symbolism, sacred history, and the sacredness of nature and cosmic religion.

1960

A68 *Myths, Dreams and Mysteries. The Encounter between Contemporary Faiths and Archaic Realities*. Translation of A58 by P. Mairet. New York: Harper and Row; and London: Harvill Press, 1960, 256 pp. Harper Torchbook ed., 1967. Republished in London: Collins Fontana Library, 1968. Harper Colophon ed., 1975.

This collection of essays consists of a Foreword added to the English edition, a Preface, and the following studies: myths of the modern world; "the Noble Savage"; "the Nostalgia for Paradise"; primitive sense-experience and mystical experience; ascension and "waking dreams"; power and holiness; Mother Earth and Cosmic Hierogamies; spiritual regeneration; religious symbolism and modern anxiety. The central theme of the book is the "encounter" of the "traditional," especially archaic and Oriental, and the "modern" Western "types of mentality." Eliade attempts to develop a hermeneutics necessary if the West is to make sense of the phenomena of "the others." The specific studies provide an excellent introduction to some of the basic characteristics of Eliade's methodology and his interpretations of myth and symbolism. These essays also contain bold normative judgments about "the human condition" and contemporary secular existence. Eliade warns that Western culture is in danger of sterile provincialism and even imminent death; but there is also some hope of the renewal of Western consciousness through a creative encounter with "the others."

A69 *Schmiede und Alchemisten*. Translation of A55 by E. von Pelet. Stuttgart: Ernst Klett Verlag, 1960, 249 pp.

A70 *Yoga. Unsterblichkeit und Freiheit*. Translation of A53 by I. Köck. Zürich and Stuttgart: Rascher Verlag, 1960, 515 pp.

1961

A71 *Images and Symbols. Studies in Religious Symbolism*. Translation of A48 by P. Mairet. New York: Sheed and Ward; and London: Harvill Press, 1961, 189 pp. Search Book paperback ed., 1969.

This book is a collection of case studies of different structural analyses of various symbolisms: symbolism of the "Centre"; Indian symbolisms of Time and Eternity; the "God Who Binds" and symbolism of Knots; symbolism of Shells. The final study is on "Symbolism and History." Eliade asserts that symbolic thought is an autonomous mode of cognition with its own structure; that symbols have their own "logic" which allows them to "fit together" to form structural systems; that essential symbolic structures are nontemporal and nonhistorical; and that a symbolic system will preserve its structure regardless of whether it is understood by the people who use it. These chapters contain some of Eliade's boldest formulations, including a description of History of Religions as becoming a "metapsychoanalysis," which produces "a more spiritual technique," and a new "maieutics," which could help to rescue the modern West from cultural provincialism and from historical and existential relativism. The controversial Foreword contains normative judgments about images and symbols, the unconscious and the imagination, and the human condition.

A72 *Das Mysterium der Wiedergeburt. Initiationsriten, ihre kulturelle und religiöse Bedeutung.* Translation of A66 by E. Hoffmann. Zürich and Stuttgart: Rascher Verlag, 1961, 264 pp.

A73 *Mythen, Träume und Mysterien.* Translation of A58 by M. Benedikt and M. Vereno. Salzburg: Otto Müller Verlag, 1961, 344 pp.

1962

A74 *The Forge and the Crucible.* Translation of A55 by S. Corrin. New York: Harper and Brothers; and London: Rider and Co., 1962, 208 pp. Enl. ed. with Postscript. *The Forge and the Crucible. The Origins and Structures of Alchemy.* Harper Torchbook ed., 1971, 230 pp. New paperback ed., Chicago: University of Chicago Press, Phoenix Books, 1978.

This is Eliade's major study on metallurgy and alchemy. It includes the following topics: mythology of the Iron Age; "the world sexualized"; "terra mater - petra genitrix"; rites and mysteries, human sacrifices, Babylonian symbolism, divine smiths, and other topics concerning metallurgy; Chinese and Indian alchemy; initiation, "arcana artis," temporality, and other topics relevant to alchemy. Throughout this study, Eliade uses a religious "scale" of interpretation. He argues that alchemy cannot be reduced to some proto-chemistry, since it is always associated with mystical traditions and since one must take seriously its goal: to perfect Matter and to conquer Time, thus allowing the alchemist to change the human mode of being and to gain immortality. The discovery of metals and techniques for manipulating metals led not only to "empirical," material, and scientific changes, but also to new symbolisms, mythologies, and rituals; in short, to new religious modes of being and worlds of meaning that shaped human history.

A75 *Méphistophélès et l'Androgyne*. Les Essais, 103. Paris: Gallimard, 1962, 275 pp. Contains Eranos Lectures published as articles from 1958 to 1961: see B148, B159, B161, B171-73, B186. English translation: *Mephistopheles and the Androgyne* A82.

A76 *Patañjali et le Yoga*. Collection Maîtres Spirituels, 27. Paris: Éditions du Seuil, 1962, 189 pp. illus. Revised extract of A41. Parts also contained in A53. English translation: *Patanjali and Yoga* A94.

1963

A77 *Aspects du mythe*. Collection Idées, 32. Paris: Gallimard, 1963, 250 pp. Contains articles published from 1956 to 1964: see B96, B142, B163, B191, B197-98, B201, B203-4, B212, B222. English translation: *Myth and Reality* A79.

A78 Eliade, M., and J.M. Kitagawa, eds. *Grundfragen der Religionswissenschaft*. Translation of A65. Salzburg: Otto Müller Verlag, 1963, 269 pp.

A79 *Myth and Reality*. Translation of A77 by W.R. Trask. World Perspectives, 31. New York: Harper and Row, 1963; and London: George Allen and Unwin, 1964, xiv + 204 pp. Harper Torchbook ed., 1968. Harper Colophon ed., 1975.

Of all Eliade's publications, this collection of essays offers the best overview of his interpretation of the nature and function of myth. This volume includes the following studies: the structure of myths; origin and cosmogonic myths; myths and rites of renewal; mythologies of "memory and forgetting"; "survivals and camouflages" of myths. There is an appendix on myths and fairy tales. For traditional religious societies, myth is not a fiction or uncritical invention of the imagination, but is a "true story" in the sense of "sacred tradition, primordial revelation, exemplary model." According to Eliade, myth is always an account of a "creation." Myth "tells how, through the deeds of Supernatural Beings, a reality came into existence." Eliade maintains that the mythic is an autonomous mode of cognition, analyzes how myth permits the transformation of chaos into a structured meaningful world, and deciphers "camouflaged" mythical survivals in contemporary secular life.

A80 *Nuvele* (Short Stories). Colecţia Destin. Madrid: Destin, 1963, 151 pp.

Collection of short stories. These are listed with dates of composition and with references to original publications: "Un om mare" (A Great Man) 1945. See H876; "Douăsprezece mii de capete de vite" (Twelve Thousand Head of Cattle) 1952. See H918; "Fata căpitanului" (The Captain's Daughter) 1955. See H933; "Ghicitor în pietre" (The Man Who Could Read Stones) 1959; "La Ţigănci" (With the Gypsies) 1959. See H952; "O fotografie veche de 14 ani" (A Fourteen Year Old Photograph) 1959. With the exception of the last, these are republished in *La Ţigănci şi alte povestiri* A92. The first two stories are translated into English as *Fantastic Tales* A93. "La Ţigănci" is translated into French in *Mircea Eliade* A122 pp. 293-312; and in *La Revue de Paris* B230; into English in *The Denver Review* B270; and into German in *Phantastische Geschichten* A128 and as B258. "O fotografie veche de 14 ani" is translated into English in *The Louisburg College Journal* B285. See A92 and A93 for annotations. See A128 for other German translations.

1964

A81 *Shamanism. Archaic Techniques of Ecstasy*. Revised and enlarged translation of A46 by W.R. Trask. Bollingen Series, 76. New York: Pantheon Books; and London: Routledge and Kegan Paul, 1964, xxiii + 610 pp. Published also as Princeton: Princeton University Press, 1970. Princeton/Bollingen Paperback ed., 1972.

This book, considered by some interpreters to be the "classical" work on shamanism, includes the following topics: the general nature and specific structure of shamanism; shamanic sicknesses and dreams, powers, costume and drum, and initiation; celestial ascents and underworld descents; magical cures and role as psychopomp; cosmology; phenomena in Central and North Asia, North and South America, Southeast Asia, Oceania, and other parts of the world. The work ends with an Epilogue and an extensive bibliography (added to the English edition). Shamanism is defined in terms of a specific structure of ecstasy. Shamanism is found throughout the world, but it is viewed in the "strict sense" of its specific structure of ecstasy (in which the shaman's "soul is believed to leave his body and ascend to the sky or descend to the underworld") as "pre-eminently a religious phenomenon of Siberia and Central Asia." Although shamans are also magicians, medicine men, and ecstatics, Eliade shows that not every magician, medicine man, or ecstatic is a shaman. The Foreword is one of the author's most important statements on his methodology. He argues that the historian of religions is a comparativist and a generalist, who integrates the findings of various specialists; that "the dialectic of the sacred" discloses a structure that is "permanent" and "universal"; that the religious life is "ahistorical," that religious experiences themselves are in some essential sense "nonhistorical," and that primordial existential experiences such as ecstasy are "constitutive of the human condition."

1965

A82 *Mephistopheles and the Androgyne. Studies in Religious Myth and Symbol*. Translation of A75 by J.M. Cohen. New York: Sheed and Ward, 1965, 223 pp. Published also as *The Two and the One*. London: Harvill Press, 1965, 223 pp. Harper Torchbook ed., as *The Two and the One*, 1969.

This collection of studies focuses on four groups or "families" of religious myths and symbols: Experiences of Mystic Light; Mephistopheles and the Androgyne or the Mystery of the Whole; Cosmic and Eschatological Renewal; Ropes and Puppets. The final study, entitled "Observations on Religious Symbolism," was annotated under A65. The Foreword is a concise formulation of the extreme relevance of the History of Religions for the contemporary West. (See A68 and A95.) The four essays on groups of myths and symbols reveal Eliade the comparativist, historian, morphologist, and phenomenologist of religion. He isolates certain basic themes and then traces them through a tremendous diversity of experiences, primarily archaic and Oriental but also modern Western phenomena. These studies suggest the fundamental unity of humankind. The essay on "Mephistopheles and the Androgyne" is the best introduction to Eliade's interpretation of the symbolism of the *coincidentia oppositorum*, which may be the symbolism he considers best suited for expressing the most spiritual experiences in the History of Religions.

A83 *Rites and Symbols of Initiation. The Mysteries of Birth and Rebirth*. Reprint of A60 [which is a trans. of A66]. New York: Harper Torchbooks, 1965, xv + 175 pp. Hardcover copies of the Harper Torchbook ed. by Peter Smith Publisher.

A84 *Le Sacré et le profane*. Collection Idées, 76. Paris: Gallimard, 1965, 187 pp. Contains articles published from 1951 to 1959: see B97, B149, B157, B163. German publication: A57. English publication: A67. French ed. adds pref. and omits final chap. of A67.

1966

A85 *Amintiri: I. Mansarda* (Recollections: I. The Attic). Colecţia Destin. Madrid: Destin, 1966, 176 pp. Autobiographical memoires of 1907 to 1928. Parts published as articles from 1963 to 1966: see H960, H968, H970, H973-74, H978-79. Chapter 5 is translated into French in *Mircea Eliade* A122 pp. 19-33.

Sequels Part II and Part III, years 1929 to 1940, remain mostly unpublished except for the following: Part II chapter 1 published in periodical *Fiinţa Românească* H967 [which is trans. into French in A122 pp. 34-46]. A fragment of Part III chapter 1 published in *Cuvântul în Exil* H969. A fragment of Part III chapter 3 published also in *Cuvântul în Exil* H976. Part III chapter 4 in *Fiinţa Românească* H986. See also the autobiographical article in *Caete de Dor* H924. See the above cross-references for annotations.

In *Amintiri: I*, Eliade recalls the impressions of his childhood experiences and adolescent ambitions. Includes recollections of family; his first discovery and relentless reading of books; the occupation of Bucharest by German soldiers; grammar school activities; vacations; adventures as a Boy Scout; his musical talent; his first writings and publications; his library (the Attic); visits and discussions with friends; university studies;

first romances; trips to Italy; work on his Master's thesis on the Italian Renaissance; his "Spiritual Itinerary" (see H195) and other publications for his generation; moods of melancholia; and, finally, his departure for India.

First glimpses into Eliade's past. A graphic representation of events that the author himself had difficulty remembering.

A86 *Kosmos und Geschichte. Der Mythos der ewigen Wiederkehr.* Reprint of A49 [which is a trans. of A43]. Rowohlt Deutsche Enzyklopädie, 260. Hamburg: Rowohlt Taschenbuchverlag, 1966, 148 pp.

1967

A87 Kitagawa, J.M., ed., in collaboration with M. Eliade and C.H. Long. *The History of Religions. Essays on the Problem of Understanding.* Essays in Divinity, 1. Chicago: University of Chicago Press, 1967, xii + 264 pp.

This volume contains 13 essays, including Eliade's "Cultural Fashions and the History of Religions." Returning to one of his frequent claims, Eliade asserts that only a historian of religions can uncover certain "secret" intentions, meanings, and significances, even in contexts that do not seem to be religious. The purpose of the essay is to determine "whether a historian of religions can decipher some hidden meanings in our so-called cultural fashions, taking as examples three recent vogues, all of which originated in Paris": the popularity of a magazine called *Planète*, of Teilhard de Chardin, and of Claude Lévi-Strauss. Eliade interprets what the popularity of these three "cultural fashions" reveals about modern dissatisfactions and nostalgias and about the contemporary spiritual and existential situation.

A88 *From Primitives to Zen. A Thematic Sourcebook of the History of Religions*. New York: Harper and Row; and London: Collins, 1967, xxv + 645 pp. Reprinted as four paperbacks: *Gods, Goddesses, and Myths of Creation* A106; *Man and the Sacred* A107; *Death, Afterlife, and Eschatology* A108; and *From Medicine Men to Muhammad* A109. Reprinted as a complete paperback ed. under original title, New York: Harper and Row; and London: Collins Fontana, 1977, xxv + 645 pp.

The religious documents in this very comprehensive sourcebook are organized under the following chapter headings: Gods, Goddesses, and Supernatural Beings; Myths of Creation and Origin; Man and the Sacred; Death, Afterlife, Eschatology; Specialists of the Sacred: From Medicine Men to Mystics and Founders of Religions; Speculations on Man and God. There is an excellent bibliography. An index of names and subjects would improve the work. The title may be misleading: As Eliade notes, "pre-literate" or "archaic" would have been better than "primitive"; and in no way does this collection culminate with Zen documents. There are several omissions, including documents from Judaism and Christianity. This sourcebook allows the reader to compare a large number of diverse texts dealing with similar themes.

A89 Comarnescu, P., M. Eliade, and I. Jianu. *Témoignages sur Brancusi*. Paris: Éditions d'Art, 1967, 71 pp.

Three separate reflections on the work of Constantin Brâncuşi, Romanian sculptor. The contemporaneity of Brâncuşi was in his ability to return to the "sources," to the themes of primitive art and folklore.

1968

A90 *Pe strada Mântuleasa* (On Mântuleasa Street). Paris: Caietele Inorogului, II, 1968, 129. Novella written from 1955 to 1967. German translation: *Auf der Mântuleasastrasse* A100. French translation: *Le Vieil homme et l'officier* A118.

A long and complex work. A story of an encounter of two antagonistic worlds: the fantastic world of an old schoolmaster and the world of his interrogators, the Communist bureaucracy of post-war Bucharest. Through the process of interrogation, the two worlds converge.

1969

A91 *Maitreyi. Nuntă în Cer* (Maitreyi. Marriage in Heaven). Introduction by D. Micu. Bucharest: Editura pentru Literatură, 1969, xliv + 315 pp. Contains A12 and A30.

Introduction of 40 pages by Micu is a thorough overview of Eliade's earlier literary achievements. See F187.

A92 *La Ţigănci şi alte povestiri* (At the Gypsies and other Short Stories). Introduction by S. Alexandrescu. Bucharest: Editura pentru Literatură, 1969, xlix + 525 pp. Contains A20, A24, A31, the short stories in A80, and two additional short stories: "Podul" (The Bridge) written in 1963, first published as H980; and "Adio!" (Good-bye!) written in 1964, first published as H975. See A80 for references to translations.

Reproduced many times, "At the Gypsies" is perhaps the most successful of the author's short stories. The main character, Gavrilescu, a piano instructor, enters the hut of the women gypsies and is asked to forget for awhile the outside world with all the troubles and anxieties it poses. Three naked girls--a Gypsy, a Greek, and a Jew--dance for him. After a matter of hours he leaves only to discover that twelve years have elapsed. When he returns home no one knows him. Possible significance: the transformation of ontological existence through a type of cosmic ritual. The Great Time of ritual and the subsequent loss or fall into time of the historical.

Alexandrescu's introduction of 40 pages, entitled "Dialectica fantasticului," is a major contribution to the understanding of the qualities of the fantastic and other motifs which can be found in both the literary and scientific writings of Eliade. See F5.

A93 Eliade, M., and M. Niculescu. *Fantastic Tales. In Rumanian and English*. Translated and edited by E. Tappe. London: Dillon's, 1969, 100 pp. The Romanian text with a parallel text in English. Contains short stories "A Great Man" and "Twelve Thousand Head of Cattle." Original Romanian in A80 and A92 also.

In the first story, a man suddenly finds himself afflicted with "macanthropy" as he rapidly outgrows, physically, the "human condition." He is forced to flee the city but reintegrates himself and nature when he returns to the mountains.

In the second narration, a businessman at midday is projected from current time into the time of an air raid some forty days earlier.

A94 *Patanjali and Yoga*. Translation of A76 by C.L. Markmann. New York: Funk and Wagnalls, 1969, viii + 216 pp. illus. Reprinted New York: Schocken Books, 1975. Parts contained in A63.

A95 *The Quest. History and Meaning in Religion.* Chicago and London: University of Chicago Press, 1969, v + 180 pp. Paperback ed., University of Chicago Press, Phoenix Books, 1975. Contains articles published from 1961 to 1967: see B183, B199, B213, B219, B231, B242. French publication: *La Nostalgie des origines* A99. German translation: *Die Sehnsucht nach dem Ursprung* A105.

This collection of essays consists of a Preface and the following studies: A New Humanism; The History of Religions in Retrospect: 1912 and After; The Quest for the "Origins" of Religion; Crisis and Renewal; Cosmogonic Myth and "Sacred History"; Paradise and Utopia: Mythical Geography and Eschatology; Initiation and the Modern World; Prolegomenon to Religious Dualism: Dyads and Polarities. The major emphasis in the first four essays is on the nature and significance of the discipline of the History of Religions. The present state of the discipline is viewed in terms of a creative "tension" between historical and phenomenological approaches. Eliade most clearly identifies himself with phenomenological approaches that are concerned with interpreting "meaning." Sociological, psychological, anthropological, and other approaches are criticized as "reductionist," since they interpret religious data in nonreligious terms and do not respect "the irreducibility of the religious." "Creative hermeneutics," the most appropriate approach for the History of Religions, will result in tremendous benefits for humankind. This hermeneutics will allow scholars to interpret the various existential situations, will make possible an "encounter" with primordial archaic and Oriental myths and symbolisms, and will lead to a deeper knowledge of humanity. It may result in a "new humanism" and a new "planetary" or universal type of culture.

1970

A96 *Two Tales of the Occult.* Translation of A31 by W.A. Coates. New York: Herder and Herder, 1970, xiii + 130 pp.

Stories of the "fantastic" in which Eliade evokes some of his own yogic experiences when in India from 1929 to 1931. Text is artistically inferior, though certain structural parallelisms become apparent. For instance, in the first story the narrator, studying in the library of Dr. Zerlendi, who had mysteriously disappeared, comes across the research manuscripts of Dr. Honigberger which describe levels of Tantric exercises. While studying these documents the narrator himself "disappears." A mélange of historical and fictitious events wherein time and space are transcended.

A97 *De Zalmoxis à Gengis-Khan. Études comparatives sur les religions et le folklore de la Dacie et de l'Europe Orientale*. Bibliothèque Historique. Paris: Payot, 1970, 252 pp. Contains articles published from 1938 to 1970: see B52, B152, B163, B165, B187, B246, B255. English translation: *Zalmoxis. The Vanishing God* A102.

1971

A98 *Noaptea de Sânziene* (Night of St. John). Paris: Ioan Cuşa, 1971, 2 vols. Written from 1949 to 1954. Parts published as articles: see H935, H994. French translation of original manuscript: *Forêt interdite* A54. English translation: *The Forbidden Forest* A119.

A99 *La Nostalgie des origines. Méthodologie et histoire des religions*. Les Essais, 157. Paris: Gallimard, 1971, 335 pp. English publication: A95 [which has Ger. trans. A105].

1972

A100 *Auf der Mântuleasastrasse*. Translation of A90 by E. Silbermann. Bibliothek Suhrkamp, 328. Frankfurt: Suhrkamp Verlag, 1972, 167 pp.

A101 *Religions australiennes: I. Religions primitives.* Translation of *Australian Religions* A103 by L. Jospin. Petite Bibliothèque, 206. Paris: Payot, 1972, 200 pp.

A102 *Zalmoxis. The Vanishing God. Comparative Studies in the Religions and Folklore of Dacia and Eastern Europe.* Translation of A97 by W.R. Trask. Chicago and London: University of Chicago Press, 1972, x + 260 pp. Paperback ed., University of Chicago Press, Phoenix Books, 1978.

The purpose of this book is to present "the essentials of the religion of the Geto-Dacians and the most important mythological traditions and folkloric creations of the Romanians." Eliade attempts to develop an interpretation of religious traditions for which there are very few historical documents. Some of the topics considered in the eight studies are the following: religious origins of the ethnic name of the Dacians; the cult of Zalmoxis; the cosmogonic myth in Romanian folklore; legends concerning the founding of Moldavia and the building of the Monastery of Arges; Romanian "shamanism"; the cult of mandragora and the gathering of medicinal herbs; and the "Mioritza," the most popular Romanian folk ballad.

1973

A103 *Australian Religions. An Introduction.* Foreword by V. Turner. Symbol, Myth, and Ritual Series. Ithaca and London: Cornell University Press, 1973, xxi + 205 pp. Based on a course given at the University of Chicago in 1964. Contains articles published from 1966 to 1968: see B227, B237-40, B250. French translation: A101.

Eliade discusses the supernatural beings of Australian religions and offers a critique of both the evolutionists, such as Tylor and Frazer, and the "romantic-decadentists," such as Lang, in the "controversy" over the "High Gods." Other topics include the nature of Australian myths and rituals, especially myths of origins and rituals that "re-create" or renew the world; "mythical geography," sacred space, and sacred time; initiation rites and secret cults; the medicine men; Australian views of death and the postexistence of the soul. Eliade argues that all attempts to discover the "origins" of religion are doomed to failure; that primitive religions are highly complex; that primitives are not only "normal and healthy" but are also highly creative; and that primitives are historical beings but are most interested in "sacred history" and not in the Western sense of history as a series of irreversible events which take place in linear historical time.

A104 *Fragments d'un journal.* Translation of parts of A8 from 1945 to 1969 by L. Badesco. Du Monde entier. Paris: Gallimard, 1973, 571 pp. Parts of original Romanian contained in articles published from 1955 to 1972: see H930, H934, H943, H953, H972, H982, H1001, H1006-7. German translation: *Im Mittelpunkt* A116. Latter part,

1957 to 1969, translated into English as *No Souvenirs* A117.

A105 *Die Sehnsucht nach dem Ursprung, von den Quellen der Humanität*. Translation of A95 by H. Bronold. Wien: Europa Verlag, 1973, 232 pp.

1974

A106 *Gods, Goddesses, and Myths of Creation*. New York: Harper and Row, 1974, xiii + 162 pp. Paperback reprint of part 1 of A88 chapters 1-2.

A107 *Man and the Sacred*. New York: Harper and Row, 1974, xiii + 173 pp. Paperback reprint of part 2 of A88 chapter 3.

A108 *Death, Afterlife, and Eschatology*. New York: Harper and Row, 1974, xi + 109 pp. Paperback reprint of part 3 of A88 chapter 4.

A109 *From Medicine Men to Muhammad*. New York: Harper and Row, 1974, xv + 217 pp. Paperback reprint of part 4 of A88 chapters 5-6.

1976

A110 *Histoire des croyances et des idées religieuses. 1. De l'âge de la pierre aux mystères d'Eleusis*. Bibliothèque Historique. Paris: Payot, 1976, 492 pp. English publication: *A History of Religious Ideas. 1. From the Stone Age to the Eleusinian Mysteries* A120. German translation: *Geschichte der religiösen Ideen. 1. Von der Steinzeit bis zu den Mysterien von Eleusis* A125.

A111 *Initiation, rites, sociétés secrètes. Naissances mystiques. Essai sur quelques types d'initiation*. Collection Idées, 332. Paris: Gallimard, 1976, 282 pp. Reprint of A66.

A112 *Myths, Rites, Symbols. A Mircea Eliade Reader*. Edited by W.C. Beane and W.G. Doty. Colophon Book. New York: Harper and Row, 1976, 2 vols., xxviii + 465 pp.

Beane and Doty have compiled an anthology of what they

consider to be the "essential" Eliade, with selections taken almost exclusively from his books. The two-volume collection is divided into three chapters: Myths--Sacred History, Time, and Intercommunication; Rites--Birth, Renewal, Religious Experience, and Technique; Symbols--Patterns, Transitions, and Paradises. Beane has a very brief introductory piece, "Understanding Eliade as Historian of Religions," and a brief concluding essay, "The Work of Mircea Eliade: Implications for a Philosophy of Humankind" (see F42 and F43). A major problem with this anthology is the length of the selections: 192 selections in about 460 pages. Many of the two-page selections are very fragmentary. Fewer and lengthier selections would improve this anthology.

A113 *Occultism, Witchcraft, and Cultural Fashions. Essays in Comparative Religions*. Chicago and London: University of Chicago Press, 1976, x + 148 pp. Paperback ed., University of Chicago Press, Phoenix Books, 1978. French translation: *Occultisme, sorcellerie et modes culturelles* A127.

This little book, written primarily for the "non-specialist," consists of six essays: "Cultural Fashions and the History of Religions" (see A87); "The World, the City, the House" focuses on sacred space and suggests its relevance for modern "desacralized" experience; "Mythologies of Death: An Introduction" describes ways traditional societies have come to terms with death and suggests a continuity from the archaic to the modern; "The Occult and the Modern World" discusses nineteenth- and twentieth-century interests in the occult and interprets the recent "occult explosion"; "Some Observations of European Witchcraft" examines the "origins" of Western witchcraft and the so-called witches' orgies and interprets some of the recent interest in witchcraft in Western culture; "Spirit, Light, and Seed" examines experiences of "mystical light" (see A82) and ritual sexuality. Eliade maintains that these diverse and perplexing modern phenomena reveal profound symbolic and mythic structures because they can be related to archaic spiritual roots.

A114 *Die Pelerine*. Translation of a Romanian manuscript written 1975, which has not been published, by E. Silbermann. Frankfurt: Suhrkamp Verlag, 1976, 96 pp. A novella.

1977

A115 *In curte la Dionis* (In the Court of Dionysus). Madrid: Caietele Inorogului, 1977, 272 pp.

Collection of short stories. These are listed below with dates of composition and with references to original publication: "Les trois grâces" 1976; "Şanţurile" (The Trenches) 1963. See H961; "Ivan" 1967. See H995; "Uniforme de general" (The General's Uniforms) 1971. See B273; "Incognito, la Buchenwald" 1974. See B288; "In curte la Dionis" 1968. See H997. "Les trois grâces" has been translated into book form as *Die drei Grazien* A123. "Ivan"; "Uniforme de general"; and "In curte la Dionis" are translated in *Phantastische Geschichten* A128.

Several of the stories contain fantastic and mysterious motifs: "In curte la Dionis" is the most obscure, with a plot that is extremely difficult to understand. The life situation of the main characters is expressed as a confluence of mysterious and mythical allusions.

"Ivan" shifts back and forth between fantasy and reality without a clear delineation of the two.

In "Uniforme de general" Antim's "true love" comes as his angel of death, fulfilling a myth that he had read as a child.

"Incognito, la Buchenwald" portrays Ieronim who, in the dust of the demolition of his family mansion, envisions a mystic transformation of Bucharest as the "New Jerusalem."

A116 *Im Mittelpunkt--Bruchstücke eines Tagebuches*. Translation of A104 by B.A. Egger. Wien: Europa Verlag, 1977, 298 pp.

A117 *No Souvenirs: Journal, 1957-1969*. Translation of the latter part of A104 by F.H. Johnson, Jr., with a new pref. New York: Harper and Row, 1977, xiv + 343 pp. London: Routledge and Kegan Paul, 1978.

This translation of the 1957 to 1969 period of A104 presents Eliade's American experiences since he first came to the University of Chicago in 1956, as well as numerous descriptions of experiences in Europe, where he spends his summers, and of extended trips to Japan and Mexico. This journal-diary is the first English publication in which Eliade freely discusses his personal feelings and views. Eliade first received recognition in Romania as a novelist. This work makes clear Eliade's view that his literary and scholarly worlds complement each other and are organically interrelated, and it reveals the emotional and intellectual basis for many of his scholarly and literary publications. The journal is lively and revealing: Eliade's thoughts about his own works; the tremendous influence of Goethe and Papini; the meetings with Jung, Tillich, and others; conversations with students; reactions to what he is reading; observations about hippies, cultural vogues, and all sorts of contemporary phenomena; feelings about his situation as a Romanian "exile."

A118 *Le Vieil homme et l'officier*. Translation of A90 by A. Guillermou. Du Monde entier. Paris: Gallimard, 1977, 189 pp.

1978

A119 *The Forbidden Forest*. Translation of A98 by M.L. Ricketts and M.P. Stevenson. Notre Dame and London: University of Notre Dame Press, 1978, xv + 596 pp.

This, Eliade's first novel to be translated into English, is considered by the author and most interpreters to be his literary masterpiece. Eliade writes that this work has been described as "realistic and psychological" and presents itself as a "historical novel," taking place between 1936 and 1948 in Bucharest and other parts of Europe and incorporating many of the author's views about the historical tragedy and destiny of the Romanian people. But a simple description of this work as a historical novel can be misleading. It is also pervaded by mystery and signs of the fantastic, by transhistorical themes and meanings. In the Preface, Eliade describes some of the symbolism of the novel, as well as his view of the importance for him of literary creativity and of the close relationship between his scholarly and literary works. The Romanian hero, Stefan, loves two women: his wife, Ioana, and a mysterious Ileana whom he meets in a forest near Bucharest on the evening of the summer solstice (Night of St. John). Many of Eliade's themes from the History of Religions are apparent in the novel: the sacred and the profane, hierophanies, the terror of history, initiation and the quest for immortality, and various basic mythic and symbolic structures and meanings. Emphasized throughout the novel is Eliade's theme that religious meanings are "hidden" or "camouflaged" in contemporary Western experiences.

A120 *A History of Religious Ideas. 1. From the Stone Age to the Eleusinian Mysteries.* Translation of A110 by W.R. Trask. Chicago and London: University of Chicago Press, 1978, xvii + 489 pp. London: Collins Publishers, 1979.

This first of a three-volume study investigates the history of religious beliefs and ideas from prehistory to the cult of Dionysus. The first two chapters, on the "Magico-Religious Behavior of the Paleanthropians" and "The Discovery of Agriculture--Mesolithic and Neolithic," are extremely important in formulating the foundations and essential structures and patterns that define much of the later History of Religions. The book includes two chapters on Israel, two chapters on pre-Buddhist India, four chapters on Greek religion, and studies on Mesopotamian, Egyptian, Iranian, and other religious developments. A lengthy critical bibliography constitutes about one-fifth of the volume. Unlike his previous synchronic, morphological studies of religious phenomena, Eliade interprets the manifestations of the sacred in chronological order. He elucidates "the major contributions to the history of religious ideas and beliefs" in terms of "crises in depth and the creations that result from them." As in previous works, the author maintains the sacred is "an element in the structure of consciousness" and not a stage in the history of consciousness; and this "historical study" is clearly guided by his morphological analysis of essential nonhistorical religious structures. What this "history" adds to the previous morphologies is a greater emphasis on the "inexhaustible newness" of religious expressions; on how the same themes and structures have been expressed throughout history in radically different ways. In short, there is a greater sense of historical change and development.

A121 *Mademoiselle Christina*. Translation of A20 by C. Levenson. Les Livres Noirs. Paris: L'Herne, 1978, 300 pp.

A122 "Textes de Mircea Eliade." A major section of *Mircea Eliade*. Edited by C. Tacou. Cahiers de L'Herne, 33. Paris: L'Herne, 1978, 409 pp. D11.

Mircea Eliade consists of French translations of texts of Eliade and a collection of articles and commentaries on Eliade. The articles and commentaries on Eliade, as well as other pertinent information about the book, are listed under D11. What follows are the texts of Eliade with cross-references to earlier publications.

"Souvenirs de jeunesse," pp. 19-33. See A85 chap. 5.
"L'Inde à vingt ans," pp. 34-46. H967; A85.
"Journal himalayen," pp. 47-60. Part of A13.
"Fragmentarium," pp. 61-78. Selections of A29.
"Architecture sacrée et symbolisme," pp. 141-56. Revision of B153.
"Le mythe de l'alchimie," pp. 157-67. B305.
"La conception de la liberté dans la pensée indienne," pp. 168-71. Part of A36; B38.
"Le folklore comme moyen de connaissance," pp. 172-81. Part of A36.
"Barabudur, temple symbolique," pp. 233-40. Part of A36.
"Sur l'érotique mystique indienne," pp. 241-45. Part of A53; B145.
"A propos d'une nouvelle philosophie de la lune," pp. 246-49. Part of A36.
"Jung, ou la Réponse à Job," pp. 250-55. B101; B299.
"Les Bohémiennes," pp. 293-312. In A80; B230.

A123 *Die drei Grazien*. Translation of the Romanian "Les trois grâces" in A115 by E. Silbermann. Bibliothek Suhrkamp, 577. Frankfurt: Suhrkamp Verlag, 1978, 102 pp.

A124 *L'Epreuve du Labyrinthe. Entretiens avec Claude-Henri Rocquet*. Collection Entretiens. Paris: Belfond, 1978. 249 pp.

Series of interviews with Eliade conducted in Paris in the summer of 1978. Eliade gives frank and revealing answers to probing and perceptive questions about his life, thought, and works. Includes photographs and a bibliography apparently condensed from that in D11.

A125 *Geschichte der religiösen Ideen. 1. Von der Steinzeit bis zu den Mysterien von Eleusis*. Translation of A110. Freiburg: Verlag Herder, 1978.

A126 *Histoire des croyances et des idées religieuses. 2. De Gautama Bouddha au triomphe du christianisme*. Bibliothèque Historique. Paris: Payot, 1978, 519 pp.

This is the second volume of the three-volume *Histoire des croyances et des idées religieuses*. The first volume, *De l'âge de la pierre aux mystères d'Eleusis* A110, was published in 1976. The third volume will be entitled *De Mohammed aux théologies athéistes contemporaines*. See A120 for an examination of Eliade's purpose and approach and the sense in which these volumes can be considered historical studies.

A127 *Occultisme, sorcellerie et modes culturelles*. Translation of A113 by J. Malaquais. Les Essais, 206. Paris: Gallimard, 1978, 183 pp.

A128 *Phantastische Geschichten*. Translation by E. Silbermann of short stories found in A80, A92, and A115. Frankfurt: Insel Verlag, 1978, 342 pp.

B

ARTICLES AND FICTION IN BOOKS AND PERIODICALS

1928

B1 "Les religions des mystères dans les publications récentes." *Logos. Revue Internationale de synthèse orthodoxe*, Bucharest (1928) 1:117-31.

Discusses various current publications concerning Mystery Religions, especially the works of V. Macchioro and R. Pettazzoni.

B2 "La vision chrétienne d'Ernesto Buonaiuti. A propos de ses derniers livres." *Logos* (1928) 1: 283-92.

1930

B3 "Problematica filozofiei indiene: linii de orientare" (The Problematics of Indian Philosophy: Lines of Orientation). *Revista de Filosofie*, Bucharest (1930) 15:50-72. Parts published in French in A21 part 2, which has further references.

First publication of part of Eliade's doctoral thesis. Outlines the origin and nature of Indian philosophy, giving some historical and philosophical variations. Includes sections on Karma and Buddhism.

B4 "Introducere în filozofia Sâmkhya" (Introduction to Samkhya Philosophy). *Revista de Filosofie* (1930) 15: 152-75. Part published in French in A21 chap. 2, which has further references.

The basic principles of Samkhya philosophy are: 1. The exterior world has ontological reality; 2. A teleological significance to the world and to experiences can be intuited; and 3. Freedom from illusion can be attained through "spiritual induction" and a logic of dialectics.

B5 "Il male e la liberazione nella filosofia Sāmkhya-Yoga" (Evil and Liberation in Samkhya-Yoga Philosophy). *Ricerche Religiose*, Rome (1930) 6:200-21. Enlarged French publication in A21 chaps. 2-3, which has further references.

In Samkhya philosophy, suffering and evil are part of the human condition as a result of the confusion of the spirit and psychomental experiences (i.e., "illusions"). Spiritual essence is attained through a dialectics of various techniques of emancipation from the pains of existence. Liberation results from a controlled transformation of mental and physical states and ultimately comes as a revelation. In Western terms, salvation embodies not only metaphysical knowledge but also a "technical will."

1931

B6 "Cunoştinţele botanice în vechea Indie" (Botanical Knowledge in Ancient India). *Buletinul Societăţii de Ştiinţe din Cluj*, Cluj (1931) 6:221-37.

Monograph on the Indian success of describing and classifying natural phenomena without appealing to the rigor and strict objectivity of Western science.

B7 "Contribuţii la psihologia Yoga" (Contributions to Yoga Psychology). *Revista de Filosofie* (1931) 16:54-76. Part published in A21 chap. 3, which has additional references.

A summary of Yogic experiences and techniques regarding the yogin's view of the structure of normal daily life; his psychological process of dissociation from this structure; and the meditative structure which leads to samādhi.

1932

B8 "Il Rituale Hindu e la vita interiore" (Hindu Ritual and Interior Life). *Ricerche Religiose* (1932) 8:486-504.

Examines the goals of Indian mysticism in the *Upanishads*,

the *Bhagavad-Gita*, and Tantrism. Human life is identified with cosmic life such that spiritual and physical exercises, even to the point of asceticism, become sacrificial material for achieving a state of the divine.

1934

B9 "America văzută de un tânăr de azi" (America as Seen by a Youth of Today). *Revista Fundaţiilor Regale*, Bucharest (1934) 1, no. 6:196-201.

Commentary on a work by D. Comarnescu, *Homo Americanus*, about a visit to the United States.

1935

B10 "Activitatea institutului de cultură comparată dela Oslo" (Activity of the Institute of Comparative Culture at Oslo). *Revista Fundaţiilor Regale* (1935) 2, no. 1:116-39. Revised and enlarged publication of H507.

Reviews monographs published by the Institute. Views it as an instrument for the advancement of a "new humanism." That is, an attempt to coordinate methods and results of scientific inquiries so that all forms of culture can be integrated into an understanding of human culture as a whole. Not a syncretism, but an understanding of the human being's place in the Cosmos as perceived by each culture within its own epoch.

B11 "Când trebue citit Paul Zarifopol" (When One Ought to Read Paul Zarifopol). *Revista Fundaţiilor Regale* (1935) 2, no. 3:658-62.

One should not confuse methods of philosophy with systems of philosophy.

B12 "Despre Italo Svevo" (Concerning Italo Svevo). *Revista Fundaţiilor Regale* (1935) 2, no. 7:201-7. Reprinted in A36 pp. 205-15.

1936

B13 "Elemente pre-ariene în hinduism" (Pre-Aryan Elements in Hinduism). *Revista Fundaţiilor Regale* (1936) 3, no. 1:

149-73. Part published in French in A21 chap. 9, which has further references.

Mysticism and popular traditions in India are evidence of a reaction against juridical forms of Brahmanism and of a quest for more personal religious experiences.

B14 "Echipele regale studenţeşti la lucru" (Royal Student Teams at Work). *Revista Fundaţiilor Regale* (1936) 3, no. 2:447-52.

B15 "Ion Ghica scriitorul" (Writer Ion Ghica). *Revista Fundaţiilor Regale* (1936) 3, no. 3:675-79.

B16 "Despre Samuel Butler" (Concerning Samuel Butler). *Revista Fundaţiilor Regale* (1936) 3, no. 4:181-90. Reprinted in A36 pp. 216-31.

B17 "Inainte de miracolul grec" (Before the Greek Miracle). *Revista Fundaţiilor Regale* (1936) 3, no. 5:397-402. Reprinted in A36 pp. 100-8.

B18 "Istoria medicinii în România" (The History of Medicine in Romania). *Revista Fundaţiilor Regale* (1936) 3, no. 6:664-69. Revised and enlarged publication of H401. Cf. A36 pp. 162-69.

B19 "Muzeul satului românesc" (Museum of the Romanian Village). *Revista Fundaţiilor Regale* (1936) 3, no. 7:193-99. Reprinted in A36 pp. 154-61.

B20 "O carte despre moarte" (A Book about Death). *Revista Fundaţiilor Regale* (1936) 3, no. 8:439-45.

Values Ion Biberi's book, *Thanatos*, as a synthesis of scientific perception and metaphysical appreciation of death of the individual. Compares to the Tibetan *Book of the Dead* which portrays the collective "fantastic" experiences of death.

B21 "Un nou fel de literatură revoluţionară" (A New Mode of Revolutionary Literature). *Revista Fundaţiilor Regale* (1936) 3, no. 11:431-36. Reprinted in A36 pp. 170-79.

B22 "Despre o 'filozofie' a lunii" (About a "Philosophy" of the Moon). *Revista Fundaţiilor Regale* (1936) 3, no. 12:655-60. Reprinted in A36 pp. 84-92.

1937

B23 "Lo Yoga e la spiritualità indiana" (Yoga and Indian Spirituality). *Asiatica*, Rome (1937) 3:229-40. Enlarged French publication in A21 chap. 3, which has further references.

Outlines major attitudes of Patañjali (Classical) Yoga as a "soteriological method" by which human beings regain their initial liberty. Indian "pessimism" of the world in general plays a positive role toward liberation.

B24 "Cosmical Homology and Yoga." *Journal of the Indian Society of Oriental Art*, Calcutta (1937) 5:188-203.

Through Yoga techniques and spirituality, all levels--physical, psychological, mental, as well as cosmic--are "homologized" and so unified. Chaos is transformed into Cosmos. Eliade's first publication in English.

B25 "Despre o etică a 'Puterii'" (Concerning an Ethics of "Power"). *Revista Fundaţiilor Regale* (1937) 4, no. 1:187-92. Reprinted in A36 pp. 180-87.

B26 "Câteva cărţi de istoria religiilor" (Some Books in the History of Religions). *Revista Fundaţiilor Regale* (1937) 4, no. 2:422-31.

Review article of A. Boissier, *Mantique babylonienne et mantique hittite*; I. Coman, *Titanul Prometheu*; and A. Christensen, *Les Gestes des Rois dans lés traditions de l'Iran antique*.

B27 "Inainte şi după miracolul biblic" (Before and After the Biblical Miracle). *Revista Fundaţiilor Regale* (1937) 4, no. 3:657-61. Reprinted in A36 pp. 109-16.

B28 "Folklorul ca instrument de cunoaştere" (Folklore as an Instrument of Knowledge). *Revista Fundaţiilor Regale* (1937) 4, no. 4:137-52. Reprinted in A36 pp. 28-49.

Eliade was greatly influenced by the works of Lucian Blaga, Rene Guénon, Ananda Coomaraswamy, Paul Mus, and others who, through a study of folkloric and ethnographic documents, deciphered symbolic meanings and cultural "styles," and who developed various "philosophies of culture." In this article Eliade sees the problem as broader than a matter of cultural comparison: folklore points to the structure and limitations of human consciousness itself. Reviewing Frazer's theory, he argues that primitive magic cannot be judged by modern laws of causality as being "superstitious" or "neurotic" since it is based on real concrete experiences which do not assume causality as the basis for understanding events. He also criticizes historicism for its "primacy of documents" and for its segregation of documents which relate miracles and other "unverifiable" phenomena from those which evidence "rational" events. He claims that folklore, having at its base actual experiences, attributes values and meanings to those experiences such that there is a certain degree of reliability to the works and they should be taken seriously. Folklore relates exceptional experiences, or events attributed exceptional values. Historicists and positivists negate these values by their very methods of investigation. Concerning afterlife, for example--the problem of "the real condition of human consciousness after death"--positivists have no say other than to deny the fact. Yet folklore from all ages and cultures values the immediate experience of death and projects beyond death to further meaningful interpretations. In this sense it is a means of knowledge and in this case, as in others, it is more instrumental than, say, positivism.

B29 "Controverse şi studii istoric-religioase" (Historical-Religious Controversies and Studies). *Revista Fundaţiilor Regale* (1937) 4, no. 5:425-30.

Review article of G.S. Marr, *Sex in Religion*; and H.M. Ransome, *The Sacred Bee in Ancient Times and Folklore*.

B30 "Ugarit şi Vechiul Testament" (Ugarit and the Old Testament). *Revista Fundaţiilor Regale* (1937) 4, no. 6: 639-44.

Review article of R. Dussaud, *Les découvertes de Ras Sharma (Ugarit) et l'Ancien Testament*.

B31 "Ananda Coomaraswamy." *Revista Fundaţiilor Regale* (1937) 4, no. 7:183-89. Reprinted in A36 pp. 265-75.

B32 "Efemeride orientale" (Oriental Ephemerides). *Revista Fundaţiilor Regale* (1937) 4, no. 8:417-23.

Review article of G. Dumézil's works from 1924 to 1935; W. Tch'ang-Tche, *La philosophie morale de Wang Yang-Ming*; and J.J. Matignon, *La Chine hermétique*.

B33 "Barabudur, templul simbolic" (Barabudur, Symbolic Temple). *Revista Fundaţiilor Regale* (1937) 4, no. 9:605-17. Reprinted in A36 pp. 50-68.

B34 "La moartea lui Rudolf Otto" (The Death of Rudolf Otto). *Revista Fundaţiilor Regale* (1937) 4, no. 9:676-79. Reprinted in A36 pp. 276-81.

B35 "Papini, istoric al literaturii italiene" (Papini, Historian of Italian Literature). *Revista Fundaţiilor Regale* (1937) 4, no. 10:175-80. Reprinted in A36 pp. 282-90.

B36 "Intre Elephantine şi Ierusalim" (Between Elephantine and Jerusalem). *Revista Fundaţiilor Regale* (1937) 4, no. 11:421-26. Reprinted in A36 pp. 117-25.

B37 "Demonologie indiană şi o legendă românească" (Indian Demonology and a Romanian Legend). *Revista Fundaţiilor Regale* (1937) 4, no. 12:644-49. French translation B50.

1938

B38 "La concezione della libertà nel pensiero indiano" (The Conception of Liberty in Indian Thought). *Asiatica* (1938) 4:345-54. Romanian publication in A36 pp. 69-83. French in A122 pp. 168-71.

The way toward Absolute Reality is to reverse and arrest the human condition, as it is performed in Brahmanic rituals and Yoga traditions. This reversal of contraries leads to a homology of Spirit and Cosmos and ultimately to a coincidence of Being and Non-Being.

B39 "Limbajele Secrete" (Secret Languages). *Revista Fundaţiilor Regale* (1938) 5, no. 1:124-41.

Takes on the problem of "secret" meanings of Tantric texts and of the works of the Islamic poet Hafiz. The key to their interpretation is that certain words have multiple symbolic significances and that they are "magical" or efficacious as well. Symbol concretizes into one expression (e.g., lotus) a polyvalence of metaphysical and psychological meanings which, as they are grasped, are also appropriated.

B40 "Lucian Blaga şi sensul culturii" (Lucian Blaga and the Meaning of Culture). *Revista Fundaţiilor Regale* (1938) 5, no. 1:162-66. Reprinted in A36 pp. 188-95.

B41 "Un amănunt din Parsifal" (A Detail from Parsifal). *Revista Fundaţiilor Regale* (1938) 5, no. 2:422-26. Reprinted in A36 pp. 196-202.

B42 "Alegorie sau 'limbaj secret'?" (Allegory or "Secret Language?"). *Revista Fundaţiilor Regale* (1938) 5, no. 3:616-32. Part 2 of B39.

Discusses mystical qualities as well as other symbolic meanings of the *Canticle of Canticles* which has been traditionally interpreted as an allegory of the relationship of Yahweh and his people. Examines Dante's *Divine Comedy* as a parallel allegory for Christianity. As "secret languages" these works annul the profane sensibility of the words and even of reality itself. Communication of such secrets constitutes a "revelation" for initiates and so promotes a state of "sacredness" among them as well as a recreation of the ontological efficacy of the secrets themselves.

B43 "Cu Prilejul unui *Shakespeare*" (On the Occasion of a Shakespeare). *Revista Fundaţiilor Regale* (1938) 5, no. 3:650-53.

Review of Haig Acterian, *Shakespeare*.

B44 "Religia evreilor nomazi" (Religion of the Nomadic Hebrews). *Revista Fundaţiilor Regale* (1938) 5, no. 4: 171-75.

Review article of E. Dhorme, *La Religion des Hébreux nomades*.

B45 "Locum refrigerii." *Revista Fundaţiilor Regale* (1938) 5, no. 5:418-22. Reprinted in A36 pp. 93-99. French translation B51.

B46 "Viaţa unui 'maestru' Tibetan" (Life of a Tibetan "Master"). *Revista Fundaţiilor Regale* (1938) 5, no. 6:668-71.

Discusses J. Bacot's studies of Milarepa and Marpa.

B47 "D'Annunzio necunoscut" (The Unknown D'Annunzio). *Revista Fundaţiilor Regale* (1938) 5, no. 7:166-71. Reprinted in A36 pp. 291-98.

B48 "Un savant rus despre literatura chineză" (A Russian Scholar on Chinese Literature). *Revista Fundaţiilor Regale* (1938) 5, no. 8:436-42. Reprinted in A36 pp. 135-44.

B49 "Metallurgy, Magic and Alchemy." *Zalmoxis. Revue des Études Religieuses*, Paris (1938) 1:85-129. Equivalent to A27. See A23 for additional references.

B50 "Notes de démonologie." *Zalmoxis* (1938) 1:197-203. Translation of B37.

Notations supporting the dualism yet functional correlativity of Good and Evil in mythology.

B51 "Locum refrigerii ..." *Zalmoxis* (1938) 1:203-8. French translation of B45.

References to the symbolic meanings of water and afterworld motifs.

B52 "Le culte de la mandragore en Roumanie." *Zalmoxis* (1938) 1:209-25. Reprinted in A97 chap. 7. English translation as B280 and in A102.

1939

B53 "Piatra şerpilor, Studiu de folklor comparat" (Snake Stones, a Study in Comparative Folklore). *Meşterul Manole*, Bucharest (1939) 1, no. 5-6:15-21.

In the process of history, the degradation of the significance of myths is due to a "decomposition of the fantastic" which results from a loss of the primordial metaphysical values of those myths.

B54 "'Treptele' lui Julien Green" (Julien Green's "Steps"). *Revista Fundaţiilor Regale* (1939) 6, no. 3:662-68. Reprinted in A36 pp. 19-27.

B55 "Cărţile populare în literatura românească" (Popular Books in Romanian Literature). *Revista Fundaţiilor Regale* (1939) 6, no. 4:132-47. French translation B64.

B56 "Moartea doctorului Gaster" (The Death of Doctor Gaster). *Revista Fundaţiilor Regale* (1939) 6, no. 5:395-99.

B57 "Insula lui Euthanasius" (Island of Euthanasius). *Revista Fundaţiilor Regale* (1939) 6, no. 7:100-9. Reprinted in A36 pp. 5-18.

B58 "D'Annunzio postum" (A Posthumous D'Annunzio). *Revista Fundaţiilor Regale* (1939) 6, no. 7:184-89. Reprinted in A36 pp. 299-306.

B59 "Vechi controverse ..." (Old Controversies). *Revista Fundaţiilor Regale* (1939) 6, no. 8:446-51. Reprinted in A36 pp. 145-53.

B60 "Simbolismul arborelui sacru" (Symbolism of the Sacred Tree). *Revista Fundaţiilor Regale* (1939) 6, no. 9: 675-80. Reprinted in A36 pp. 126-34.

B61 "Mediterana şi Oceanul Indian" (Mediterranean and Indian Ocean). *Revista Fundaţiilor Regale* (1939) 6, no. 10: 203-8.

Review of works of C. Autran.

B62 "Ierburile de sub cruce" (Herbs at the Foot of the Cross). *Revista Fundaţiilor Regale* (1939) 6, no. 11:353-69.

Examines the qualities of plant motifs in various traditions.

B63 "Greşelile de tipar" (Typographical Errors). *Revista Fundaţiilor Regale* (1939) 6, no. 12:663-67.

Laments typographical mistakes.

B64 "Les livres populaires dans la littérature roumaine." *Zalmoxis* (1939) 2:63-78. Translation of B55.

Review article of N. Cartojan, *Cărţile populare în literatură românească*. Eliade compares popular interest in literature to folkloric creations, and sees contrary processes at work in each: On the one hand, there is a degradation of the "fantastic" due to a localization or ethnization of certain universal values; on the other hand, there develops a categorization of historical individuals and events into types and episodes. Within these processes, or within the works themselves, one can find archaic, primitive theories and attitudes.

B65 "Notes sur le symbolisme aquatique." *Zalmoxis* (1939) 2: 131-52. Reprinted in A48 chap. 4. Translations: German in A61. English in A71.

1940

B66 "Imagini dintr'o România aspră" (Images of a Hardy Romania). *Revista Fundaţiilor Regale* (1940) 7, no. 1: 191-95.

Review of G. Bogza, *Ţări de piatră, de foc şi de pământ.*

B67 "Un Roman '1900'" (A Novel, "1900"). *Revista Fundaţiilor Regale* (1940) 7, no. 2:427-31.

Review of T. Scorţescu, *Concina prădată.*

B68 "Tărâmul nevăzut" (Unseen Realm). *Revista Fundaţiilor Regale* (1940) 7, no. 3:506-27; 4:34-54. Published also as A31, which has further references.

B69 "Comentarii italiene" (Italian Commentaries). *Revista Fundaţiilor Regale* (1940) 7, no. 7:189-94.

Examines contributions of G. Papini and G. Dauli.

B70 "La Mandragore et les mythes de la 'naissance miraculeuse.'" *Zalmoxis* (1940-42) 3:3-38.

Attests to the universality of plant motifs which symbolize in many cultures one's solidarity with nature and yet also one's sacrificial rebirth or transfiguration.

1946

B71 "Le problème du chamanisme." *Revue de l'Histoire des Religions* (1946) 131:5-52. Contains material for A46 chaps. 1-4. Cf. German in A59 and English in A81.

1947

B72 "Les sacrifices grecs et les rites des peuples primitifs." *Revue de l'Histoire des Religions* (1947-48) 133:225-30.

Review of article by K. Meuli, "Griechische Opferbräuche," in *Phyllobolia für Peter von der Mühll zum 60 Geburtstag.*

B73 "Le 'dieu lieur' et le symbolisme des noeuds." *Revue de l'Histoire des Religions* (1947-48) 134:5-36. Reprinted in A48 chap. 3. Translations: German in A61. English in A71.

1948

B74 "*Dūrohana* and the 'waking dream.'" In *Art and Thought*. Ed. by K.B. Iyer. London: Luzac, 1948, pp. 209-13. Reprinted in A68 part of chap. 5. Original French in A58. German in A73.

B75 "Science, idéalisme et phénomènes paranormaux." *Critique. Revue Générale des Publications Françaises et Étrangères* (1948) 23:315-23.

Review article of works of E. de Martino, particularly *Il Mondo magico*.

B76 "La mythologie primitive." *Critique* (1948) 27:708-17.

Review article of R. Pettazzoni, *Miti e Leggende*; M. Leenhardt, *Do Kamo*; and F.K. Numazawa, *Die Weltanfänge in der japanischen Mythologie*.

B77 "Origines et diffusion de la civilisation." *Critique* (1948) 29:897-908. Romanian publication H893.

Review article of P. Laviosa Zambotti, *Origini e Diffusione della Civiltà*. Of interest are the different notions of "history" that Eliade raises: resistance to time; periodic regeneration of origins; terror of history; epiphany of history; social history; historicism; fall into history.

1949

B78 "Les Sept Pas du Bouddha." In *Acts du XXIe Congrès international des orientalistes*. Paris: Société Asiatique, 1949, pp. 209-10; and in *Pro Regno, Pro Sanctuario: Hommage van der Leeuw*. Ed. by W.J. Kooiman and J.M. van Veen. Nijkerk: 1950, pp. 169-75. Published also as B86. Reprinted in A58 part of chap. 5. Translations: English in A68. German in A73.

B79 "La vigne mystique." *L'Amour de l'Art* (Dec. 1949) pp. 39-45.

Very brief. Summary from several works.

B80 "Pour une histoire générale des religions indo-européennes." *Annales. Economies. Sociétés. Civilisations* (1949) 4:183-91.

The works of G. Dumézil are valuable not only for a history of Indo-European religions but also for a philosophy of culture and for a philosophy of history as well.

B81 "Introduction au tantrisme." In *Approches de l'Inde*. Dir. by J. Masui. Marseille: Cahiers du Sud, 1949, pp. 132-44.

An introduction to the various forms and practices of Tantrism, stressing the relationship of guru and disciple, the multivalence of secret languages and texts, and the identification of contraries. Transformation of concrete carnal condition into divine cosmic life.

B82 "Des méthodes de l'ascetisme hindou." *Le Courrier des Indes*, Paris (1949), no. 2.

B83 "La souveraineté et la religion indo-européennes." *Critique* (1949) 35:342-49.

Review article of G. Dumézil, *Mitra-Varuna*, and A. Coomaraswamy, *Spiritual Authority and Temporal Power in the Indian Theory of Government*.

B84 "Phénoménologie de la religion et sociologie religieuse." *Critique* (1949) 39:713-20.

Review article of G. van der Leeuw, *La Religion dans son Essence et ses Manifestations*; J. Wach, *Sociology of Religion*; and G. Mensching, *Soziologie der Religion*. Phenomenology suspends attempts at "origins" and "causes" and views various phenomena *sui generis*. Yet religious phenomena are conditioned by socio-historical factors as practical expressions, and even degradations, of the sacred. While no religious fact rests outside of history, many religious phenomena resist history as a profane modality.

B85 "Shamanism." In *Forgotten Religions*. Ed. by V. Ferm. New York: Philosophical Library, 1949, pp. 297-308. Translation of material contained in A46. Cf. A81 and German A59.

B86 "Sapta padani kramati." In *The Munshi Diamond Jubilee Commemoration Volume. Part I: Bhāratīya Vidyā*.

Poona: 1949, vol. 9, pp. 180-88. Published also as B78, which has further references.

B87 "Mythes et Réalité." *Recherches et Debats*. Supplement philosophique: bimestriel dactylographie (1949) 3, nos. 9-11 and 14-15.

1950

B88 "Actualité de la mythologie." *Critique* (1950) 43:236-43.

Review article of contributions to *Eranos-Jahrbuch* vol. 17, *Der Mensch und die Mythische Welt*; and vol. 18, *Aus der Welt der Urbilder*.

For the primitive, myth constitutes a mode of knowledge of being in the world as a revelation of the structure of reality and of the ultimate sacredness of life. Generally myths are cosmogonies which depict what happened in the beginning, before Time. So myths reveal the "first forms" or atemporal models--archetypes. Archetypes of a similar order are camouflaged in modern systems of thought, both scientific and philosophical.

B89 "Eminescu, o poeta da raça romena" (Eminescu, A Poet of the Roman Race). In M. Eminescu's *Poesias*. Translated by V. Buescu. Lisbon: Fernandes, 1950, pp. 21-32.

1951

B90 "Le double visage de l'Asie et la tradition orientale de la culture roumain." *Bulletin du Centre Roumain de Recherches* (1951) 1:38-44.

B91 "Redécouverte du symbolisme." *Combat: de la Résistance à la Révolution* (Dec. 27, 1951). Published also in A48 foreword. Translations: German in A61. English in A71.

B92 "L'Europe et les rideaux." *Comprendre* (1951) 3:115-22; and in *La Revue de Culture Européenne* (1952) 2:117-23. German translation B104.

A classification of the vastly different geographical, religious, and political orientations of European and East European peoples. Despite Romania's proximity to nations of such different accord, Romania has preserved her "latin temperament" by continuing her own popular customs and folkloric traditions.

B93 "Psychologie et histoire des religions: à propos du symbolisme du 'Centre.'" *Eranos-Jahrbuch* (1951) 19: 247-82. Published also as B106 and in A48 chap. 1. Translations: English as B125 and in A71. German in A61.

B94 "Eléments chamaniques dans le Lamaïsme." *France-Asie*, Saigon (1951) 61-62:96-105. Reprinted from A46 chap. 12. Cf. German in A59 and English in A81.

B95 "Einführende Betrachtungen über den Schamanismus." *Paideuma* (1951) 5:87-97. Contains material for A59. See original French in A46 and revised English in A81.

B96 "Mythes cosmogoniques et guérisons magiques." An abstract in *Proceedings of the 7th International Congress for the History of Religions*. Amsterdam: North-Holland Pub. Co., 1951, pp. 180-81. Original text revised in A77 parts of chaps. 2 and 5. Translations of original: German as B144. English in A79.

B97 "Le Dieu lointain dans les religions primitives." *Témoignages. Cahiers de la Pierre-qui-vire* (1951) 28: 22-27. Revised in A84 part of chap. 3. Revised translations: German in A57. English in A67.

1952

B98 "Mythe et histoire dans la littérature orale." *Bulletin du Centre Roumain de Recherches* (1952) 1:26-31. Part of B141.

B99 "Mythes indiens du temps." *Combat* (March 13, 1952). Part of B103. Cf. B102.

B100 "Le Bouddhisme et l'Occident." *Combat* (Aug. 7, 1952).

B101 "Rencontre avec Jung." *Combat* (Oct. 9, 1952). Reprinted in A122 pp. 250-55. See English B299.

B102 "Le temps et l'éternité dans la pensée indienne." *Eranos-Jahrbuch* (1952) 20:219-52. Reprinted in A48 chap. 2. Condensed as B103. Translations: German in A61. English as B150 and in A71.

B103 "Symbolisme indien de l'abolition du temps." *Journal de Psychologie* (1952) 45:430-38. Condensed version of B102.

B104 "Von der Unteilbarkeit Europas." *Merkur* (1952) 58:1101-10. Translation of B92.

B105 "Chasteté, sexualité et vie mystique chez les primitifs." *Mystique et Continence*, Études Carmélitaines (1952) pp. 29-50. Part published in A46 chap. 3. Translations: German in A59. English in A81.

B106 "Le Symbolisme du 'Centre.'" *Revue de Culture Européenne* (1952) 2:227-39. Published also as B93, which has additional references.

1953

B107 "Le symbolisme religieux et la valorisation de l'angoisse." In *L'Angoisse du temps présent et les devoirs de l'esprit*. Rencontres internationales de Genève. Neuchâtel: Baconnière, 1953, pp. 55-71, and "Discussion" pp. 211-24, 335-39. Reprinted without "Discussion" in A58 chap. 9. Translations: English in A68. German in A73.

B108 "The Yearning for Paradise in Primitive Tradition." *Diogenes* (1953) 3:18-30. Reprinted in *Daedalus* (1959) 88:255-67; in *Myth and Mythmaking*. Ed. by H.A. Murray. New York: Braziller, 1960, pp. 61-75; in *The Making of Myth*. Ed. by R.M. Ohmann. New York: G.P. Putnam's Sons, 1960, pp. 84-98; and in A68 chap. 3. French publication B109 and in A58. German translation B110 and in A73.

B109 "La nostalgie du Paradis dans les traditions primitives." *Diogène* (1953) 3:31-45. English publication B108. See B108 for further references.

B110 "Das Heimweh nach dem Paradies in den Uberlieferungen der primitiven Völker." *Diogenes* (1953) 3:301-15. Translation of B109. See B108.

B111 "Puissance et Sacralité dans l'histoire des religions." *Eranos-Jahrbuch* (1953) 21:11-44. Reprinted in A58 chap. 6. Translations: English in A68. German in A73.

B112 "Apport de la synthèse: René Grousset." *France-Asie* (1953) 88-89:827-28.

B113 "Les mythes du monde moderne." *La Nouvelle Revue Française* (1953) 1:440-58. Reprinted in A58 chap. 1. Translations: German B122 and in A73. English B185, B229, and in A68.

B114 "Dos tradiciones culturales y la situacion actual de la cultura rumana." *Revista Oriente*, Madrid (1953) 3: 213-18. Translation of H875. English publication B195.

B115 "Le problème des origines du Yoga." In *Yoga. Science de l'homme intégral*. Marseille: Cahiers du Sud, 1953, pp. 11-20. English publication B119.

B116 "Chamanisme et techniques yogiques indiennes." In *Yoga. Science de l'homme intégral*. Marseille: Cahiers du Sud, 1953, pp. 98-115. English publication B120.

1954

B117 "Symbolisme et histoire des religions." *Critique* (1954) 83:323-37.

Review article of G. Tucci, *Teoria e Pratica del "Mandala"*; O. Höfler, *Germanische Sakralkönigtum. I*; C. Hentze, *Bronzegerät, Kultbauten, Religion im ältesten China der Shangzeit*; and A. Bulling, *The Meaning of China's Most Ancient Art*.

B118 "La Terre-Mère et les hiérogamies cosmiques." *Eranos-Jahrbuch* (1954) 22:57-95. Reprinted in A58 chap. 7. Translations: English B138 and in A68. German in A73.

B119 "The Problem of the Origins of Yoga." In *Forms and Techniques of Altruistic and Spiritual Growth*. Ed. by P.A. Sorokin. Boston: Beacon Press, 1954, pp. 63-70. French B115.

Yoga evidences pre-Aryan features which were later assimilated by Brahmanism and Hinduism. As a primarily ascetic practice, Yoga represents a "ritual interiorization" of Brahmanic sacrificial acts, and functions ultimately as a metaphysics. The "jivan-mukta," one who is paradoxically "freed in life," probably best exemplifies the archaic dimension of Indian spirituality.

B120 "Shamanism and Indian Yoga Techniques." In *Forms and Techniques of Altruistic and Spiritual Growth*. Ed. by P.A. Sorokin. Boston: Beacon Press, 1954, pp. 70-84. French B116.

Outlines differences between the goals and techniques of shamanism and Yoga. Concludes with the example of a "jivan-mukta," one who expresses ultimate paradox.

B121 "Der Mythos der ewigen Wiederkehr." In *Handbuch der Weltgeschichte*. Ed. by A. Randa. Olten: Verlag Otto Walter, 1954, vol. 1, cols. 189-92. Condensed translation of A43 chaps. 1-2. Cf. German in A49 and English in A51.

B122 "Die Mythen in der modernen Welt." *Merkur* (1954) 8: 724-35. Translation of B113, which has further references.

B123 "Eranos." *Nimbus*, London (1954) 2:57-58. Condensed French translation B133. Cf. B179.

Report on Eranos conferences at Ascona from first meeting in 1933 to 1954. Includes the names of several participating scholars from different disciplines.

B124 "Expérience sensorielle et expérience mystique chez les primitifs." *Nos Sens et Dieu*, Études Carmélitaines (1954) pp. 70-99. Reprinted as B300 and in A58 chap. 4. See also B267. Translations: English in A68. German in A73.

B125 "Psychology and Comparative Religion: A Study of the Symbolism of the Centre." In *Selection*. Ed. by C. Hastings and D. Nicholl. New York and London: Sheed and Ward, 1954, vol. 2, pp. 17-43. Translation of B93, which has additional references.

B126 "Les représentations de la mort chez les primitifs." *Témoignages. Cahiers de la Pierre-qui-vire* (1954) 41:166-74.

For primitives death is not simply a natural phenomenon; it is rather a consequence of a "fall" *in illo tempore*, in Mythical Times of the Beginning. Dying is a form of passage to a new ontological level of existence, a reintegration into the Cosmos, a rebirth. This is the structure of most initiations.

1955

B127 "Aspects initiatiques de l'alchimie occidentale." *Archivio di Filosofia. Studi di Filosofia della Religione* (1955) 2:215-25. Part published in A55 chap. 14. Translations: German in A69. English in A74.

B128 "Preistoria unui motiv folkloric românesc" (Prehistory of a Romanian Folkloric Motif). *Buletinul Bibliotecii Române*, Freiburg (1955) 3:41-54. Revised and enlarged French publication B187, which has additional references.

B129 "Techniques de l'extase et langages secrets." In *Conferenze*. Rome: Istituto Italiano per il Medio ed Estremo Oriente, 1955, vol. 2, pp. 57-79.

Renounces theories that shamanism is mainly a manifestation of a mental disorder or a regression to a less evolved state. Perceives shamanistic imitation of the acts and sounds of animals as a "secret language" based upon and leading to further experiences of ecstasy. This "language" functions to reveal the secrets of Nature and to contact the realm of the Supernatural by freeing the shaman or his initiate from the human condition to that beatitude of Mythical paradisiac time. Today ecstatic experiences are "concretized" as similar secret languages in poetic expression, for instance, and in various linguistic processes themselves.

B129a "Culture européenne et 'personnes déplacées.'" *Bulletin Européen*, Rome (1955) 6, no. 6-7:7-8. Published also (unsigned) in *Revue de Culture Européen* (1955) no. 4.

B130 "Nouvel An, peau neuve." *Le Courrier de l'Unesco* (1955) 8, no. 12:7, 32. Condensed publication of A43 chap. 2. See English B147 and in A51. German in A49.

B131 "Mythologie et histoire des religions." *Diogène* (1955) 9:99-116.

Review article of several works of R. Pettazzoni; M.P. Nilsson, *La Religion populaire dans la Grèce antique*; and G. Germain, *Genèse de l'Odyssée*.

According to Eliade, the historian of religions' proper discipline is to decipher atemporal constants of religious experience and of resulting structures that are irreducible to historicity. One's role is to integrate the findings of specialized disciplines such as ethnology, sociology, psychology, and history strictly speaking. In this vein, Eliade agrees with Pettazzoni that all religious phenomena are necessarily conditioned by historical factors, though rightfully they must be considered as religious. Hence a tension exists between history and phenomenology. Also, myth is "true history" because it is "sacred" and that which is "real" is that which is "exemplary" in myths and in human religious activity.

B132 "Note sur Jung et l'alchimie." *Le Disque Vert*, Paris (1955) pp. 97-109. Published also in A55 note N. Translations: German in A69. English in A74.

B133 "Les danseurs passent, la danse reste." *Du*, Zürich (1955) 15:60, 62. Condensed translation of B123.

B134 "Smiths, Shamans and Mystagogues." *East and West* (1955) 6:206-15. Reprinted in A74 chaps. 8-10. French publication in A55. German translation in A69.

B135 "Mystère et régénération spirituelle dans les religions extra-européennes." *Eranos-Jahrbuch* (1955) 23:57-98. Reprinted in A58 chap. 8. Translations: English as B215 and in A68. German in A73.

B136 "Le mythe du Bon Sauvage." *La Nouvelle Revue Française* (1955) 3:229-49. Reprinted in A58 chap. 2. Translations: English in A68. German in A73.

B137 "Note sur l'alchimie indienne." *Rencontre Orient-Occident*, Geneva (1955) 1:3-10. Published also in A55 chap. 12. Translations: German in A69. English in A74.

B138 "Terra Mater and Cosmic Hierogamies." *Spring*, New York (1955) pp. 15-40. Translation of B118, which has further references.

B139 "Symbolisme et rituels métallurgiques babyloniens." In *Studien zur analytischen Psychologie C.G. Jung*. Ed. by C.G. Jung Institute. Zürich: Rascher Verlag, 1955, vol. 2, pp. 42-46. Published also in A55 chap. 7. Translations: German in A69. English in A74.

B139a "Echapper à la mort: des religions primitives à l'alchimie." *Verité et Vie* (1955) 27, no. 248:6-10.

1956

B140 "Masse und Mythos." In *Handbuch der Weltgeschichte*. Ed. by A. Randa. Olten: Verlag Otto Walter, 1956, vol. 2, cols. 2302-4. Condensed translation of A51.

B141 "Littérature orale." In *Histoire des Littératures. I: Littératures anciennes orientales et orales*. Encyclopédie de la Pléiade. Ed. by R. Queneau. Paris: Gallimard, 1956, pp. 3-26. Contains B98.

For primitives there are profane stories as well as desacralized forms of oral literature. However, those narratives which are recounted in a sacred context, such as during initiation rituals and popular feasts, are considered to be true and real and, concurrently, are imitated and repeated as models of human behavior and as explications of the human condition. As collective creations, certain forms of oral literature found to be similar among variant cultures point to a "collective conscience," of which the solution of origins is impossible. In history the dialectic process of these collective creations moves basically in two directions: 1. ethnicization or historicization of mythical archetypes into more individual and personal events as, for example, in the hero ballad; and 2. the remythization or assimilation of historical personalities and events into their archetypal equivalents.

B142 "Les savants et les contes de fées." *La Nouvelle Revue Française* (1956) 4:884-91. Reprinted in A77 app. 1. English translation in A79.

B143 "Symbolisme du 'vol magique.'" *Numen* (1956) 3:1-13. Reprinted in A58 part of chap. 5. Translations: German as B160 and in A73. English in A68.

B144 "Kosmogonische Mythen und magische Heilungen." *Paideuma* (1956) 6:194-204. Translation of B96.

B145 "Note sur l'érotique mystique indienne." *La Table Ronde* (1956) 97:28-33. Reprinted from A53 part of chap. 6. Reprinted in A122 pp. 241-45. See English in A63 and German in A70.

B146 "Terra Mater--Petra Genitrix." *La Tour Saint-Jacques* (1956) 5:2-9. Published also in A55 chap. 4. Translations: German in A69. English in A74.

B147 "Rituals and Symbols of Time Reborn." *The Unesco Courier* (Feb. 1956) pp. 7, 32. Condensed publication of A51 chap. 2. See French B130, which has additional references.

1957

B148 "Étude comparative sur le 'Rope Trick.'" In *Akten des Vierundzwanzigsten Internationalen Orientalistenkongress*. Ed. by H. Franke. Wiesbaden: Deutsche Morgenländische, 1957, pp. 562-64. Revised as B170. Fully revised in A75 part of chap. 4. English revised translation in A82.

B149 "La vertu créatrice du mythe." *Eranos-Jahrbuch* (1957) 25:59-85. Parts reprinted in A84 chap. 2 and in A97 chap. 5. Translations: German in A57. English in A67 and A102.

B150 "Time and Eternity in Indian Thought." In *Man and Time*. Ed. by J. Campbell. Eranos Yearbook, 3; Bollingen Series, 30. New York: Pantheon Books, 1957, pp. 173-200. Translation of B102, which has additional references.

B151 *Die Religion in Geschichte und Gegenwart. Handwörtenbuch für Theologie und Religionswissenschaft*. Ed. by H.V. Campenhausen, E. Dinkler, *et al*. Tübingen: Mohr, 1957-65, 7 vols. Articles: "Bauopfer"; "Berge, heilige, I"; "Chaos"; "Drache"; "Ei"; "Erde"; "Initiation"; "Lebensbaum, I"; "Mond"; "Neujahr"; "Pferd"; "Rites de passage"; "Schamanismus"; "Yoga."

B152 "Manole et le Monastère d'Argeş." *Revue des Études Roumaines* (1957) 3-4:7-28. Reprinted in A97 chap. 5. English translation in A102. Cf. A35.

B153 "Centre du monde, temple, maison." In *Le Symbolisme cosmique des monuments religieux*. Ed. by G. Tucci. Rome: Istituto Italiano per il Medio ed Estremo Oriente, 1957, pp. 57-82. Revised in A122 pp. 141-56. Part revised as B244.

A very stimulating article in which the author recalls the works of Ananda Coomaraswamy, Paul Mus, Guiseppe Tucci, Stella Kramrisch, Carl Hentze and others that had impressed on his own way of thinking some fundamental themes of architectonic symbolism, and of symbolism in general. Eliade understands that architectural structures cannot be reduced simply to geometrical design or to historical diffusion, which would seem to be very logical scientifically. Many of these structures, each in its own way, reveal the "Centre of the World," although many such centers would be absurd empirically. These structures constitute a "sacred zone" and as structures give meaning and orientation within profane, unstructured, and chaotic zones. The sacred building or space, and especially its construction, constitutes a rupture from the ordinary and a communication with transcendent realities. A temple, for instance, is both a visible and spiritual intersection of the three cosmic zones and so is an *Axis mundi* that functions as a point of passage from one zone to another and as a homologation of those zones. Symbolically, it reaches to the significance of Creation, and its construction is an act of Creation or a reinactment of Creation. It is therefore both a cosmology and a soteriology.

1958

B154 "Bi-Unité et Totalité dans la pensée indienne." *Acta Philosophica et Theologica*, Rome (1958) 1:7-13. Part of B161, which has further references.

B155 "Mystique de la lumière." *L'Age Nouveau* (Nov.-Dec. 1958) pp. 27-34. Part of B159.

B156 "Religione dei Turco-Mongoli" (Religions of the Turks-Mongols). *Le Civiltà dell'Oriente* (1958) 3:849-68.

In reviewing the religions of the Turks and Mongols not yet converted to Buddhism or Islam, the author outlines archaic "primitive" elements, such as belief in the Sky God, the active pantheon of "sons" and "messengers," and especially the practice of shamanism. Studying the structure and function of these archaic expressions, he reconstructs their cosmology. Shamanism in particular is an attempt to experiment, or to technically "achieve," the cosmological "theory."

B157 "Prestiges du mythe cosmogonique." *Diogène* (1958) 23: 3-17. Part contained in B163. Revised in A84 chap. 1. Revised translations: German in A57. English as B158 and in A67.

B158 "The Prestige of the Cosmogonic Myth." *Diogenes* (1958) 23:1-13; and in *The Divinity School News*, University of Chicago (1959) 26:1-12. Revised translation of B157. For further references see B157 and B163.

B159 "Significations de la 'lumière intérieure.'" *Eranos-Jahrbuch* (1958) 26:189-242. Part published as B155. Reprinted in A75 chap. 1. English translation in A82.

1959

B160 "Der magische Flug." *Antaios. Zeitschrift für eine freie Welt* (1959) 1:1-12. Translation of B143, which has further references.

B161 "La *coincidentia oppositorum* et le mystère de la totalité." *Eranos-Jahrbuch* (1959) 27:195-236. Part published as B154. Reprinted in A75 chap. 2. English translation in A82.

B162 "Methodological Remarks on the Study of Religious Symbolism." In *The History of Religions. Essays in Methodology*. Ed. by M. Eliade and J.M. Kitagawa. Chicago: University of Chicago Press, 1959, pp. 86-107. A65. Part published as B177. Another English version (a translation of part of A75) in A82 chap. 5. Translations: German as B166 (condensed) and in A78. French in A75. See A65 for annotation.

B163 "Structure et fonction du mythe cosmogonique." In *La Naissance du Monde*. Sources Orientales, 1. Paris: Seuil, 1959, pp. 471-95. Contains part of B157. Also contains condensed part of A97 chap. 3. Parts revised in A77 chap. 2 and in A84 chaps. 1-2. Translations: German as B215a and part in A57 chaps. 1-2. Parts revised in English as B158; in A67 chaps. 1-2; in A79 chap. 2; and in A102 chap. 3.

B164 "Les thèmes initiatiques dans les grandes religions." *La Nouvelle Revue Française* (1959) 7:390-407, 629-47. Reprinted in A66 chap. 6. Translations: English in A60. German in A72.

B165 "Les Daces et les Loups." *Numen* (1959) 6:15-31. See Romanian H941. Revised publication B188. Reprinted in A97 chap. 1. English translation in A102.

1960

B166 "Betrachtungen über die religiöse Symbolik." *Antaios* (1960) 2:1-12. Condensed translation of B162, which has additional references.

B167 "Alchemie und Zeitlichkeit." *Antaios* (1960) 2:180-88. Reprinted from A69 chap. 15. Cf. French in A55 and English in A74.

B168 "Götter und Bilder." *Antaios* (1960) 2:485-501. A translation. See English B181 and French B221.

B169 "Structures and Changes in the History of Religion." In *City Invincible*. Ed. by C. Kraeling and R. Adams. Chicago: University of Chicago Press, 1960, pp. 351-66. Translation from French.

There are constants in religious experience, but they undergo numerous variations and modifications. The author analyzes the structure of an "original," celestial, Supreme Being and then examines the changes and new existential situations that gave rise to the disappearance of this Supreme Being and the emergence of new, more dynamic divine figures. He also shows how "the discovery of agriculture" gave rise to modifications in religious structures. Finally, he examines changes in expressions and images without corresponding modifications in the underlying structures. In short, in order to develop an adequate hermeneutics, the scholar must be sensitive to the complex dynamic relationships between structure and change in the history of religions.

B170 "Remarques sur le 'rope trick.'" In *Culture in History. Essays in Honour of Paul Radin*. Ed. by S. Diamond. New York: Columbia University Press, 1960, pp. 541-51. Revision of B148, which has further references.

B171 "Dimensions religieuses du renouvellement cosmique." *Eranos-Jahrbuch* (1960) 28:241-75. Reprinted in A75 part of chap. 3. English translation in A82.

B172 "Les Américains en Océanie et le nudisme eschatologique." *La Nouvelle Revue Française* (1960) 8:58-74. Reprinted in A75 part of chap. 3. Translations: German as B180. English in A82.

B173 "Le 'miracle de la corde' et la préhistoire du spectacle." *La Nouvelle Revue Française* (1960) 8:682-93. Published also as B182. Revised in A75 part of chap. 4. English publication B174, which is revised in A82.

B174 "Spiritual Thread, sūtrātman, Catena aurea." *Paideuma* (1960) 7:225-34; in *Festgabe für Herman Lommel*. Ed. by B. Schlerath and O. Harrassowitz. Wiesbaden: 1960, pp. 47-56; and in *The University of Chicago Committee on South Asian Studies*. Reprint Series, 9. 1960. See French B173 for further references.

B175 "History and the Cyclical View of Time." *Perspectives*, Notre Dame (1960) 5:11-14.

A short summary of author's understanding of various perceptions of time among archaic or primitive peoples; India; Greece and Rome; Judeo and Christian traditions; the Middle Ages; more modern theories of "history"; historicism; and existentialist philosophers.

B176 "Le symbolisme des ténèbres dans les religions archaïques." *Polarités du symbole*, Études Carmélitaines, 39 (1960) pp. 15-28.

An extremely significant article for grasping Eliade's understanding of symbolism and his hermeneutics of "deciphering" symbols. He begins by claiming that for archaic societies all important symbols are religious symbols, since the latter are concurrently "hierophanies" and "ontophanies." That is, symbols manifest the sacred and constitute what is real, even to the point of a coherent yet presystematic cosmology. On their own, symbols reveal "transcendence" and "liberty" to many peoples of predialectic, prephilosophic vocabularies. Because of their revelatory and efficatory function, symbols are quite different from concepts (of "liberty," etc.). Symbols, in a concrete yet also spiritual way, offer preliterate persons the opportunity to surpass the human condition.

Structurally, symbols are multivalent and always retain necessary cosmic valences. A light or form in the shadows, for instance, can signify not only the creation of the World but also the appearance of man, the beginning of History. In a ritual context the same symbolism refers to both death and resurrection, which in itself is a repetition of a cosmogony. Shadow symbolism, in sum, consists of three simultaneous categories: cosmology, anthropocosmology, and anthropology.

Functionally, therefore, symbols translate the human condition into cosmic terms, and *vice versa*, such that solidarity and confidence exists between the two. This leads the individual person or culture to a comprehension of the universal, as expressed in concrete exemplary terms. "Par conséquent, 'vivre' un symbole et en déchiffrer correctement le message équivaut à accéder à l'universel. Transformer une expérience individuelle par le symbolisme équivaut à l'ouvrir vers l'Esprit."

B177 "The Structure of Religious Symbolism." In *Proceedings of the IXth International Congress for the History of Religions*. Tokyo: Maruzen, 1960, pp. 506-12. Part of B162.

B178 "Impressions of Japan." In *Proceedings of the IXth International Congress for the History of Religions*. Tokyo: Maruzen, 1960, pp. 838-40.

B179 "Encounters at Ascona." In *Spiritual Disciplines*. Ed. by J. Campbell. Eranos Yearbook, 4; Bollingen Series, 30. New York: Pantheon Books, 1960, pp. xvii-xxi. Cf. B123.

Describes characteristics and contributions of Eranos gatherings at Ascona: a bringing together of scholars from different disciplines concerned with "the human mind and spirit"; an encounter and confrontation with the unknown, leading to new "breakthroughs," new universes of spiritual meanings; hope that a "new humanism" might emerge from such encounters; need for an intelligent and sympathetic hermeneutics; interest in spiritual disciplines and mystical techniques as revealing "conquests of the human spirit" neglected in the recent West.

1961

B180 "Die Amerikaner in Ozeanien und der eschatologische Nacktkult." *Antaios* (1961) 3:201-14. Translation of B172, which has further references.

B181 "Divinities: Art and the Divine." In *Encyclopedia of World Art*. London and New York: McGraw-Hill, 1961, vol. 4, cols. 382-87. Translations: German B168. French B221.

Art among archaic and folk cultures, which lack philosophical vocabularies, translates religious experiences and metaphysical conceptions of the world into concrete expressive forms. On the other hand, God, it is believed, reveals himself to man in forms without limiting himself to those forms.

B182 "Mythes et symboles de la corde." *Eranos-Jahrbuch* (1961) 29:109-37. Published also as B173, which has additional references.

B183 "History of Religions and a New Humanism." *History of Religions* (1961) 1:1-8. Reprinted in *Criterion* (1961) 1:8-11. Revised in A95 chap. 1. Translations: German as B189 and in A105. Revised French in A99.

A good introduction to Eliade's view of the nature and significance of the History of Religions. The discipline is defined by a creative "tension" between historical and phenomenological approaches, although the emphasis is on phenomenological approaches concerned with structures and meanings. Much of the article is what Eliade takes to be various "antireductionist" claims for the "irreducible" and "autonomous" nature of the approach of the History of Religions. Also emphasizes the possible cultural benefits of a "creative hermeneutics" which may lead to a "new humanism." See A95 for additional annotation.

B184 "Recent Works on Shamanism. A Review Article." *History of Religions* (1961) 1:152-86.

Attempts to update the essential bibliography on shamanism since Eliade wrote *Le Chamanisme et les techniques archaïques de l'extase* A46. The review article also provides a summary of his views of shamanism.

B185 "The Myths of the Modern World." *Jubilee* (1961) 8:16-20. Reprinted as B229. Translation of B113, which has additional references.

B186 "Note pour un humanisme." *La Nouvelle Revue Française* (1961) 9:872-78. Reprinted in A75 foreword. English translation in A82.

B187 "Mythologies asiatiques et folklore sud-est européen, Le plongeon cosmogonique." *Revue de l'Histoire des Religions* (1961) 160:157-212. See Romanian B128. Revised as B192. Fully revised in A97 chap. 3. Revised English translation in A102.

B188 "Les Loups et les Daces, Introduction à une histoire religieuse de la Dacie." *Revue des Études Roumaines*

(1961) 7-8:225-28. Revision of B165, which has further references.

1962

B189 "Gedanken zu einem neuen Humanismus." *Antaios* (1962) 4: 113-19. Translation of B183, which has further references.

B190 "Marginalien zum Wesen der Maske." *Antaios* (1962) 4: 396-404. Revised English publication B210.

B191 "Les élites modernes tentent de retrouver, par l'initiation, un monde perdu." *Arts* (Dec. 5, 1962) p. 5. Excerpt from A77 chap. 9. Cf. English in A79.

B192 "Le Créateur et son 'Ombre.'" *Eranos-Jahrbuch* (1962) 30: 211-39. See Romanian B128. Revision of B187, which has additional references.

B193 "'Cargo-cults' and Cosmic Regeneration." In *Millennial Dreams in Action*. Ed. by S.L. Thrupp. The Hague: Mouton, 1962, pp. 139-43. Revised in A82 part of chap. 3. French publication in A75.

1963

B194 "Die Mythologie des Erinnerns und des Vergessens." *Antaios* (1963) 5:28-48. Translation of B198, which has further references.

B195 "Two Spiritual Traditions in Rumania." *Arena*, London (1963) 11:15-25. Translation, see B114. Original Romanian H875.

Describes the Romanian character as a polarity of contrary historical tendencies that revolve around an ecumenical vision of life. As tensions expand, greater syntheses and levels of values result. This is particularly true of the Romanian diaspora.

B196 "Survivals and Camouflages of Myths." *Diogenes* (1963) 41:1-25. Reprinted in A79 chap. 9. See French publication B197.

B197 "Survivances et camouflage des mythes." *Diogène* (1963) 41:3-27. Reprinted in A77 chap. 9. See English publication B196.

B198 "Mythologies of Memory and Forgetting." *History of Religions* (1963) 2:329-44. Reprinted in A79 chap. 7. French publication B201 and in A77. German translation B194.

B199 "The History of Religions in Retrospect: 1912-1962." *The Journal of Bible and Religion* (1963) 31:98-109. Revised publication in A95 chap. 2. Translations: French in A99. German in A105.

A good overview of the History of Religions during a fifty-year period. During the twentieth century, the History of Religions became highly specialized, and here Eliade formulates scholarly contributions in terms of five major approaches: the sociological, psychological, ethnological, historical, and phenomenological. See A95 for additional annotation.

B200 "Yoga and Modern Philosophy." *Journal of General Education* (1963) 15:124-37. Reprinted from A63 parts of intro. and chaps. 1-2. Cf. French in A53 and German in A70.

B201 "Mythologie de la mémoire et de l'oubli." *La Nouvelle Revue Française* (1963) 11:597-620. Reprinted in A77 chap. 7. See English B198, which has further references.

B202 "La méthode de Roger Godel." In *Roger Godel. De l'humanisme à l'humain*. Paris: Les Belles Lettres, 1963, pp. 99-105.

Review article primarily of Godel's *Essais sur l'expérience liberatrice*. Godel, a specialist in cardiology, was concerned with problems of the spirit as well as the heart. A scientist and practitioner, he also applied himself to larger questions of epistemology in science, transcendence of thought, freedom. He was interested in the *jivan-mukta* who can live "on the level of a tension of complementaries: pure consciousness and lived experience."

1964

B203 "Introduction à l'étude des mythes." *Acta Philosophica et Theologica* (1964) 2:145-59. Reprinted from A77 chap. 1. Cf. English in A79.

B204 "Myth and Reality." In *Alienation, The Cultural Climate of Modern Man*. Ed. with intro. by G. Sykes. New York: Braziller, 1964, vol. 2, pp. 748-53. Reprinted from A79 parts of chaps. 4 and 9. French publication in A77.

B205 "Die Suche nach den 'Ursprüngen der Religion.'" *Antaios* (1964) 6:1-18. Translation of B213, which has additional references.

B206 "Notes sur le journal d'Ernst Jünger." *Antaios* (1964) 6:488-92.

Comments on Jünger's *Journal* and its literary style.

B207 "The Pattern of Initiation." In *Bear, Man and God*. Ed. by F.L. Utley. New York: Random House, 1964, pp. 190-93. Reprinted from A68 part of chap. 8. French publication in A58. German translation in A73.

B208 "Rosa del Conte: *Mihail Eminescu o dell'Assoluto*." *Belfagor. Rassegna di varia umanità* (1964) 19:367-71.

A review article. Eminescu's works left a profound impression on Eliade's own thought and spiritual development even from a very early age. Here Eliade acclaims Eminescu not as a "systematic philosopher" but as a magnificent poet and encyclopedist whose creations reveal a passion for hermeticism, magic, and archaic Romanian folkloric traditions. Eminescu had a cosmic imagination and an obsession with time. He was a "universal man" in whom was incarnated a "coexistence of contraries."

B209 "Beauty and Faith." In *Bridges of Human Understanding*. Ed. by J. Nef. New York: University Publishers, 1964, pp. 121-23.

A brief reflection on the artistic genius of Marc Chagall.

B210 "Masks: Mythical and Ritual Origins." In *Encyclopedia of World Art*. London and New York: McGraw-Hill, 1964, vol.

9, cols. 520-25. German B190.

Analyzes different kinds of "magico-religious transformation brought about by wearing masks." Claims that masks are always bound up with idea of time: wearer transcends earthly time and "personal temporal identity," thus becoming something "other."

B211 "Paradis et Utopie, Géographie mythique et eschatologie." *Eranos-Jahrbuch* (1964) 32:211-34. Revised in A99 chap. 6. Translations: English as B231 and revised in A95. German in A105.

B212 "Mythologie, ontologie, histoire." In *Festschrift für Ad. E. Jensen*. Ed. by E. Haberland. Munich: Klaus Renner, 1964, vol. 1, pp. 123-33. Also published in A77 chap. 6. English translation in A79.

B213 "The Quest for the 'Origins' of Religion." *History of Religions* (1964) 4:154-69. Revised in A95 chap. 3. Translations: French in A99. German as B205 and in A105.

Formulates a wide-ranging and thought-provoking essay around the theme of the human nostalgia and obsession for "origins." The nineteenth-century antireligious positivism and the nineteenth-century interest in religious phenomena were similar in their nostalgia for the primordial, for the absolute origins. In addition, Müller, Tylor, Lang, Schmidt, Freud, and others tended to use positivistic approaches in their quest for the origins of religion. One now realizes that the origins of religion cannot be reached. While recognizing that all data are historical, Eliade criticizes modern historicism or historical reductionism. One must ask what historically conditioned documents reveal about the meaning of religious experience and about the nature of the human being. See A95 for additional annotation.

B214 "Shamanism in Southeast Asia and Oceania." *International Journal of Parapsychology* (1964) 6, no. 3:329-61. Published also in A81 chap. 10, which is a translation of the French in A46. German translation in A59.

B215 "Mystery and Spiritual Regeneration in Extra-European Religions." In *Man and Transformation*. Ed. by J. Campbell. Eranos Yearbook, 5; Bollingen Series, 30. New York: Pantheon Books, 1964, pp. 3-36. Translation of B135, which has further references.

B215a "Gefüge und Funktion der Schöpfungsmythen." In *Die Schöpfungsmythen*. Zurich: Benziger Verlag Einsiedeln, 1964, foreword, pp. 9-34. Translation of B163.

B216 "Sur la permanence du sacré dans l'art contemporain." *XXe Siècle* (1964) 26:3-10. Translations: German B217. English B218.

1965

B217 "Notizen über das Heilige in der modernen Kunst." *Antaios* (1965) 7:305-9. Translation of B216, which has additional references.

B218 "The Sacred and the Modern Artist." *Criterion* (1965) 4:22-24. Translation of B216, which has additional references.

Modern artists are no longer interested in traditional religious art, but the "sacred" has not completely disappeared from modern art. It is "camouflaged in forms, purposes and meanings which are apparently 'profane.'" Specific characteristics of modern art can be given religious interpretations, especially by relating them to archaic "cosmic religion."

B219 "Crisis and Renewal in History of Religions." *History of Religions* (1965) 5:1-17; and in *New Theology No. 4*. Ed. by M.E. Marty and D.G. Peerman. New York: Macmillan, 1967, pp. 19-38. Revised in A95 chap. 4. Translations: French in A99. German as B232 and in A105.

One of Eliade's most important essays on the present state of the History of Religions. The discipline is now in crisis. He says that excessive specialization has resulted in timidity, cautiousness, inhibition, and provincialism, with a resultant loss of creativity and cultural synthesis. Nevertheless, there is the possibility for renewal, especially through "creative hermeneutics." Only when the History of Religions realizes itself as a synthetic, integrative, total discipline can it be truly creative. Such a creative hermeneutics will lead to the creation of new cultural values and to the opening of Western thought to new perspectives and to the possibilities of a universal type of culture. See A95 for additional annotation.

B220 "L'initiation et le monde moderne." In *Initiation*. Ed. by C.J. Bleeker. International Association for the History of Religions, 1964. Leiden: Brill, 1965, pp. 1-14. Revised in A99 chap. 7. Revised English publication in A95. German translation in A105.

B221 "Les mythes qui deviennent des idoles." *Janus. L'Homme, son histoire et son avenir* (1965) 5:59-63. Revised translation. See German B168 and English B181.

B222 "Archaic Myth and Historical Man." *McCormick Quarterly*. Special Supplement: *Myth and Modern Man* (1965) 18:23-36. Condensed publication of A79 chaps. 1-2, and of A67 chap. 4. Part published in German in A57. French publication in A77 and in A84.

B223 "The Oddest Graduate School in the United States." *The University of Chicago Magazine* (1965) 57:18-22.

1966

B224 "In Memoriam: Paul Tillich." *Criterion* (1966) 5:10-15. Revised as B226.

B225 "Initiation Dreams and Visions Among the Siberian Shamans." In *The Dream and Human Societies*. Ed. by G.E. von Grunebaum and R. Callois. Los Angeles and Berkeley: University of California Press, 1966, pp. 331-40. Translation of B243, which has further references.

B226 "Paul Tillich and the History of Religions." In *The Future of Religions*. Ed. by J.C. Brauer. New York: Harper and Row, 1966, pp. 31-36. Revision of B224.

A tribute to Tillich, pointing to his interest in the History of Religions; his need for dialogue with many religions; and his propensity for systematization. He was concerned with "existential history," or *Geschichte*, and in that sense he was a foremost thinker of his times.

B227 "Australian Religions, Part I: An Introduction." *History of Religions* (1966) 6:108-34. Reprinted in A103 chap. 1. French translation in A101.

B228 "Significations du mythe." In *Le Langage II*. Ed. by Société de Philosophie de Langue Française. Geneva:

1966, pp. 167-79, and "Discussion," pp. 184-87. Revised in A99 chap. 5. English publication without "Discussion" as B242, which is revised in A95. German translation as B233, which is revised in A105.

B229 "Myths, Dreams and Mysteries." In *Myth and Symbol*. Ed. by F.W. Dillistone. London: Society for the Publication of Christian Knowledge, 1966, pp. 35-50. Reprint of B185. See B113.

B230 "Les Bohémiennes." *La Revue de Paris* (Dec. 1966) pp. 29-58. Reprinted in A122 pp. 293-312. Translation of short story "La Ţigănci" in A80, which has additional references. See English B270.

B231 "Paradise and Utopia, Mythical Geography and Eschatology." In *Utopias and Utopian Thought*. Ed. by F.E. Manuel. Boston: Houghton Mifflin, 1966, pp. 260-80. Translation of B211, which has additional references.

1967

B232 "Krisis und Erneuerung der Religionswissenschaft." *Antaios* (1967) 9:1-20. Translation of B219, which has additional references.

B233 "Schöpfungsmythos und Heilsgeschichte." *Antaios* (1967) 9:329-45. Translation of B228, which has further references.

B234 "Historical Events and Structural Meaning in Tension." *Criterion* (1967) 6:29-31.

While reporting on the status of his various research projects, Eliade formulates the central methodological problems and issues facing the historian of religions. He reveals some of his own methodological and epistemological position.

B235 *Encyclopaedia Britannica*. Chicago: Encyclopaedia Britannica, 1967, 24 vols. Articles: "Dualism"; "Myth"; "Shamanism." Latter two are condensed from A79 chaps. 1-4 and 6; and from A81 chaps. 9-10 and 15. Cf. French in A77 and A46. German in A81.

B236 *Encyclopedia of Philosophy*. Ed. by P. Edwards. New York: Macmillan, 1967, 8 vols. Articles: "Blaga,

Lucian"; "Ionescu, Nae"; "Rădulescu-Motru, Constantin"; and "Rumanian Philosophy."

B237 "On Understanding Primitive Religions." In *Glaube, Geist, Geschichte. Festschrift für Ernst Benz*. Ed. by G. Müller and W. Zeller. Leiden: Brill, 1967, pp. 498-505. Reprinted in A103 pref. Translations: French in A101. German as B247.

Claims little progress has been made in understanding "primitive" (archaic, traditional, preliterate) religions. Criticizes earlier naturalistic and later historical approaches. They have not given rise to an adequate hermeneutics. The nature and creativity of primitive religions can only be understood by a hermeneutics that recognizes the religious basis and religious frame of reference of primitive religions. See A103 for additional annotation.

B238 "Australian Religions, Part II: An Introduction." *History of Religions* (1967) 6:208-35. Reprinted in A103 chap. 2. French translation in A101.

B239 "Australian Religions, Part III: Initiation Rites and Secret Cults." *History of Religions* (1967) 7:61-90. Reprinted in A103 chap. 3. French translation in A101.

B240 "Australian Religions, Part IV: The Medicine Men and Their Supernatural Models." *History of Religions* (1967) 7:159-83. Reprinted in A103 chap. 4. French translation in A101.

B241 "Cultural Fashions and the History of Religions." In *The History of Religions. Essays on the Problem of Understanding*. Ed. by J.M. Kitagawa. Essays in Divinity, 1. Chicago: University of Chicago Press, 1967, pp. 21-38. A87. Published also as Monday Evening Papers, 8. Middletown, Conn.: Center for Advanced Studies, Wesleyan University, 1967, 22 pp.; and in A113 chap. 1. French in A127. See A87 for annotation.

B242 "Cosmogonic Myth and 'Sacred History.'" *Religious Studies* (1967) 2:171-83. Revised in A95 chap. 5. See French publication B228, which has additional references.

B243 "Rêves et vision initiatiques chez les chamans sibériens." In *Le Rêve et les sociétés humaines*. Ed. by G.E. von

Grunebaum and R. Callois. Paris: Gallimard, 1967, pp. 315-23. Reprinted from A46 part of chap. 2. Translations: German in A59. English as B225 and in A81.

B244 "Briser le toit de la maison, Symbolisme architectonique et physiologie subtile." In *Studies in Mysticism and Religion*. Ed. by E.E. Urbach *et al*. Jerusalem: Magnes Press, 1967, pp. 131-39. Revised part of B153.

B245 "Marc Chagall et l'amour du cosmos." *XXe Siècle* (1967) 29:137-39.

1968

B246 "'Chamanisme' chez les Roumains?" *Acta Historica*, Rome (1968) 8:147-57. Reprinted in A97 chap. 6. English translation in A102.

B247 "Zum verständnis primitiver Religionen." *Antaios* (1968) 10:337-45. Translation of B237, which has additional references.

B248 *Encyclopaedia Universalis*. France: Encyclopaedia Universalis, 1968- . Articles: "Ancêtres (Culte des)"; "Chamanisme"; "Création: Les mythes de la création"; "Déluge (Mythes du)"; "Dieux et Déesses"; "Enfers et Paradis."

B249 "Mythes de combat et de repos, dyades et polarités." *Eranos-Jahrbuch* (1968) 36:59-111. Reprinted in A99 chap. 8. English publication in A95. German translation in A105.

B250 "Australian Religions, Part V: Death, Eschatology, and Some Conclusions." *History of Religions* (1968) 7: 244-68. Reprinted in A103 chap. 5. French translation in A101.

B251 "The Forge and the Crucible: A Postscript." *History of Religions* (1968) 8:74-88. Reprinted as the "Postscript" in the new ed. of *The Forge and the Crucible* A74, Harper Torchbooks, 1971, pp. 179-99.

Attempts to update the essential bibliography on the religious meanings of metallurgy and alchemy since he wrote *Forgerons et alchimistes* A55. Briefly summarizes his own views on these topics.

B252 "Comparative Religion: Its Past and Future." In *Knowledge and the Future of Man*. Ed. by W.J. Ong. New York: Holt, Rinehart and Winston, 1968, pp. 245-54. Revised and enlarged in A95 parts of chaps. 1, 3-4. Translations: French in A99. German in A105.

B253 "Notes on the Symbolism of the Arrow." In *Religions in Antiquity. Essays in Memory of Erwin Ramsdell Goodenough*. Ed. by J. Neusner. Leiden: Brill, 1968, pp. 463-75.

Discusses certain aspects of arrow symbolism. After reviewing several categories of phenomena involving arrow symbolism, the article focuses on "myths of the chain of arrows" and "arrows in mystical techniques and mystical imagination."

1969

B254 "South American High Gods, Part I." *History of Religions* (1969) 8:338-54.

Based on a course given in 1964. With the exception of the last section which concerns the Araucanians of Chile and Argentina, this essay analyzes the High Gods of the Fuegians. A comparative analysis of the three Fuegian tribes reveals the complexity of their High Gods and the coexistence of other religious phenomena with the belief in High Gods. For Part II, see B263.

B255 "Dragoş et la 'chasse rituelle.'" *Revue des Études Roumaines* (1969) 11-12:31-59. Reprinted in A97 chap. 4. English translation in A102.

1970

B256 "Alchemy and Science in China." *History of Religions* (1970) 10:178-82.

Review article of N. Sivin, *Chinese Alchemy: Preliminary Studies*.

B257 "The Meaning of Myth." In *Man, Myth and Magic. An Illustrated Encyclopedia of the Supernatural*. Ed. by R. Cavendish. London: Purnell, for BPC Publishing, 1970, vol. 1, no. 8, pp. 213-16. Condensed summary of several works.

B258 "Bei den Zigeunerinnen." In *Die Schwartze Grube und andere rumänische Erzählungen*. Stuttgart: Horst Erdmann Verlag, 1970, pp. 214-49. Translation of "La Ţigănci" in A80, which has additional references.

B259 "Notes for a Dialogue." In *The Theology of Altizer. Critique and Response*. Ed. by J.B. Cobb. Philadelphia: Westminster, 1970, pp. 234-41.

Discusses Thomas Altizer's *Mircea Eliade and the Dialectic of the Sacred* D3 by formulating six points of disagreement. For example, Eliade says he does not want to establish the archaic and the Oriental as the "model" for the modern West and does not call for some "return" to a premodern mode of existence. Most significant is the claim that Altizer has misunderstood the dialectic of the sacred, since it does not consist of establishing the sacred by abolishing the profane within which the sacred manifests itself.

1971

B260 "Space--Sacred and Profane." *The Center Magazine* (1971) 41:53-54. Condensed from A67 chap. 1. Cf. German in A57 and French in A84.

B261 "A Cosmic Territorial Imperative?" *Center Report* (1971) 4, no. 2:22-26.

Illustrations of sacred, cosmic, and meaningful "existential worlds" in which persons and societies live. Examples: the world of a professor; Jews and the Temple; a Bororo village in Brazil; Romulus and the founding of Rome; Angkor in Cambodia; Brancusi's art.

B262 "L'impossible désacralisation." *La France Catholique* (March 12, 1971). Extract from A99.

B263 "South American High Gods, Part II." *History of Religions* (1971) 10:234-66.

Based on a course given in 1964. Unlike Part I with its focus on the High Gods of the Fuegians, this essay consists of very brief descriptions of the beliefs of the Botocado, the Tupi-Guarani, various Cariban and numerous other tribes. More extensive treatments are given of the Tacana of Bolivia and the Kogi of Colombia. The most detailed presentation is taken from Reichel-Dolmatoff's research on the Desana, a small Amazonian tribe. The richness and complexity of the morphology of South American High Gods becomes evident. For Part I, see B254.

B264 "Spirit, Light, and Seed." *History of Religions* (1971) 11:1-30. Reprinted in A113 chap. 6. French in A127.

B265 "Shaman." In *Man, Myth and Magic. An Illustrated Encyclopedia of the Supernatural*. Ed. by R. Cavendish. London: Purnell, for BPC Publishing, 1971, vol. 6, no. 91, pp. 2546-49. Condensed summary of several works.

1972

B266 "Zalmoxis." *History of Religions* (1972) 11:257-302. Translation of A97 chap. 2. Published also in A102.

B267 "Expériences mystiques chez les primitifs: le chamanisme." In *Encyclopédie des mystiques*. Dir. by M.M. Davy and R. Laffont, 1972, pp. 1-35. Summary article of B124, which has additional references.

B268 "Gayōmart et la Mandragore." In *Ex orbe religionum. Studia Geo Widengren*. Leiden: Brill, 1972, vol. 2, pp. 65-74. Part revised as B286.

Notes on Gayōmart in Iranian mythology and mandragora plant motif. Presents several archaic themes with cultural parallelisms and interpretations.

1973

B269 "The Sacred in the Secular World." *Cultural Hermeneutics* (1973) 1:101-13. (The title of the journal was changed to *Philosophy and Social Criticism* in 1978.)

In some respects, this is one of the author's most important methodological articles. Eliade has stated that he has intentionally avoided formulating his methodology. However, in the first half of this essay, he presents some very explicit formulations. The emphasis is on phenomenology and synchronicity. The historian of religions "must become a phenomenologist of religion" because of his or her concern for meaning, which is given through the intentionality of structure.

"The structure of the sacred in the human consciousness is built on the structure of synchronicity, as opposed to the diachronic structure of radical historicism." The second half of the essay deals with the important role of the sacred in the modern secular world and related topics found throughout the author's writings.

B270 "With the Gypsy Girls." *Denver Review* (1973) 8, no. 2: 13-58. Translation of short story "La Ţigănci" in A80, which has additional references. See A92 for annotation.

B271 "Myth, Nineteenth and Twentieth Centuries." In *Dictionary of the History of Ideas*. New York: Scribners, 1973, vol. 3, pp. 307-18.

Attempts to delineate the "important theories of myth from the late nineteenth century to the present day": Müller, Tylor, and Lang; astral-mythology and Pan-Babylonianism; "the priority of ritual" (Harrison, Cornford, Murray, Hocart, etc.); British and Scandinavian "Myth and Ritual" schools; Freud and Jung; "from Bachofen to cultural morphology" (Frobenius, Jensen, W. Otto, etc.); "recent trends in history of religions" (Malinowski, Pettazzoni, a good summary of Eliade on myth, etc.); "philosophers and myth" (Cassirer, Langer, Gusdorf, Ricoeur, Durand, etc.); "the folkloristic approach"; Lévi-Strauss. Ends with a useful bibliography.

B272 "On the Terror of History." In *Dimensions of Man*. Ed. by H.P. Simonson and J.B. Magee. New York: Harper and Row, 1973, pp. 164-68. Reprinted from A51 parts of chap. 4.

B273 "Uniforme de general." *Ethos*, Paris (1973) 1:26-59. Reprinted in A115.

B274 "Notes on the Căluşari." In *The Gaster Festschrift. The Journal of the Ancient Near Eastern Society of Columbia University* (1973) 5:115-22.

Examines a popular Romanian dance, the *căluş* (derived from the Romanian term for "horse"), especially by analyzing the origin and function of the *căluşari* and the meaning of the mythico-ritual scenario associated with this group of dancers.

B275 "Dictionaries and Encyclopedias." *History of Religions* (1973) 12:288-95.

Review article of *Dictionary of Comparative Religion*, edited by S.G.F. Brandon; *Enciclopedia delle religioni*, first three volumes of six-volume encyclopedia, planned and organized by A. di Nola. Eliade estimates that A. di Nola wrote at least 80 percent of the text. When all six volumes are published, "*Enciclopedia delle religioni* will constitute the largest and the most up-to-date presentation of primitive religion published thus far."

B276 "Occultism and Freemasonry in Eighteenth Century Europe." *History of Religions* (1973) 13:89-91.

Review article of R. Le Forestier, *La Franc-Maçonnerie Templiere et Occultiste aux XVIIIe et XIXe siècle.*

B277 "The Dragon and the Shaman. Notes on a South American Mythology." In *Man and his Salvation. Studies in Memory of S.G.F. Brandon*. Ed. by E.J. Sharpe and J.R. Hinnells. Manchester: Manchester University Press, 1973, pp. 99-105.

Discusses some relations between myth and "history" in the Peruvian tribe of the Campa. Analyzes how the cosmogonic myth and other myths of origin allow the Campa to integrate a real historical event, such as being conquered by Spanish invaders, into a sacred history; this gives meaning to the tragic event and provides a framework for further historical actions.

B278 "The Comparative Study of Religions." In *Marxism, Communism and Western Society. A Comparative Encyclopedia*. Ed. by C.D. Kernig. New York: Herder and Herder, 1973, vol. 7, pp. 163-66. Summation taken from several works.

B279 "Myth." In *Readings on the Sociology of Religion*. Ed. by T. O'Dea and J. O'Dea. Englewood Cliffs, N.J.: Prentice-Hall, 1973, pp. 70-78. Reprinted from A79 chap. 1. Cf. French in A77.

B280 "The Cult of the Mandragora in Romania." *The University of Chicago Magazine* (1973), 65, no. 4:8-16. Reprinted from A102 chap. 7. French as B52 and in A97.

1974

B281 "Mitologiás de la muerte: una introducción" (Mythologies of Death: An Introduction). *Dialogos*, Mexico (1974) 58:4-10. See B302.

B282 "On the Slavic Matriarchy." *History of Religions* (1974) 14:74-78.

Review article of E. Gasparini, *Il Matriarcato Slavo. Antropologia Culturale dei Protoslavi*.

B283 "On Prehistoric Religions." *History of Religions* (1974) 14:140-47.

Review article of A. Marshak, *The Roots of Civilization. The Cognitive Beginnings of Man's First Art, Symbol, and Notation*; J. Cauvin, *Religions néolithiques de Syro-Palestine. Documents*; S.I. Rudenko, *Frozen Tombs of Siberia. The Pazyryk Burials of Iron-Age Horsemen*, trans. with a pref. by M.W. Thompson. Eliade claims that "Marshak has succeeded in disclosing a new dimension of *Homo sapiens*' mode of being in the world."

B284 "The Occult and the Modern World." *Journal of the Philadelphia Association for Psychoanalysis* (1974) 1, no. 3:195-213. Reprinted in A113 chap. 4; and in *The University of Chicago Magazine* (Summer 1976) pp. 18-21. French in A127.

B285 "A Fourteen Year Old Photograph." *The Louisburg College Journal* (1974) 8:3-15. Translation of short story "O fotografie veche de 14 ani" in A80.

B286 "Adam, le Christ et la Mandragore." In *Mélanges d'Histoire des Religions. Offerts à Henri-Charles Puech*. Paris: Sous le patronage et avec le concours du Collège de France et de la section des Sciences Religieuses de l'École Pratique des Hautes Études, 1974, pp. 611-15. Revised part of B268.

1975

B287 "Le Macranthrope." *Cahiers de l'Est* (1975) 2:5-25. Translation of short story "Um om mare" in A80 and as H876. English in A93.

B288 "Incognito la Buchenwald." *Ethos* (1975) 2:85-106. Reprinted in A115.

B289 "Some Observations on European Witchcraft." *History of Religions* (1975) 14:149-72. Reprinted in A113 chap. 5. Part published as B292. French in A127.

Discusses two controversial problems: the "origins" of Western witchcraft and the so-called witches' orgies. The History of Religions reveals the inadequacy of past accounts of the origins of Western witchcraft. Comparative analysis discloses most of the same features in Indo-Tibetan yoga and magic, Romanian folkloric parallels, etc., and helps one to understand the complexity and meaning of Western witchcraft. The real or imaginary witches' orgies reveal a protest against the dominant religious and social institutions and a religious nostalgia to return to an archaic non-Christian mode of being. Contemporary youth culture discloses some similar dissatisfactions and nostalgias.

B290 "Orphée et l'orphisme." In *Sens et existence: en hommage à Paul Ricoeur*. Dir. by G.B. Madison. Paris: Éditions du Seuil, 1975, pp. 46-59. Reprinted in A126 pp. 176-91.

1976

B291 "What the Symbols Reveal." In *Eros and Nihilism*. Ed. by C.P. Bigger and D.B. Convay. Dubuque, Iowa: Kendall/Hunt Pub. Co., 1976, pp. 127-29. Extracts from A68, A82, A83.

B292 "Some European Secret Cults." In *Festgabe für Otto Hofler zum 75 Geburtstag*. Wien: Wilhelm Branmiller, 1976, pp. 190-204. Part of B289, which has additional references.

B293 "Recent Works on Prehistoric Religion." *History of Religions* (1976) 16:178-85.

Review article of E. Anati, *Evoluzione e stile nell' arte rupestre camuna; Symposium International sur les Religions de la Prêhistoire, Valcamonica, 18-23 Septembre 1972*, published under the direction of E. Anati; and M. Gimbutas, *The Gods and Goddesses of Old Europe: 7000-3500 B.C. Myths, Legends and Cult Images*.

B294 "Myths and Mythical Thought." In *Myths*. By A. Eliot, with contributions by M. Eliade and J. Campbell. New York and Maidenhead, England: McGraw-Hill, 1976, pp. 12-29. French translation as B297.

Large, rather expensive book with many spectacular color photographs. Eliade's essay is a good introduction to his views of the nature and function of myth, with a delineation of the major mythic themes.

B295 "Nostalgia for Paradise." *Parabola. Myth and the Quest for Meaning* (1976) 1, no. 1:6-15. Adapted from A71 chap. 1. Cf. French in A48 and German in A61.

B296 "Sacred Tradition and Modern Man. A Conversation with Mircea Eliade." *Parabola* (1976) 1, no. 3:74-80.

Briefly discusses initiation, esotericism, myth, alchemy, various aspects of contemporary secular society, and the possibility for a "resanctification" of work. In response to a question as to which tradition has most deeply influenced him, Eliade replies: "I consider myself deeply influenced, I can almost say 'formed' or 'shaped,' by the Indian tradition."

B297 "Les mythes et la pensée mythique." In *L'univers fantastique des mythes*. By A. Eliot, with contributions by M. Eliade and J. Campbell. Paris: Les Presses de la Connaissance, 1976, pp. 12-29. Translation of B294.

1977

B298 "Réception de M. Mircea Eliade. Discours." *Académie Royale de Langue et de Littérature Françaises*, Bruxelles (Feb. 19, 1977) pp. 16-26. Translated into Romanian as H1021.

B299 "Eliade's Interview for 'Combat.'" In *C.G. Jung Speaking. Interviews and Encounters*. Ed. by W. McGuire and R.F.C. Hull. Bollingen Series, 97. Princeton: Princeton University Press, 1977, pp. 225-34. Revised translation of B101, which is reprinted in A122 pp. 250-55.

B300 "Le chamanisme et la découverte 'primitive' de l'extase." In *Les Corps à prodiges*. Paris: Tchou, 1977, pp. 19-52. Reprint of B124, which has additional references.

B301 "Religions." *International Social Science Journal* (1977) 29, no. 4:615-27. Condensed summary, mainly of A95 chap. 2.

B302 "Mythologies of Death: An Introduction." In *Religious Encounters with Death. Insights from the History and Anthropology of Religions*. Ed. by F.E. Reynolds and E.H. Waugh. University Park: Pennsylvania State University Press, 1977, pp. 13-23. Reprinted from A113 chap. 3. French in A127. Cf. B281.

1978

B303 "Literary Imagination and Religious Structure." *Criterion* (1978) 17, no. 2:30-34. Part published also as part of Preface to *The Forbidden Forest* A119.

A refreshing article in which Eliade reveals the interdependency of his literary imagination and his work as a historian of religions. The writing of fiction, particularly narratives, is for him an "experience in method" and "an *instrument of knowledge*." He, like other writers, believes in "the objectivity and the intellectual value of the *mundus imaginalis*" that is also expressed, say, in dreams, myths, and rituals.

B304 "Les religions dont nous heritons. Un dialogue entre Mircea Eliade et Georges Dumézil." *Les Nouvelles Littéraires* (Oct. 27, 1978) 56, no. 2658:17-18.

B305 "The Myth of Alchemy." *Parabola* (1978) 3, no. 3:7-23. French publication in A122 pp. 157-67.

An excellent introduction to many of the myths, rituals, techniques, and themes analyzed in *The Forge and the Crucible* A74. Updates his analysis with research that has been published in the 1960s and 1970s. A major topic in this article, which did not appear in A74, although it has been incorporated in the text of the 1977 French ed., is the decisive role alchemy played "in the cultural metamorphosis that made possible the triumph of the natural sciences and the industrial revolution." Analyzes Newton's attempt to integrate alchemy and the Hermetic tradition with mechanical philosophy. In modern science, "the triumph of Newton's mechanics abolished Newton's own scientific ideal."

B306 "Eugene Ionescu and 'Le Nostalgie du Paradis.'" In *The Two Faces of Ionescu*. Ed. by R.C. Lamont and M.G. Friedman. Troy, N.Y.: The Whitston Publishing Co., 1978, pp. 25-33.

C

OTHER WRITINGS: PREFACES, FOREWORDS, JOURNALS FOUNDED AND EDITED, TRANSLATIONS, AND BOOK REVIEWS

1926

C1 *Revista Universitară*. University of Bucharest, 1926, three issues only. Founded and edited.

1934

C2 Lawrence, T.E. *Revolta în deşert*. Bucharest: Fundaţia Regală pentru Literatură şi Artă, 1934, 2 vols. Translation of *Revolt in the Desert*.

1938

C3 *Zalmoxis. Revue des Études Religieuses*. Paris: Librairie Orientaliste Paul Geuthner, 1938 to 1942, three volumes only. Journal founded and edited.

C4 *Zalmoxis* (1938) 1:226-49. Reviews of the following:

R. Pettazzoni, *La confessione dei peccati*
C. Hentze, *Frühchinesische Bronzen und Kultdarstellungen*
R. Dussaud, *Les Découvertes de Ras Shamra (Ugarit) et l'Ancien Testament*
A. Coomaraswamy, *Elements of Buddhist Iconography*
H.M. Ransome, *The Sacred Bee in Ancient Times and Folklore*
A. Boissier, *Mantique babylonienne et mantique hittite*
A. Christensen, *Les Gestes des Rois dans les traditions de l'Iran antique*
G. Dumézil, *Flamen-Brahman*

Wang Tch'ang-Tche, *La Philosophie morale de Wang Yang-ming*
G.S. Marr, *Sex in Religion. An Historical Survey*
J. Bacot, *La Vie de Marpa le "traducteur"*
F. Cumont, *L'Egypte des astrologues*

1939

C5 *Zalmoxis* (1939) 2:168-69. Reviews of:

A. Coomaraswamy, *The Rig Veda as Land-Nâma-Bók*
A.C. March, *A Buddhist Bibliography*

C6 Buck, P. *Inger Luptător*. Bucharest: Fundaţia Regală pentru Literatură şi Artă, 1939, 264 pp. Translation of *Fighting Angel*.

1948

C7 *Critique. Revue Générale des Publications Françaises et Etrangères* (1948) 29:897-908. Review of:

P. Laviosa Zambotti, *Les Origines et la diffusion de la civilisation*

C8 *Luceafărul. Revista Scriitorilor Români în Exil*. Paris, 1948- . Journal founded and edited.

C9 *Revue de l'Histoire des Religions* (1948) 133-34:211-14, 222-26. Reviews of:

E.D. van Buren, *Symbols of the Gods in Mesopotamian Art*
F.K. Numazawa, *Die Weltanfänge in der japanischen Mythologie*
R. Pettazzoni, *Miti e Leggende*

1949

C10 *Bibliotheca Orientalis* (1949) 6, no. 6:192-93. Review of:

G.R. Levy, *The Gate of Horn*

C11 Laviosa Zambotti, P. *Les Origines et la diffusion de la civilisation*. Translated by J. Gouillard. Paris: Payot, 1949, 468 pp. Preface.

C12 *Paru* (1949) 51:104-5. Review of:

G. Dumézil, *Loki*

C13 *Revue de l'Histoire des Religions* (1949) 135-36:105-8, 115-17, 122-24. Reviews of:

E. de Martino, *Il mondo magico*
Art and Thought (Coomaraswamy Festschrift)
A. Runeberg, *Witches, Demons and Fertility Magic*

1950

C14 *Revue de l'Histoire des Religions* (1950) 137-38:108-10, 219-21, 253-55. Reviews of:

G. van der Leeuw, *La Religion dans son essence et ses manifestations*
C. Hentze, *Die Sakralbronzen und ihre Bedeutung in der frühchinesischen Kulturen*
H. Webster, *Taboo*

1951

C15 *Revue de l'Histoire des Religions* (1951) 139-40:117-18, 120-21, 246-49. Reviews of:

L. Vannicelli, *La religione dei Lolo*
W. Koppers, *Die Bhil in Zentralindien*
A.E. Jensen, *Mythe, Mensch und Umwelt*
M. Bouteiller, *Chamanisme et guérison magique*

1952

C16 *Critique* (1952) 8:810-11. Review of:

A. Franck-Duquesne, *Création et procréation. Métaphysique, théologie et mystique du couple humain*

C17 Godel, R. *Essais sur l'expérience libératrice*. Les Essais, 54. Paris: Gallimard, 1952, 342 pp. Preface.

C18 Vulliaud, P. *La Fin du monde*. Paris: Payot, 1952, 240 pp. Preface.

1953

C19 Gaster, T. *Les plus anciens contes de l'humanité*. Translated by S.M. Guillemin. Paris: Payot, 1953, 207 pp. Preface.

1954

C20 *Critique* (1954) 89:904-7. Review of:

H. von Beit, *Symbolik des Märchens. Versuch einer Deutung*

C21 *La Revue de Culture Européenne* (1954) 9-10:75-77. Reviews of:

C.G. Jung, *Psychology and Alchemy*
E. Frauwallner, *Geschichte der indischen Philosophie*
F. von der Leyen, *Die Welt der Märchen*

C22 *Revue de l'Histoire des Religions* (1954) 145-46:110-15, 127-28, 236-40. Reviews of:

U. Harva, *Die religiöse Vorstellungen der Mordvinen*
A.E. Wilhelm-Hooijbergh, *Peccatum. Sin and Guilt in Ancient Rome*
Archiv für Völkerkunde, 6-7
A.E. Jensen, *Mythos und Kult bei Naturvölker*
Kultur und Sprache

1955

C23 *La Nouvelle Revue Française* (June 1955) pp. 1096-99. Review of:

H. Corbin, *Avicenne et le Récit visionnaire*

C24 *Revue de l'Histoire des Religions* (1955) 147-48:101-6, 118-20, 240-41, 262-63, 267. Reviews of:

M. Haavic, *Väinämöinen, Eternal Saga*
H. Hartmann, *Der Totenkult in Irland*
G. Ränk, *Die heilige Hinterecke im Hauskult der Völker Nordosteuropas und Nordasiens*
W. Müller, *Die blane Hütte*
R. Girard, *Le Popol-Vuh*
E. Anderson, *Les Kuta*
Publication de l'Institut Italien d'Extrême Orient

1956

C25 *La Nouvelle Revue Française* (Aug. 1956) pp. 336-38. Review of:

G. Dumézil, *Aspects de la fonction guerrière chez les Indo-Européens*

C26 *La Tour Saint-Jacques* (July 1956) pp. 94-95. Reviews of:

Schamanengeschichte aus Sibirien
R.J. Forbes, *Studies in Ancient Technology*
C. Lévi-Strauss, *Tristes tropiques*

1958

C27 *Revue de l'Histoire des Religions* (1958) 153-54:118-20, 268-70. Reviews of:

H. Baumann, *Das doppelte Geschlecht*
W.E. Mühlmann, *Arioi und Mamaia*
W. Müller, *Weltbild und Kult der Kwakiutl-Indianer*
W. Schmidt, *Das Mutterrecht*

1959

C28 *Antaios. Zeitschrift für eine freie Welt*. Stuttgart: Klett Verlag, 1959- . Journal founded and edited in collaboration with E. Jünger.

1960

C29 *Revue de l'Histoire des Religions* (1960) 157-58:220-24. Reviews of:

H. Biezais, *Die Hauptgöttinnen der alten Letten*
F. Hancar, *Das Pferd in prähistorischer und früher historischer Zeit*

1961

C30 *History of Religions. An International Journal for Comparative Historical Studies*. University of Chicago

Press, 1961- . Journal founded and edited in collaboration with J.M. Kitagawa and C.H. Long.

1962

C31 *Journal of the American Oriental Society* (1962) 82:216-18. Review of:

S.N. Kramer, *Mythologies of the Ancient World*

C32 *The Journal of Religion* (1962) 42:238-39. Review of:

G. Papini, *Tutte le Opere*, Part 1

C33 Racoveanu, G. *Omenia şi "Frumseţea cea dintâi."* Freising: Editura Cuvântul, 1962, 23 pp. Foreword.

C34 Séjourné, L. *El universo de Quetzalcóatl*. Translated by A. Orfila Reynal. Mexico and Buenos Aires: Fondo de Cultura Económica, 1962, x + 205 pp. Preface.

1963

C35 Leeuw, G. van der. *Sacred and Profane Beauty. The Holy in Art*. Translated by D.E. Green. New York: Holt, Rinehart and Winston; and London: Weidenfeld and Nicolson, 1963, 357 pp. Preface.

1965

C36 Bolle, K.W. *The Persistence of Religion*. Studies in the History of Religions, Supplement to *Numen*, 8. Leiden: Brill, 1965, xviii + 134 pp. Preface.

1966

C37 *Commentary* (1966) 41, no. 3:95-96, 98. Review of:

G.G. Scholem, *On the Kabbalah and Its Symbolism*

C38 *The Journal of Religion* (1966) 46:333-34. Review of:

G. Papini, *Tutte le Opere*, Part 2

1968

C39 Munson, T.N. *Reflective Theology. Philosophical Orientations in Religion*. New Haven and London: Yale University Press, 1968, xv + 211 pp. Reprinted: Westport, Conn.: Greenwood Press, 1976. Preface.

1970

C40 Dumézil, G. *Archaic Roman Religion*. Translated by P. Krapp. Chicago and London: University of Chicago Press, 1970, 2 vols. Foreword to vol. 1.

1971

C41 Uscatescu, G., ed. *Symposion Heidegger*. Madrid: Destin, 1971, 87 pp. Preface.

1972

C42 Feldman, B., and R.D. Richardson. *The Rise of Modern Mythology, 1680-1860*. Bloomington and London: Indiana University Press, 1972, xxvii + 564 pp. Foreword.

1975

C43 Beane, W.C., and W.G. Doty, eds. *Myths, Rites, Symbols: A Mircea Eliade Reader*. Colophon Book. New York: Harper and Row, 1976, 2 vols. A112. Preface.

1978

C44 Allen, D. *Structure and Creativity in Religion. Hermeneutics in Mircea Eliade's Phenomenology and New Directions*. Religion and Reason, 14. The Hague: Mouton Publishers, 1978, xviii + 266 pp. Foreword.

Part 2
Works about Mircea Eliade

D

BOOKS

D1 Allen, D. *Structure and Creativity in Religion. Hermeneutics in Mircea Eliade's Phenomenology and New Directions.* Religion and Reason, 14. The Hague, Paris, and New York: Mouton Publishers, 1978, xviii + 266 pp.

This first major study by a philosopher of Eliade's works presents an evaluative formulation of his hermeneutical framework, grounding his methodology in his understanding of symbolism and relating his history and phenomenology of religion to various methodological problems and concepts in phenomenological philosophy. Part 1 provides a brief but rather comprehensive introduction to the major anthropological, sociological, psychological, phenomenological, and other approaches in the History of Religions during the nineteenth and twentieth centuries. Part 2 formulates the key methodological notions that provide the foundation for Eliade's phenomenology: "the dialectic of the sacred and the profane" and the "autonomous," universal, coherent, structural systems of symbolic associations. Part 3, which often goes beyond anything Eliade has written, formulates new criteria for evaluating religious phenomena, identifying the "transconscious," providing the basis for a phenomenological induction, verifying primary symbolic structures, and creating new philosophical anthropologies.

D2 ———. *Mircea Eliade et le phénomène de la religion.* Paris: Payot Éditions, forthcoming.

D3 Altizer, T.J.J. *Mircea Eliade and the Dialectic of the Sacred.* Philadelphia: Westminster Press, 1963, 219 pp. Reprinted: Westport, Conn.: Greenwood Press, 1975.

Altizer's study was the first book written on Eliade's history and phenomenology of religion. The author is "employing Eliade as a route to a new form of theology."

The first half of the book "attempts to elucidate Eliade's understanding of the sacred, and in doing so, it explores various philosophical and theological implications of his thought about which he himself has chosen to be silent." The first four chapters are on Understanding the Sacred, Archaic Religion, Christianity and Archaic Religion, and the Coincidence of Opposites. The second half of the book only infrequently mentions Eliade. Altizer believes that Eliade's dialectical understanding of the sacred and of the *coincidentia oppositorum* offers possibilities for making the sacred meaningful to modern profane consciousness. He contends that Eliade's History of Religions is largely based on an archaic and Oriental framework and is not adequate for historical Christianity or our present historical situation. Altizer's interpretation has been criticized, both by Eliade (B259) and others (D1, D2, F251, F253).

D4 Culianu, I.P. *Mircea Eliade*. Assisi: Cittadella Editrice, 1978, 186 pp.

Consists of the following main sections (translated from Italian): 1. The Philosopher's Stone (1921-1943); 2. Techniques of Salvation (Yoga, Shamanism, Alchemy); 3. Structure of the Interior Life; 4. Morphology of the Sacred and Religious History; 5. Myth and Philosophy.

D5 Devi, Maitreyi. *It Does Not Die. A Romance*. A Writers Workshop Saffronbird Book. Translation from Bengali *Na Hanyaté*, published by Manisha Granthalaya, 1974. Calcutta: P. Lal; and Connecticut: Inter-Culture Associates, 1976, 274 pp.

The author is the daughter of Surendranath Dasgupta, under whom Eliade studied and in whose house Eliade lived in 1930. During that time, Eliade had an intimate relationship with the author. This "autobiographical novel" makes clear that she felt that *Maitreyi* A12 made her "a victim of unpleasant lies." "Your book is a nightmare for me." Much of this work is her attempt to present her side of the story, the relationship as she viewed it. Although this work is a novel, the author makes little if any effort to disguise individuals, dates, places, and events.

D6 Duch, L. *Ciencia de la religión y mito. Estudios sobre la interpretación del mito*. Scripta et documenta, 22. Montserrat: Abadia, 1974, 284 pp.

This manuscript was presented as a dissertation to the Faculty of Catholic Theology of Eberhard-Karls-University of Tübingen. Over half of the book is devoted to a study of Eliade. After extensive formulations of the sacred and the profane and symbolism, the major section analyzes Eliade's interpretation of myth.

D7 Dudley, G., III. *Religion on Trial. Mircea Eliade and His Critics*. Philadelphia: Temple University Press, 1977, vii + 183 pp.

Mircea Eliade's methodology is proposed as the "leading candidate" to bring about some sense of unity and development in contemporary History of Religions. But Dudley shows that Eliade cannot unify all of the present methodological approaches since he has been continually criticized and dismissed by the "empiricists" and he cannot meet their minimal criteria for a "scientific" approach. Chapter 2 provides a valuable introduction to many of Eliade's basic concepts and values. Chapter 3 argues Eliade's History of Religions is highly normative, since it rests on a privileged ontological status granted to the "archaic ontology." Chapter 4 traces the basis of Eliade's "archaic ontology" to India and, more particularly, to Patañjali's Yoga. In the controversial final chapter, Dudley identifies Eliade as an "antihistorian" of religions within a tradition of French, deductive, synchronic, systematic approaches. He argues Eliade should avoid the confusion and contradictions in his writings arising from his frequent insistence that he is using an empirical and historical method. It is only when Eliade and his followers are clear about such an "antihistorical" "research program" that one can examine the full potential of this overall theory of religion.

D8 Kitagawa, J., and C. Long, eds. *Myths and Symbols. Studies in Honor of Mircea Eliade*. Chicago and London: University of Chicago Press, 1969, xii + 438 pp.

This *Festschrift* of twenty essays is divided into three sections: phenomenological and theoretical studies, historical studies, and literary studies. There is also a seventeen-page bibliography. Only six of the essays concern Eliade's works. With the exception of Mircea Popescu, "Eliade and Folklore," all of the studies dealing with Eliade are in the literary section: Virgil Ierunca, "The Literary Work of Mircea Eliade" (French publication in D11);

Günther Spaltmann, "Authenticity and Experience of Time: Remarks on Mircea Eliade's Literary Works"; Vintila Horia, "The Forest as Mandala: Notes concerning a Novel by Mircea Eliade"; George Uscatescu, "Time and Destiny in the Novels of Mircea Eliade"; E.M. Cioran, "Beginnings of a Friendship" (French publication in D11), which presents different aspects of Eliade's background and personality. Most readers outside Romania, and especially those familiar only with his English publications, have simply identified Eliade as a historian and phenomenologist of religion. This volume is significant for introducing readers to the extremely important literary dimension of his creativity.

D9 Lugarini, L. *Il Tema del sacro e la mentalita arcaica. R. Otto e M. Eliade*. L'Aquila: Japadre.

* Murăraşu, D. *Haşdeu. Ediţia Mircea Eliade*. Bucharest: Tiparul Universitar, 1938, 67 pp. See F199.

D10 Saliba, J.A. *"Homo Religiosus" in Mircea Eliade. An Anthropological Evaluation*. Supplementa ad Numen, altera series: dissertationes ad historiam religionum pertinentes, vol. 5. Leiden: E.J. Brill, 1976, vi + 210 pp.

This book "is written by a religious believer with the simple aim of examining whether Eliade's interpretation of the religions of nonliterate societies conforms to contemporary anthropological research." The overall impression that one gains from this study is that Eliade's interpretation of *homo religiosus* is extremely inadequate when evaluated in light of contemporary anthropology in Great Britain and the United States. Saliba formulates many serious criticisms of Eliade's History of Religions: Eliade lacks a rigorous methodology; he makes numerous factual errors and is not sensitive to historical evidence; he makes uncritical generalizations and pays insufficient attention to cultural and social contexts; etc. The potential strengths of this study are usually negated by its glaring weaknesses, especially its superficial treatment of methodological and other issues and its frequent misinterpretations of Eliade's position.

D11 Tacou, C., ed. *Mircea Eliade*. Cahiers de L'Herne, 33. Paris: L'Herne, 1978, 409 pp. A122.

Contains the most important collection of articles and commentaries on Eliade yet assembled. After a useful "repères biographiques," the volume is divided into five sections: Textes de Mircea Eliade; Phénoménologie et Herméneutique; Spiritualité et régénération; Souvenirs, rencontres, traces; Les voies du fantastique. The work ends with a nineteen-page "bibliographie." Although it contains a number of mistakes, this is the most comprehensive bibliography of Eliade published through 1978. For "Textes de Mircea Eliade," see A122. Following is a list of the articles and commentaries with cross-references to earlier publications, as they are arranged according to sectional titles:

"Phénoménologie et Herméneutique"

J. Ries, "Histoire des religions, phénoménologie, herméneutique," pp. 81-87.
G. Dumézil, "Le message avant la mort," pp. 88-91.
G. Durand, "Eliade ou l'anthropologie profonde," pp. 92-96.
D. Rasmussen, "Herméneutique structurale et philosophie," pp. 97-104. F242.
C. Noica, "Hiérophanie et sacralité," pp. 105-9.
M.L. Ricketts, "Mircea Eliade et la mort de Dieu," pp. 110-19. F252.
S. Reno, "Hiérophanie, symbole et expériences," pp. 120-27. F247.
D. Allen, "L'analyse phénoménologique de l'expérience religieuse," pp. 128-38. F13.

"Spiritualité et régénération"

M. de Gandillac, "Répétition et renaissance," pp. 185-93.
M. Borie, "De l'herméneutique à la régénération par le théâtre," pp. 194-202.
I.P. Culianu, "L'anthropologie philosophique," pp. 203-11.
P. Pasquier, "L'amer festin, histoire des religions et spiritualité," pp. 212-19.
M. Lobet, "La chronique souterraine de l'humanité," pp. 220-23. F153.
C. Long, "Le sens de l'oeuvre de Mircea Eliade pour l'homme moderne," pp. 224-30. F158.

"Souvenirs, rencontres, traces"

E.M. Cioran, "Les débuts d'une amitié," pp. 259-63. D8.
A. Rosetti, "Eliade au temps jadis...," pp. 264-65.
A. Cioranesco, "A Bucharest, un lycée," pp. 266-69.
H. Corbin, E. Ionesco, M. Meslin, P. Ricoeur, "Mircea Eliade," pp. 270-77.

G. Taraghi, "Rencontre," pp. 278-79.
Correspondance, pp. 280-89.

"Les voies du fantastique"

V. Ierunca, "L'oeuvre littéraire," pp. 315-29. D8.
J. Biès, "Chamanisme et littérature," pp. 330-40.
S. Al-George, "Temps, histoire et destin," pp. 341-46.
W.R. Comstock, "Mythe et cinéma contemporain," pp. 347-49.
S. Vierne, "La littérature sous la lumière des mythes," pp. 350-54.
J. Masui, "Mythes et symboles," pp. 355-63. F181.
M. Calinescu, "Imagination et sens," pp. 364-74. F59.
W.A. Coates, "Littérature fantastique: métaphysique et occulte," pp. 375-80.
I. Bălu, "Les débuts littéraires de Mircea Eliade," pp. 381-89.

E

DISSERTATIONS

E1 Allen, D. *The History of Religions and Eliade's Phenomenology*. Ph.D., Vanderbilt University, 1971, xi + 367 pp.

E2 Avens, R. *Mircea Eliade's Conception of the Polarity "Sacred-Profane" in Archaic Religions and in Christianity*. Ph.D., Fordham University, 1971, 251 pp.

E3 Charpentier, A. *Sens et fonction du sacré selon Mircea Eliade*. Thèse de Licence en Sciences religieuses, Université Catholique de Louvain, 1975, 220 pp.

E4 Deprit, R. *Le Symbole chez Mircea Eliade et chez Claude Lévi-Strauss. Etude Comparée*. Thèse de Licence, Université Catholique de Louvain, 1974-1975, 224 pp.

E5 Di Nardo, M.A. *The Study of the Role of Symbol in the Writings of Karl Rahner, Mircea Eliade and H. Richard Niebuhr. Some Implications for Contemporary Catechesis*. Ph.D., The Catholic University of America, 1971, 304 pp.

E6 Doeing, D.A. *A Biography of Mircea Eliade's Spiritual and Intellectual Development from 1917 to 1940*. Ph.D., University of Ottawa, 1975, xviii + 351 pp.

E7 Duch, L. *Ciencia de la religion y mito. Estudios sobre la interpretación del mito con especial atención de mircea eliade*. Ph.D., Eberhard-Karls-Universität of Tübingen, Faculty of Catholic Theology, 1974, 284 pp.

E8 Duchêne, H. *Le Thème du Temps dans l'oeuvre de Mircea Eliade*. Ph.D., Université Catholique de Louvain, Faculty of Philosophy and Letters, 1965, 199 pp.

E9 Dudley, G., III. *Mircea Eliade and the Recovery of Archaic Religions. A Critical Assessment of Eliade's Vision and*

Method for the History of Religions. Ph.D., University of Pennsylvania, 1972, 463 pp.

E10 Franssen, J. *Notion et fonction du mythe selon Mircea Eliade*. Thèse de Licence en Sciences religieuses, Université Catholique de Louvain, 1975, xvi + 166 pp.

E11 Greenberg, L. *Mircea Eliade's Mythology. A Descriptive Analytical Study*. M.A., McGill University, 1977, 100 pp.

E12 Hagon, C. *L'Homme religieux et le symbolisme du Centre selon Mircea Eliade*. Thèse de Licence en Sciences religieuses, Université Catholique de Louvain, 1977-1978, 207 pp.

E13 Janssens, J.P. *Dialectique du sacré et du profane selon Mircea Eliade*. Thèse de Licence en Sciences religieuses, Université Catholique de Louvain, 1978.

E14 Kraay, R.W. *Symbols in Paradox. A Theory of Communication based on the Writings of Mircea Eliade*. Ph.D., University of Iowa, 1977, 229 pp.

E15 Lebrun, R. *L'Homo religiosus selon Mircea Eliade*. Thèse de Licence en Sciences religieuses, Université Catholique de Louvain, 1974, 158 pp.

E16 Saliba, J.A. *The Concept of "Homo Religiosus" in the Works of Mircea Eliade. An Anthropological Evaluation for Religious Studies*. Ph.D., The Catholic University of America, 1971, 338 pp.

E17 Saracino, A. *Mircea Eliade, Novelle*. Ph.D., Università di Bari, Faculty of Letters, 1966, 488 pp.

E18 Scagno, R. *Religiosità cosmica e cultura tradizionale nel pensiero di Mircea Eliade*. Tesi di Laurea, Università degli Studi di Torino, Faculty of Letters and Philosophy, 1972-1973, 352 pp.

E19 Schreiber, D. *The Value of History and of Jesus Christ in the Works of Mircea Eliade*. Union Theological Seminary (Richmond, Virginia), 1969, 139 pp.

E20 Shippee, A.W. *Mircea Eliade's Concept of Myth. A Study of Its Possible Relevancy to an Understanding of Islam*. Ph.D., Hartford Seminary Foundation, 1974, viii + 248 pp.

E21 Slater, R.G. *The Role of Myth in Religion. A Study of Mircea Eliade's Phenomenology of Religion.* Toronto, 1973, 151 pp.

E22 Velz, E. *Le Paradoxe de la Rédemption (Erlösung) ici et maintenant. En prenant comme "modèle" F. Nietzsche interprété principalement à la lumière des oeuvres de Mircea Eliade.* Ph.D., Université Catholique de Louvain, 1974, xl + 630 pp.

E23 Welbon, G.R. *Mircea Eliade's Image of Man. An Anthropogeny by a Historian of Religions.* M.A., Northwestern University, 1960.

E24 Wheeler, C. *Contrasting Modes of Archaic and Modern Consciousness according to Mircea Eliade.* M.A., Georgetown University, 1971, 83 pp.

E25 Yarian, S.O. *Mircea Eliade and a "New Humanism."* Ph.D., Brown University, 1970, 229 pp.

F

ARTICLES

F1 Acterian, H. "Discuţii." *Ulise* (1932) 1, no. 2:12.

F2 ———. "Mircea Eliade pornograf?" *Vremea* (1937) 10, no. 492:9.

F3 Ahlberg, A. "Mircea Eliade och de religiösa symbolerna." *Svenska Dagbladet* (Sept. 21, 1966).

F4 Alexandrescu, S. "Nawoord." In *De Mântuleasa-straat* I43 pp. 141-53.

F5 ———. "Dialectica fantasticului." In *La Ţigănci* A92 pp. v-1.

Alexandrescu offers a detailed analysis of several stories of the volume *La Ţigănci* that he considers to be of the type "fantastic." Parallels are given between the dialectics of sacred and profane in Eliade's literature and in his work as a historian of religions. Also relates his work to Romanian folklore and to the themes of the great Romanian poet Eminescu. Whereas in Eliade's prewar writings the sacred appears distinct from the profane, his postwar stories reveal the sacred fully camouflaged in the profane, as best exemplified by the short story "La Ţigănci."

F6 ———. "Mircea Eliade, scriitor." *Luceafărul* (March 9 and 16, 1968) 11, nos. 10 and 11.

Discusses Eliade's accomplishments as essayist and novelist. Traces the theme of birth and rebirth from essays of the 1930s to his later concerns as a historian of religions.

F7 ———. "Een gesprek met de Roemeense romanschrijver en antropoloog." *Vrij Nederland*, Amsterdam (March 20, 1976) 37:31.

F8 ———. "Mircea Eliade en de menselijke bronnen." *Vrij Nederland* (March 20, 1976) 37:31.

F9 Al-George, S. "Temps, histoire et destin." In *Mircea Eliade* D11 pp. 341-46.

F10 Allen, D. "A Phenomenological Evaluation of Religious Mysticism." *Darshana International* (July 1972) 12, no. 3:71-78. Rev. in D1 part of chap. 7.

Investigates the type of religious experience Eliade evaluates as the "highest" spiritual manifestation: suggests criteria used to evaluate, provides illustrations, and finally identifies this "most elevated" type of experience. Concludes that Eliade's evaluation is at least partially based on an assumed ontological position much more characteristic of Eastern mysticism than Western religious traditions.

F11 ———. "Mircea Eliade's Phenomenological Analysis of Religious Experience." *Journal of Religion* (1972) 52, no. 2:170-86. Translated as F13 which appears in D11. Rev. and enl. in D1 chap. 4.

Presents a phenomenological analysis which focuses on the dialectic of the sacred, taken as the key methodological principle for distinguishing religious phenomena. Analyzes the irreducibility of the sacred, religion and the sacred, and the structure of the dialectic of the sacred.

F12 ———. "Givenness and Creativity." *Journal of Thought* (1973) 8, no. 4:270-78. Rev. in D1 as part of chap. 6.

Formulates a certain ambiguity in Eliade's analysis of religious experience: on the one hand, the major emphasis on the passive reception of, or "givenness" of, universal structures; on the other hand, a sense of active creativity on the part of religious persons. Suggests a dynamic interaction between universal and particular, passive and active, in terms of a "constituted given."

F13 ———. "L'analyse phénoménologique de l'expérience religieuse." In *Mircea Eliade* D11 pp. 128-38. Translation of F11.

F14 Altizer, T.J.J. "Mircea Eliade and the Recovery of the Sacred." *Christian Scholar* (1962) 45:267-89.

Claims there is a "disastrous contradiction" in Eliade's thought derived from giving two contrary meanings to "time." Suggests Eliade has not seen the radical implications of his own dialectic of the sacred for the contemporary human situation. The analysis in this article is repeated in Altizer's *Mircea Eliade and the Dialectic of the Sacred* D3.

F15 ———. "The Religious Meaning of Myth and Symbol." In *Truth, Myth, and Symbol*. Ed. by T. Altizer, W. Beardslee, and J. Young. Englewood Cliffs, N.J.: Prentice-Hall, 1962, pp. 87-108.

"It is the purpose of this paper to challenge Eliade's correlation of man, the cosmos, and the sacred, in his understanding of the religious meaning of myth and symbol." By identifying the religious symbol with the archaic symbol, Eliade cannot account for the symbol in the higher religions or its meaning in our historical situation. An excellent challenge to the overall adequacy of Eliade's interpretation of myth and symbol.

F16 Alvarez de Miranda, A. "Un tratato de Historia de las Religiones." *Cuadernos Hispanoamericanos*, Madrid (1955) 61:109-12.

F17 Amariu, C. "Mircea Eliade: 'Souvenirs.'" *La Nation Roumaine* (Jan. 1968) 242:2.

F18 Anér, K. "Mytens man." *Vår Lösen. Kristen Kulturtidshrift*, Uppsala (Oct. 1965) pp. 355-57.

F19 Angelescu, N. "Generaţie fără maeştrii." *Vremea*(1937) 10, no. 495:3.

F20 "L'angoisse revalorisée par les civilisations religieuxes selon M. Mircea Eliade." *Le Courrier*, Geneva (Sept. 6, 1953) p. 5.

F21 Arc, A. "Spre un nou umanism." *Fiinţa Românească* (1963) 1:102-4.

F22 "Atentatul moral împotriva lui Mircea Eliade." *Vremea* (1937) 10, no. 491:5.

F23 Baciu, S. "Mircea Eliade e sua obra." *Correio da Manhã*, Rio de Janeiro (Feb. 2, 1952).

F24 Baconsky, L. "Mircea Eliade. În perspectiva unei restituiri." *Steaua*, Cluj (May 1970) 21, no. 5 (244): 54-58.

F25 Bagdanavičius, V. "Mircea Eliade, Žmonijos religinių simbolių tyrinėtojas." *Aidai. Mênesinis Kulturos Zurnalas*, New York (1969) 3:115-27.

F26 Bail, J. "The Spiritual Revolution, Thomas Merton, Shunryo Suzuki, Mircea Eliade." *The Book Review, An Alternative Magazine from San Francisco* (March 1971) 18:6-9, 32-33, 38.

F27 Baird, R.D. *Category Formation and the History of Religions*. Religion and Reason, 1. The Hague: Mouton, 1971. See especially pp. 74-91. The analysis is the same as F28.

Using an empirical-historical approach, Baird contends that Eliade's approach is ahistorical and that an analysis of his phenomenology of symbolism reveals that his History of Religions "is as normative as theology because it is based on an assumed ontology which is neither historically derived nor descriptively verifiable." Good challenge to Eliade's history and phenomenology of religion. One could counter that Baird's notion of verification is narrow, inadequate, and outdated.

F28 ———. "Normative Elements in Eliade's Phenomenology of Symbolism." *Union Seminary Quarterly Review* (1970) 25: 505-16. Revised as part of F27.

F29 Balandier, G. "Mircea Eliade, chroniqueur de l'humanité." *Les Nouvelles Littéraires* (July 5, 1978) 56, no. 2642: 10.

F30 Balotă, N. "Un hermeneut al secolului XX: Mircea Eliade, explorator al mitului." In *Euphorion*, 1969, pp. 412-48.

F31 ———. "Mitologie şi romanesc." *Familia* (Nov. 1967) 3, no. 2:16.

F32 ———. "Mircea Eliade şi etosul cunoaşterii." *Viaţa Românească* (March 1977) 30, no. 3:53-55.

F32a Baltag, C. "Recuperarea sensurilor." *Secolul 20* (1978) 205-6:57-58.

F33 Baltazar, C. "Intre scriitor şi editor." *România Literară* (1932) 1, no. 26:1-2.

F34 ———. "Intre originalitate şi autenticitate." *România Literară* (1933) 2, no. 60:4.

F35 ———. "Cartea inimii mele." *România Literară* (1933) 2, no 63:1-2.

F36 ———. "Lectorii lui Maitreyi." *România Literară* (1933) 2, no. 76:4.

F37 Bălu, I. "Les débuts littéraires de Mircea Eliade." In *Mircea Eliade* D11 pp. 381-89. Translation of F38.

Studies Eliade's earliest literary writings located only in Romania.

F37a ———. "Mircea Eliade şi 'Experienţa Indiei.'" *România Literară* (Feb. 8, 1979) pp. 20-21.

F38 ———. "Mircea Eliade, prozator. Începuturile." *Steaua* (Oct. 1969) 20, no. 10 (237):71-78. Translated as F37 which appears in D11.

F39 Bănulescu, Ş. "Mircea Eliade în 'Amintiri.'" *Ramuri* (Jan. 15, 1968) 5, no. 1:2-3.

F40 ———. "Pe dimensiunea timpului interior, o nuvelă de Mircea Eliade." *Secolul 20* (Sept. 1967) 9:22-24.

F41 Barbu, E. "Acasă la Mircea Eliade." *Luceafărul* (Feb. 3, 1968) 11, no. 5:4.

F42 Beane, W.C. "Understanding Eliade as Historian of Religions." In *Myths, Rites, Symbols* A112 vols. 1 and 2, pp. xxiii-xxviii.

F43 ———. "The Work of Mircea Eliade: Implications for a Philosophy of Humankind." In *Myths, Rites, Symbols* A112 vol. 2, pp. 461-65.

F44 Bharati, A. "Über Eliades Yogaauffassung." *Zeitschrift für Religions und Geistesgeschichte* (1960) 12:176-79.

F45 Biès, J. "Chamanisme et littérature." In *Mircea Eliade* D11 pp. 330-40.

F46 Bîrlea, O. "Mircea Eliade." In *Istoria folcloristicei româneşti*. Bucharest: Ed. enciclopedia română, 1974, pp. 540-42.

F47 Bogza, G. "Cu d. Mircea Eliade de vorbă despre reportaj." *Vremea* (1934) 7, no. 335:5.

F48 Bolle, K.W. *The Freedom of Man in Myth*. Nashville: Vanderbilt University Press, 1968, 199 pp.

The major focus of chapter 3, "Themes and Ideas" (of Myths), is on Eliade's analysis of cosmogonic myths.

F49 Bologa, V. "Documente: Mircea Eliade şi istoriografia medicală clujeană." *Steaua* (Dec. 1969) 20, no. 12 (239): 176-90.

Correspondence between student Eliade and Professor Bologa concerning history of science, particularly that of alchemy.

F50 Borie, M. "De l'herméneutique à la régénération par le théâtre." In *Mircea Eliade* D11 pp. 194-202.

F51 Bosio, F. "Implicazioni filosofiche della storia delle religioni in Mircea Eliade." *Il Pensiero*, Rome, Urbino (1969) 14:71-76.

F52 Botez, A., and O. Nistor. "Studenţii despre Mircea Eliade." *Vremea* (1937) 10, no. 492:9.

F53 Breu, G. "Teacher: Shamans? Hippies? They're All Creative to the World's Leading Historian of Religions." *People Weekly* (March 27, 1978) 9, no. 12:43, 49.

F54 Brezianu, B. "Confluenţa Brâncuşi-Eliade." *Secolul 20* (1976) 89-91:172-74.

Introduction to Eliade's play "Coloana nesfârşită" H1004.

F55 Bucur, M. "Un umanist în acest veac." *Luceafărul* (Sept. 30, 1978) 21, no. 39:8.

F56 "Buletin Bio-bibliografic: Mircea Eliade." *Viaţa Literară* (1933) 8, no. 146:2.

F57 Calinescu, M. "Mircea Eliade's Journals." *The Denver Quarterly* (1977) 12, no. 1:313-15.

Review article of *Fragments d'un journal* A104 = *No Souvenirs* A117. Identifies main themes as Eliade's existential situation of exile from postwar Romania; the imaginative and creative qualities of his hermeneutics in the History of Religions; and the complimentarity of his literary and scientific achievements.

F58 ———. "Imagination and Meaning: Aesthetic Attitudes and Ideas in Mircea Eliade's Thought." *Journal of Religion* (Jan. 1977) 57, no. 1:1-15. Translated as F59 which appears in D11.

Claims "Eliade's weltanschauung is largely an aesthetic one." Characteristics of this aesthetic, existential orientation include the following: "ambiguity," "unrecognizable" meanings, "integration," consciousness of richness and diversity beyond the "camouflage"; creativity, intellectual expansiveness, and vitality; interpretation as opposing all tendencies toward reduction and conceived as a "totalizing activity, as an attempt to grasp the organic whole." Claims the opposite of frequent criticisms that Eliade ignores differences and reduces the diversity of his data. Totally supportive of Eliade.

F59 ———. "Imagination et sens." In *Mircea Eliade* D11 pp. 364-74. Translation of F58.

F60 ———. "The Disguises of Miracle: Notes on Mircea Eliade's Fiction." *World Literature Today* (1978) 52, no. 4:558-64.

F61 Cantoni, G. "Mircea Eliade e la mitologia della storia." *L'Osservatore Romano* (Oct. 11, 1968) 234:3, 7.

F62 Carrouges, M. "L'Asie mystique et la condition humaine." *Monde Nouveau* (March 1955) pp. 106-9.

F63 Cavicchioli, G. "L'eterno ritorno." *Valori*, Bologna (Jan.-Feb. 1951) 2, no. 1:10-21.

F64 "Cazul Mircea Eliade, Precizările D'lui Prof. S. Megedinţi." *Vremea* (1937) 9, no. 492:8.

F65 "Cele 7 premii literare (140.000 lei) sau Minunile telefonului." *Viaţa Literară* (1934) 8, no. 151:3-4.

F66 "Ce ne spun librarii din capitală." *Viaţa Literară* (1934) 8, no. 157:3.

F67 Chirnoagă, M. "Portret: Mircea Eliade." *Viaţa*, Bucharest (March 25, 1944).

F68 Chorão, J.B. "Um Latino do Oriente." *Brotéria*, Lisbon (Oct.-Dec. 1975) 101, no. 10-12:374-78.

F69 Christian, V. "Maitreyi de Mircea Eliade." *România Literară* (1933) 2, no. 63:1-2.

F70 Cioculescu, Ş. "Aspecte Epice Contemporane." *Revista Fundaţiilor Regale* (1935) 2, no. 1:152-68.

Includes commentary on *Lumina ce se stinge* A15.

F71 ———. "Mircea Eliade." *România Literară* (1978) 11, no. 35:7.

F72 ———. "Un 'Itinerariu Spiritual.'" *Viaţa Literară* (1928) 3, no. 86:1, 3.

F73 ———. "Intre ortodoxie şi spiritualitate." *Viaţa Literară* (1928) 3, no. 94:1-2.

F74 Cioran, E. "Les débuts d'une amitié." In *Mircea Eliade* D11 pp. 259-63. Translation of F75 which appears in D8.

F75 ———. "Beginnings of a Friendship." In *Myths and Symbols. Studies in Honor of Mircea Eliade* D8 pp. 407-14. Translated as F74 which appears in D11.

F76 ———. "Crima bătrânilor." *Vremea* (1937) 10, no. 492:9.

F77 Cioranescu, A. "A Bucharest, un lycée." In *Mircea Eliade* D11 pp. 266-69.

F78 Clément, C. "Mircea Eliade, un 'chamane' moderne." *Le Matin*, Paris (Sept. 26, 1978) 490:25.

F79 Clonaru, C. "Generaţia." *Floarea de foc* (1936) 3, no. 20:1.

F80 Coates, W.A. "Littérature fantastique: métaphysique et occulte." In *Mircea Eliade* D11 pp. 375-80.

F81 Comarnescu, P. "Epistemologia dragostii la Mircea Eliade." *România Literară* (1933) 2, no. 81:1-2.

F82 ———. "Mircea Eliade, romancier al exasperării." *România Literară* (1934) 3, no. 334:4.

F83 Comstock, W.R. "Mythe et cinéma contemporain." In *Mircea Eliade* D11 pp. 347-49.

F84 Constantinescu, P. "Momente în cultura română în 1935." *Vremea* (1936) 9, no. 419:9.

F85 ———. "Anul literar." *Vremea* (1937) 9, no. 469:12.

F86 "Criza cărţii aşa cum o vede Mircea Eliade." *Preocupări Literare* (1938) 3, no. 2:81.

F87 Culianu, I.P. "Mircea Eliade a 70 anni (1907)." *Biserica Româneasca* (Jan.-June 1977) p. 6. See also *Limite* (Aug. 1978) no. 26-27.

F88 ———. "L'anthropologie philosophique." In *Mircea Eliade* D11 pp. 203-11. Note: author listed as I.P. Coulianou.

F89 "Curier." *Floarea de foc* (1933) 2, nos. 2:8; 3:8.

F90 "Curier Literar." *Viaţa Literară* (1930) 5, nos. 126:4; 128:4; 132:4, 8; 145:4.

F91 Damaschin, V. "Romanul românesc de azi." *Floarea de foc* (1936) 3, no. 17:2.

F92 ———. "Esseul, meditaţia, literatură actuală." *România Literară* (1933) 2, no. 83:4.

F92a Dan, S.P. "Mircea Eliade." In Dan, *Proza fantastică românească*. Bucharest: Ed. Minerva, 1975, pp. 235-47.

F93 Daniélou, J. "Témoignage sur Mircea Eliade." *Revue des Études Roumaines* (1961) 7-8:217-18.

F94 Deleanu, P.C. "Apendice la clipa de faţă a tineretului românesc." *Ideea Românească* (1935) 1, no. 2-4:173-74.

F95 Demetrio y Radaza, F. *Symbols in Comparative Religion and the Georgics*. Logos, 3. Manila: Loyola House of Studies, Ateneo de Manila University, 1968, 146 pp.

Chapter 2, entitled "Mircea Eliade: His Methodology and a Critique," consists of Eliade's basic assumptions, his analysis of hierophanies and symbols, his relationship to phenomenology, his analysis of symbol, objections to his methodology, and a defense of his methodology. The chapters "The Symbol" and "Cosmic Symbols: The Earth and Symbols Related to the Earth" rely heavily on Eliade's interpretation of symbolism. The chapters "Cosmic Symbols of the Earth in the *Georgics*" and "Water Divinities in the *Georgics*" make considerable use of Eliade's analysis of certain symbols.

F96 "Despre bazaconia generaţiei de ultima ora." *Pana Literară* (1933) 1, no. 1:1.

F97 "Despre domnii Pericle, Tatu şi ... Eliade." *Azi* (1937) 6, no. 27:2525-26.

F98 "De vorbă cu domnul Mircea Eliade." *Reporter* (1934) 2, no. 10:5.

F99 "De vorbă cu domnul Mircea Eliade." *România Literară* (1934) 3, no. 89:3.

F100 "Dl. Mircea Eliade pornograf." *Adevĕrul Literar şi Artistic* (1937) 18, no. 862:18.

F101 "Dl. Mircea Eliade şi S.S.R." *Adevĕrul Literar şi Artistic* (1937) 18, no. 863:18.

F102 Donescu, C. "Conflictul dintre generaţii." *Vremea* (1937) 10, no. 494:3.

F103 Dudley, G. "Mircea Eliade as the 'Anti-Historian' of Religions." *Journal of the American Academy of Religion* (1976) 44, no. 2:345-59.

Very controversial and creative interpretation of Eliade that treats his History of Religions as an "anti-historical" synchronic approach to religious phenomena that can be situated within the French tradition of paradigms and deductive reasoning. There is an interesting comparison between Foucault and Eliade. The entire analysis of this article can be found in greatly expanded form in D7.

F104 Dumézil, G. "Le message avant la mort." In *Mircea Eliade* D11 pp. 88-91.

F105 Dumitrescu-Buşulenga, Z. "Un filozof de miturilor." *Seculol 20* (Sept. 1967) 9:4-5.

F105a ———. "Istorie şi mit: de la romantiei la Mircea Eliade." *Seculol 20* (1978) 205-6:45-51.

F106 Durand, G. "Eliade ou l'anthropologie profonde." In *Mircea Eliade* D11 pp. 92-96.

F107 "Eliade e o universo mítico." *Jornal do Brasil*, Rio de Janeiro (Sept. 17, 1972) p. 6.

F108 Etienne, J. "La morphologie du sacré: remarques sur le *Traité* de Mircea Eliade." In *Miscellanea Albert Dondeyne, Ephemerides Theologicae Louvanienses*, 1974, pp. 233-40.

F109 "Felicitări." *Solia*, Detroit (April 28, 1968) 33, no. 9:2.

F109a Filip, T. "Lumea prin care am trecut. Mircea Eliade şi Mihail Sebastian în corespondenţă cu Petru Comarnescu." *Manuscriptum* (1978) 9, no. 4:158-67.

Documentation of letters of Eliade to Comarnescu in 1929.

F110 Florescu, N. "Mircea Eliade şi literatura populară." *Iaşul Literar* (April 1970) 4:64-66.

F111 ———. "Mircea Eliade--şi 'romanul' enigmaticei R ..." *Manuscriptum* (1972) 3, no. 3:132-40.

Documentation identifying the person Rica Botez (with whom Eliade had a relationship, 1926 through 1928), characterized as "R" in the autobiographical novels *Gaudeamus* A7 and *Şantier* A19, and in *Amintiri: I* A85.

F112 Frenkel, V. "Mircea Eliade ed alcuni studiosi del suo tempo." *ACME. Annali della Facoltà di Lettere e Filosofia dell'Università degli Studi di Milano* (1975) 28:173-88.

Compares the method of Eliade with those of R. Guénon, C.G. Jung, K. Kerényi, G. van der Leeuw, R. Otto, and T.J.J. Altizer.

F113 Frye, N. "World Enough Without Time." *The Hudson Review* (1959) 12:423-31.

While briefly reviewing five books and one article, Frye focuses on the theme of the revolt against "life in time" with the need to surmount the world of time. His attempt to relate Eliade's analysis to modern literary criticism and literature is interesting and includes criticisms. Unfortunately, it also reveals his ignorance of Eliade's literary career: "Mr. Eliade has little interest in literature, and it is perhaps unreasonable to expect him to extend his already enormous erudition to include it."

F114 Gandillac, M. de. "Répétition et renaissance." In *Mircea Eliade* D11 pp. 185-93.

F115 Gerbore, P. "Le religioni." *Roma* (Dec. 27, 1957).

F116 Gombrich, R. "Eliade on Buddhism." *Religious Studies* (1974) 10:225-31.

Contends that the treatment of early Buddhism in *Yoga. Immortality and Freedom* A63 leaves much to be desired. After questioning associations of the Buddha with shamanistic practices, Gombrich focuses on chapter 5, "Yoga Techniques in Buddhism," offers numerous criticisms, and concludes that these criticisms "cast doubt on the chapter's value as a contribution to our understanding of early Buddhism."

F117 Graziella, S. "Mircea Eliade." *Vremea* (1934) 7, no. 323:9.

F117a Grigoriu, T. "Popas la Mircea Eliade." *Secolul 20* (1978) 205-6:190-91.

F118 Grozea, E. "Romanul românesc in anul 1934." *Viaţa Literară* (1935) 9, no. 165:5.

F119 Hamilton, K. "'Homo Religiosus' and Historical Faith." *Journal of Bible and Religion* (1965) 33:213-22.

Argues that Eliade's *homo religiosus*, while adequate for archaic religion, is inadequate for the debate about religion and Christianity. Offers some good criticisms. Unfortunately, the entire formulation is based on *The Sacred and the Profane* A67, and the author writes from a highly normative, faith-oriented, "religionless," Christian, theological stance and assumes Eliade is offering an alternative theology. Thus, he fails to appreciate the basically descriptive, phenomenological dimension of much of Eliade's interpretation.

F120 Handoca, M. "Mircea Eliade. Mitul jertfei creatoare." *Manuscriptum* (1974) 5, no. 14:27-28.

Introduction to the play *Iphigenia* (see H1012 and A47).

F121 Hecht, R., and M.G. Bradford, eds. *Mircea Eliade. A Bibliography*. Santa Barbara: University of California Library and the Institute of Religious Studies, 1974, 22 pp. Revision of F239.

F122 Hof, H. "Religionsfenomelog med budskap: Mircea Eliade." *Vår Lösen* (June 1965) pp. 251-56.

F123 Holban, A. "Dificultatea în literatură. In marginea lui Mircea Eliade." *Viaţa Literară* (1936) 11, no. 9:3.

F124 Horia, V. "The Forest as Mandala. Notes concerning a Novel by Mircea Eliade." In *Myths and Symbols. Studies in Honor of Mircea Eliade* D8 pp. 387-95.

F125 Hudson, W.M. "Eliade's Contributions to the Study of Myth." In *Tire Shrinker to Dragster*. Ed. by Texas Folklore Society. Austin: Encino Press, 1968, pp. 218-41.

Summary and sympathetic formulation of a tremendous number of topics in Eliade's History of Religions. The major emphasis is on his analysis of symbolism, and this is related to his view of myth, which is distinguished from those of some past investigators.

F126 Ierunca, V. "Mircea Eliade." *Exil et Liberté* (May 1954) p. 3.

F127 ———. "Foaie verde lui Mircea Eliade." *Fiinţa Românească* (1964) 2:47-48. A poem.

F128 ———. "L'oeuvre littéraire." In *Mircea Eliade* D11 pp. 315-29. Translation of F129 which appears in D8.

F129 ———. "The Literary Work of Mircea Eliade." In *Myths and Symbols. Studies in Honor of Mircea Eliade* D8 pp. 343-63. Translated as F128 which appears in D11.

F130 Ilovici, M. "Falimentul trecutei generaţii." *Litere* (1933) 1, no. 2:1-2.

F131 ———. "Cunoaşterea experienţialist-ontologică." *România Literară* (1933) 2, no. 57:2.

F132 Ionescu, E. "Mircea Eliade şi 'Şantierul.'" *Ideea Românească* (1935) 1, no. 2-4:148-54.

F133 Ionescu, T., and S. Baciu. "De vorba cu 'tânăra generaţie.'" *Viaţa Literară* (1938) 13, no. 14:1, 3.

F134 Jans, A. "Visages de Roumanie et de Grèce." *Le Soir* (May 15, 1954).

F135 ———. "Mircea Eliade, le Roumain." *La Vie Littéraire* (May 15, 1954) p. 7.

F136 Jebeleanu, E. "Autenticitate sau substanţialism?" *România Literară* (1933) 2, no. 60:1.

F137 Jerome. "Revista Revistelor." *România Literară* (1932) 1, no. 4:4.

F138 Jianu, I. "Amintiri despre Mircea Eliade." *Destin* (1968) 16:133-39.

F139 ———. "O monografie despre Mircea Eliade." *Fiinţa Românească* (1965) 3:132-34.

F139a Jung, C.G. "Letter to Eliade." In *Letters*. Ed. by G. Adler and A. Jaffe. Bollingen Series, 95. Princeton: Princeton University Press, 1975, vol. 2, pp. 210-12.

F140 Kanters, R. "Mircea Eliade écrit en trois langues." *L'Express* (April 27, 1956).

F141 Kijowski, A. "Wizja ludzkości nieomylnej." *Twórczość* (1965) 21, no. 10:143-48.

An introduction to Eliade's understanding of the nature and functions of myth among archaic, classical, and modern societies.

F142 Kim, J.J. "Hierophany and History." *Journal of the American Academy of Religion* (1972) 40, no. 3:334-48.

By stressing a phenomenology of archaic religions, Eliade and others have, it appears, created difficulties in the interpretation of the more historical and modern World Religions. However, his concept of "central hierophany," which Kim calls "ontological locus," can be very useful for a hermeneutics of current religions.

F143 Koga, T. "Shūkyōkenkyū niokeru Hōhōronteki Kadai no Ichishiten" (A Viewpoint of Methodological Problems in the History of Religions). *Hikakushisō-kenkyū* (Dec. 1976) 3:90-98.

F144 ———. "Rekishi no Shinwaronteki Kōsatsu" (A Mythological View of History). *Ōtani-daigaku Kenkyū-nenpō* (1976) 29:52-90.

F145 ———. "Shōchō to Rekishi" (Symbol and History). *Tetsugakuronshū*, Ōtani University (1975), 22:14-26.

F146 La Barre, W. *The Ghost Dance. The Origin of Religion.* New York: Doubleday, 1970; London: George Allen and Unwin, 1972, 677 pp. See pp. 38-39, 177, 366-67, etc.

There is little utilization of Eliade's own thought in the text, but La Barre lists many of his works on shamanism in the notes at the end of chapters.

F147 "La ce lucrează scriitorii nostri." *Viaţa Literară* (1934) 8, nos. 152:4; 153:4; 154:4.

F148 Laviosa Zambotti, P. "La scienza delle religioni e il trionfo del metodo storico." *Rivista di Scienze Preistoriche*, Florence (1949) 4:83-95.

Applies themes in *Traité d'histoire des religions* A44 to Palethnological research, particularly of the Near East.

F149 ———. "Ancora sul metodo in Paletnologia." *Rivista di Scienze Preistoriche* (1952) 7, no. 3-4:131-54.

Deals with the theory expressed in *Le Chamanisme* A46 in an analysis of the Supreme Being in the Paleolithic Age and the concept of "Centre" in the Agricultural Age.

F150 Leach, E. "Sermons by a Man on a Ladder." *New York Review of Books* (Oct. 20, 1966) 7, no. 6:28-31.

A strange essay in which it is not clear to what extent Leach wants to be taken seriously or is just being cute. Eliade is condemned for bad historiography, bad ethnography, bad method, bad psychology, and a confusion of terms. Unfortunately, most of Leach's personal attacks are so vicious and petty and his criticisms so based on misunderstanding or ignorance that the reader may fail to appreciate a few serious challenges. For example, he claims that Eliade attaches importance to the symbols as such and not to their structural relations. See rebuttal by Ricketts, F254.

F151 Lillin, A. "Arhetip şi mediu în nuvela 'La Ţigănci' de Mircea Eliade." *Orizont*, Timişoara (Jan. 1968) 19, no. 1:45-52.

Confused commentary on "La Ţigănci."

F152 Lobet, M. "Réception de M. Mircea Eliade." *Académie Royale de Langue et de Littérature Françaises* (Feb. 19, 1977) pp. 3-15.

F153 ———. "Mircea Eliade et la chronique souterraine de l'humanité." *Revue Générale* (April 1975) pp. 41-46. Reprinted in *Mircea Eliade* D11 pp. 220-23.

Review article of *Fragments d'un journal* A104.

F154 Loghin, G.D. "Ceva despre Mircea Eliade." *Jurnalul Literar* (1939) 1, no. 36:1-2.

F155 Long, C.H. "The Significance for Modern Man of Mircea Eliade's Work." In *Cosmic Piety. Modern Man and the Meaning of the Universe*. Ed. by C. Derrick. New York: P.J. Kenedy and Sons, 1967, pp. 131-44. Translated as F158 which appears in D11.

Extolls Eliade's interdisciplinary aptitude and his role as hermeneut in dealing with crises of the modern world, especially through his interpretation of symbols and his insistence upon the metaphysical and existential relevance for modern man of the archaic imagination in an age of historicism.

F156 ———. "The Meaning of Religion in the Contemporary Study of the History of Religions." *Criterion*, University of Chicago (1963) 2, no. 2:23-26.

Compares orientations of Eliade with those of R. Otto, J. Wach, G. van der Leeuw, and J. Kitagawa.

F157 ———. "Recent Developments in the History of Religions Field." *Divinity School News*, Chicago (1959) 26, no. 2:8-12.

Gives mostly background information related to Eliade's interest in the study of religion and his appointment as chairman of the History of Religions Field at the University of Chicago. Also briefly reviews his scholarly works which were available in English at the time.

F158 ———. "Le sens de l'oeuvre de Mircea Eliade pour l'homme moderne." In *Mircea Eliade* D11 pp. 224-30. Translation of F155.

F159 Lorinţ, F.E. "L'Ouverture vers la mort dans la *Forêt interdite* de Mircea Eliade." *International Journal of Rumanian Studies*, Lisse, Netherlands (1976) 1, no. 1-2:101-8.

Death is identified as a central theme of *Forêt interdite* A54 and is interpreted as a form of initiation based upon Romanian folkloric motifs.

F160 Lotreanu, I. "Pasiunea culturii"; "Aspecte ale mitului"; and "Probleme ale prozei." Series of weekly articles in *Săptămîna*, Bucharest, begun in April 1978.

F161 Lovinescu, M. "Ghicitor în pietre." *Fiinţa Românească* (1964) 2:111-13.

F162 Luyster, R. "The Study of Myth: Two Approaches." *Journal of Bible and Religion* (1966) 34, no. 3:235-43.

Briefly analyzes, contrasts, and evaluates two approaches to the study of myth: Eliade's phenomenology and "the pluralists" in anthropology, especially "Boas-oriented American anthropologists." The analysis, save for the final two paragraphs, is totally sympathetic to Eliade's phenomenological approach and critical of this anthropological approach and its criticisms of Eliade.

F163 Maguire, J.J. "The New Look in Comparative Religion." *Perspectives*, Notre Dame (1960) 5, no. 3:8-10.

F164 Mairet, P. "The Primordial Myths: A Note on the Works of Professor Mircea Eliade." *The Aryan Path*, Bombay (1963) 34:8-12.

Outlines a few of Eliade's mythic and symbolic themes with very little analysis. Mentions that some of the "most universal mythological motifs" were revealed through the study of shamanism and that one keeps finding the reappearance of "archetypal" religious notions, such as viewing the human condition as a "fall" from some earlier state of bliss.

F165 Malandra, W.W. "The Concept of Movement in History of Religions." *Numen* (1967) 14:23-69.

Emphasizes the dynamic, interdisciplinary, and ever-changing climate of the History of Religions from the viewpoints of van der Leeuw, Pettazzoni, and Eliade. Examines Eliade's understanding of archetypes and symbols, and his call for hermeneutics.

F166 Manolescu, F. "Mircea Eliade: Romanul 'experienţialist.'" *Analele Universităţii Bucureşti, Limbă şi Literatură Română* (1969) 18, no. 2:131-39.

A study of Eliade's "Indian literature": *Isabel* A9, *Şantier* A19, and *Maitreyi* A12. Interprets these novels as "experientialist": that is, the author intended to write about his own experiences--whether factual or imaginary--in an "authentic," "non-literary" way.

F167 Manolescu, N. "Insemnări disparate despre Mircea Eliade." *Tribuna* (Feb. 5, 1970) 14, no. 6 (680).

F168 Manoliu, P. "Cu Papini, Unamuno şi Maitreyi despre Mircea Eliade." *România Literară* (1933) 2, no. 67:3.

F169 Manu, A. "Ce face şi unde e Mircea Eliade?" *Seara*, Bucharest (Nov. 17, 1943).

F170 Manu, E. "Citînd jurnalul lui Mircea Eliade." *Luceafărul* (June 3, 1978) 21, no. 22:3.

F171 ———. "Brâncuşi intr'o viziune originală." *Săptămîna* (Feb. 6, 1976) no. 270.

F172 ———. "Mircea Eliade, scriitorul." *Săptămîna* (March 25, 1977) no. 329:3.

F173 Mărgineanu, N. "Gândirea simbolică în opera lui Mircea Eliade." *Steaua* (Dec. 1967) 18, no. 11:62-68.

A Marxist critique of Eliade's "magico-religious thought."

F174 Margul, T. "Mircea Eliade jako teoretyk świetości i mitu." *Euhemer*, Warsaw (1961) 5:36-52.

F175 Marino, A. "Brancuşi interprété par Mircea Eliade." *Cahiers Roumains d'êtudes littéraires* (1976) 3:161-62. Romanian publication in *Omajiu lui Brâncuşi*. Sibiu: Tribuna, 1976, pp. 53-54.

F176 ———. "Hermeneutica lui Mircea Eliade." *Revista de istorie şi teorie literară*, Bucharest (1977) 26, nos. 2:223-50; 3:371-99.

An exciting study of the major features of Eliade's hermeneutics in History of Religions. Analyzes the possibility of a hermeneutics of archaic and popular religions; the language and significance of terms used in such a hermeneutics; the notion of meaning and the role of interpretation; and the resulting possibility of understanding. It discusses Eliade's method further in terms of "circular hermeneutics"; intuitive and objective qualities; integration of documentation; the explicative and demonstrative nature of hermeneutics; the dialectical character of phenomena and their interpretation; archetypes, patterns, symbols; logic or "systematics" of archetypes and symbols; schemes and typologies; "homologization and totalization"; the role of history and the dialectic past-present; and Eliade's overwhelming nostalgia for the universal and creative dimension of human culture and of his own work.

F177 ———. "Mircea Eliade şi metoda hermeneutică." *Tribuna*, Cluj (March 10, 1977) 10:10.

F178 Martinescu, P. "Săracul scriitor român." *Vremea* (1934) 7, no. 359:6.

F179 ———. "Eliade exemplu de generozitate şi camaraderie." *Vremea* (1937) 10, no. 492:10.

F180 Maschke, G. "Eine intellektuelle Energie, so sensibel wie gefrässig." *Frankfurter Allgemeine Zeitung* (Dec. 13, 1977) no. 289.

F181 Masui, D. "Mythes et symboles selon Mircea Eliade." *Les Cahiers du Sud* (1952) 316:478-90. Reprinted in *Mircea Eliade*, D11 pp. 355-63.

Exposition of some philosophical implications behind Eliade's study of myths and symbols.

F182 Mateescu, M. "Atentat împotriva generaţiei lui Eliade." *Vremea* (1937) 10, no. 494:3.

F183 Mauriac, C. "Avec Mircea Eliade de la sociologie à la métaphysique." *Le Figaro* (Sept. 2, 1959).

F184 Maxim, I. "Amintirile lui Mircea Eliade." *Viaţa Românească* (May 1978) 31, no. 5:45-49.

F185 Mehedinţi, S. "Cazul Mircea Eliade." *Vremea* (1937) 10, no. 492:8.

F186 Micu, D. "Présence roumaine de Mircea Eliade." *Cahiers roumains d'études littéraires* (1974) 2:136-39.

F187 ———. "Introducere" to *Maitreyi. Nuntă în Cer* A91 pp. v-xliv. Part published also as "Proza lui Mircea Eliade." *Analele Universităţii Bucureşti. Limbă şi Literatură Română*, Bucharest (1968) 18:95-116. Part translated into English as "Mircea Eliade as a Romanian Writer," *Analele Universităţii Bucureşti. Limbă şi Literatură Română* (1977) 26:63-71; and in *Romanian Bulletin*, New York (1978) 7, nos. 5:7-8;

6:6-7; 7-8:6-7.

Micu, employing Eliade's autobiography, *Amintiri* A85, and documentation of earlier works, elucidates Eliade's youthful ambition to imitate such scholars as Voltaire, Goethe, Balzac, Hasdeu, Iorga, Papini, and others. Eliade was especially influenced by Professor Nae Ionescu at the University of Bucharest, when Eliade was a student and later as his colleague, and on the newspaper *Cuvântul* to which both contributed articles regularly. Particular attention is given to those articles of 1927 entitled "Itinerariu spiritual" (see H195) in which Eliade outlined the enthusiastic goals of his generation. Micu further examines Eliade's "post-Indian" novels, indicating their autobiographical elements. He sees in them the influence of Eliade's Indian studies and his younger struggle toward "nietzschean freedom."

F188 ———. "O sinteză de istorie şi spiritualităţii arhaice." *Steaua* (Feb. 1977) 28:22-27.

Comments on *Histoire des croyances* vol. 1. A110.

F189 ———. "Mircea Eliade." In Zaciu, *Scriitori români*. Bucharest: Ed. Ştiinţifica şi Enciclopedică, 1978, pp. 203-8.

F190 Mihail, P. "D-nul Mircea Eliade a plecat în India sau cum a rămas 'Generaţia' fără şef." *Vremea* (1928) 1, no. 41:2.

F191 "Mircea Eliade." *Viaţa Literară* (1933) 146:2.

F192 "Mircea Eliade, Doctor Honoris Causa la Sorbona." *Micro Magazin* (April 1977) p. 11.

F193 "Mircea Eliade: 'Le grand-père céleste a sombré dans l'oubli.'" *La Vie Internationale*, Geneva (Sept. 6, 1966) 208:5.

F194 "M. Mircea Eliade parle ..." *Les Dernières nouvelles d'Alsace* (Nov. 17, 1954) p. 15.

F195 Molinski, B. "Humanistyka, Religioznawstwo i Mit samotnego czlowieka Uwagi o twórezości Mircea Eliadego." In *Sacrum, mit, historia*, Warsaw (1970) pp. 11-29.

F196 Morretta, A. "La riscoperta del simbolo." *La Fiera Letteraria*, Rome (July 14, 1957) pp. 5-6.

F197 Munson, T. "Freedom: A Philosophical Reflection on Spirituality." *Philosophy Today* (1967) 11:47-54.

Inspired by *Yoga. Immortality and Freedom* A63. A reflection on the problematics of the notion of "freedom" and the process of "despiritualization" in the western world as interpreted by Nietzsche, Descartes, Hume, Hegel, and others.

F198 ———. *Reflective Theology. Philosophical Orientations in Religion.* New Haven: Yale University Press, 1968, 211 pp. Reprinted: Westport, Conn.: Greenwood Press, 1976. See pp. 135, 138-39, 148, 159-61, 164-65, 184-87 etc.

A small part of chapter 7, "The History and Phenomenology of Religion," is devoted to a consideration of several of Eliade's concepts. There is an interesting comparison of Eliade and Sartre in chapter 8, "The Fate of Commitment."

F199 Murăraşu, D. *Haşdeu. Ediţia Mircea Eliade.* Bucharest: Tiparul Universitar, 1938, 67 pp.

Author comments on A25: B.P. Hasdeu, *Scrieri literare, morale şi politice*, edited by Eliade. Since the length of this book is equivalent to a 30- or 40-page journal article, it is listed under F.

F200 Mureşanu, M. "Mircea Eliade şi o noua tematica în romanul modern." *Inşir'te mărgărite*, Rio de Janeiro (1956-1957) 6-7, no. 21-26:38-41.

Notes on *Forêt interdite* A54.

F201 Murty, K.S. "Yoga: The Path to Freedom from Suffering." *Review of Metaphysics* (1961) 15:118-24.

Extrapolations on *Yoga. Immortality and Freedom* A63.

F202 Musceleanu, M. "Lirica unui gânditor." *Gând, Vers, Critică, Proză* (1935) 2, no. 7:3.

F203 Myers, L. "A Technique of Ecstasy." *Sewanee Review* (1966) 74:717-22.

F204 "Myths for Moderns." *Times Literary Supplement* (Feb. 10, 1966) no. 3337:102.

Brief commentary on several of Eliade's works.

F205 Nakamura, K. "Seishinsekai no Kakudai" (Expansion of the Spiritual World). *Kōza Shūkyōgaku*, Tokyo, Tokyo-daigakushuppankai (1978) 5.

F206 ———. "M. Eliāde niokeru Shūkyōgaku to Bungaku" (History of Religions and Literature in M. Eliade). *Shūkyōkenkyū* (March 1976) 49, no. 3:33-35.

F207 ———. "Shūkyōgaku niokeru Tsūjiteki Kenkyū no arikata" (Diachronic Research in the History of Religions). *Shūkyōkenkyū* (Dec. 1976) 50, no. 3:23-24.

F208 Navarro, E. "Um encontro com Mircea Eliade." *A Voz* (Dec. 27, 1942).

F209 Negoiţescu, I. "Mircea Eliade--sau de la fantastic la oniric." *Viaţa Românească* (Feb. 1970) 23:71-77.

A leading Romanian literary critic examines Eliade's literature of the type "fantastic," comparing prewar and postwar compositions.

F210 Niculescu, M. "Un om al tainei." *Destin* (1968) 16:114-16.

F211 Noica, C. "Hiérophanie et sacralité." In *Mircea Eliade* D11 pp. 105-9.

F212 ———. "'Yoga' şi autorul ei." *Revista Fundaţiilor Regale* (1937) 4, no. 1:202-11.

F213 ———. "Adevăratul înţeles al 'Sacrului.'" *Săptămîna* (Dec. 5, 12, 19, 1975) nos. 261-63.

F214 ———. "Rânduri despre un pornograf." *Vremea* (1937) 10, no. 492.

F215 ———. "Mircea Eliade erudit." *Vremea* (1937) 10, no. 492:8.

F216 "Omagii internaţionale lui Mircea Eliade." *Tribuna* (1978) 22, no. 26:3.

F217 Oprea, A. "Mircea Eliade: Tehnica epifaniei şi vârstele creaţiei." In Oprea, *Mitul "faurului aburit."* Bucharest: Ed. Albatros, 1974, pp. 167-83.

Discusses Eliade's prewar novels and essays and his autobiography *Amintiri* A85. Interprets his style as "epiphanic": that he writes when "inspired" and this results in "romantic," quasi-religious or revelatory expressions.

F218 Pan, G.O. "Mircea Eliade." *Azi* (1937) 6, no. 30:2803-4.

F219 Papadima, O. "Mircea Eliade." *Gândirea* (1934) 13, no. 8:367.

F220 Pasquier, P. "L'amer festin ou Histoire des religions et Spiritualité." In *Mircea Eliade* D11 pp. 212-19.

F221 Patri, A. "Mircea Eliade nous parle des méthodes de l'ascétisme indou." *Paru* (1948) 46:49-54.

F222 Păunescu, A. "Mircea Eliade." *Contemporanul* (March 10 and 17, 1972) no. 11.

Interview repudiated by Eliade because of unauthorized changes in the original text.

F223 Penner, H. "Bedeutung und Probleme der religiösen Symbolik bei Tillich und Eliade." *Antaios* (1967) 9: 127-43.

F224 Pernet, H. "Rencontre avec Mircea Eliade." *Gazette de Lausanne* (Sept. 1961) p. 3.

F225 Petrascincu, A.M. "Il mondo misterioso del pensiero orientale." *Il Momento*, Rome (May 19, 1952) p. 3.

F226 Petrasincu, D. "Anul literar 1932." *Discobolul* (1933) 5:3.

F227 Pettazzoni, R. "Il Metodo." *Studi e Materiali di Storia delle Religioni*, University of Rome (1960) 31:31-55.

Notes and comments (dated) on *Le Mythe de l'éternel retour* A43; *Images et symboles* A48; and *Mythes, rêves et mystères* A58.

F228 Pimenta, A. "Romenia erudita: Mircea Eliade." *A Voz* (June 17, 1943).

F229 Piru, A. "Literatură fantastică." *România Literară* (1968) 1, nos. 5:12-13 and 6:1.

Relates some short stories of Eliade to folkloric themes.

F230 Pleşu, A. "Mircea Eliade şi hermeneutica artelor." *Secolul 20* (1978) 205-6:59-64.

F230a Popa, D.R. "Mircea Eliade şi cercetarea religiilor." *Tribuna României* (1977) 6, no. 104:6.

F231 Popescu, M. "L'odissea dei poeli romeni." *Folla*, Rome (June 21, 1964) 1, no. 17:12-13.

F232 ———. "Eliade and Folklore." In *Myths and Symbols. Studies in Honor of Mircea Eliade* D8 pp. 81-90.

F233 ———. "O mare prezenţă românească în exil: Mircea Eliade." *Revista Scriitorilor Români* (1966) 5:138-39.

F234 Popovici, C.L. "Umanism şi exotism." *Destin* (1964) 13-14:172-74.

F235 Porumbacu, V. "Maitreye regăsită." *Secolul 20* (1973) 7, no. 150:138-39.

F236 Posteucă, V. "Naştere şi renaştere de Mircea Eliade." *America*, Cleveland (Dec. 2, 1958) pp. 1-2; and (Dec. 9, 1958) p. 2.

F237 ———. "Mircea Eliade şi gândirea americană." *Cuvântul în Exil* (1966) 46-47:3.

F238 Preda, G. "Viaţa indiană. De vorbă cu D-nul Mircea Eliade." *Viaţa Literară* (1933) 8, no. 145:1-2.

F239 Pritchard, A., and D.E. Fitch. *Mircea Eliade: A Check-List of His Publications in the History of Religions.* Santa Barbara: University of California, 1968, 50 pp. Revised and updated by R. Hecht and M.G. Bradford as *Mircea Eliade. A Bibliography* F121.

F240 Progoff, I. "Culture and Being: Mircea Eliade's Studies in Religion." *International Journal of Parapsychology* (1960) 2, no. 3:47-60.

Eliade's work is in the forefront of the reevaluation of spiritual reality. His interpretations of the sacred, as seen in his studies of religious initiation, help one to understand the nature of human existence and the need for a new initiation to establish contact with a sacred dimension that is relevant to and necessary for modern civilization.

F241 Radian, E. "Reviste şi moravuri literare în anul 1934." *Frize* (1934) 1, no. 10:1.

F242 Rasmussen, D. "Herméneutique structurale et philosophie." In *Mircea Eliade* D11 pp. 97-104. Translation of F243.

F243 ———. "Mircea Eliade: Structural Hermeneutics and Philosophy." *Philosophy Today* (1968) 12:138-46. Reprinted in Rasmussen, *Symbol and Interpretation*. The Hague: Martinus Nijhoff, 1974, chap. 2. Translated as F242 which appears in D11.

Excellent analysis, which is one of the rare efforts by a philosopher to take Eliade's work seriously. Clarifies the hermeneutic movement from the appearance of the sacred (involving principles of the irreducibility and dialectic of the sacred) to the understanding of the sacred on the basis of structural and morphological principles. Suggests how this hermeneutic procedure might serve as a method for philosophic reflection.

F244 Ray, R.A. "Is Eliade's Metapsychoanalysis an End Run around Bultmann's Demythologization?" In *Myth and the Crisis of Historical Consciousness*. Ed. by L.W. Gibbs and W.T. Stevenson. Missoula, Mont.: Scholars Press, University of Montana, 1975, pp. 57-74.

F245 "Réception de Mircea Eliade." *La Libre Belgique* (Feb. 22, 1977).

F246 Rei, D. "Fra storicismo ed ermeneutica religiosa: note su Mircea Eliade." *Rivista di storia e litteratura religiosa*, Florence (1973) pp. 535-62.

Discusses Eliade's hermeneutics under the following headings (translated): Eliade in Italy; Religions and History; Archaic and Modern; Modernity and Sacrality; Modern Historicism and Archaic Ontology; the History of Religions and the Dialectic of the Sacred; and the Freedom of Moderns.

F247 Reno, S.J. "Hiérophanie, symbole et expériences." In *Mircea Eliade* D11 pp. 120-27. Translation of F248.

F248 ———. "Eliade's Progressional View of Hierophanies." *Religious Studies* (1972) 8:153-60. Translated as F247 which appears in D11.

This very controversial interpretation claims Eliade has a "progressional view" of hierophanies based on a Christian theological position in which hierophanies can be arranged in some hierarchical order from the most elementary to the supreme Incarnation of Jesus Christ. Relies very heavily on a few pages in *Patterns in Comparative Religion* A62.

F249 Revol, E.L. "Aproximación a la obra de Mircea Eliade." *La Torre*, Puerto Rico (1953) 1, no. 3:153-63.

Short essay on hierophany and symbol and other themes common to Eliade's work.

F250 Ricardi, F. "L'interpretazione del sacro nell'opera di M. Eliade." *Rivista di Filosofia Neo-scolastica* (1969) 61:509-35; and (1970) 62:133-62.

A very good introduction to Eliade's hermeneutics. The first part of the study includes sections on the sacred and the profane; sacred space; sacred time and repetition; myth; the sacred and primitive ontology; the sacred and existence. The second part: Christianity; the experience of the secular person; the language of symbols; the History of Religions and a hermeneutics of the sacred.

F251 Ricketts, M.L. "Eliade and Altizer: Very Different Outlooks." *Christian Advocate* (Oct. 1967) pp. 11-12.

Although Altizer and Eliade have frequently been associated, "two men could not represent more opposite positions with respect to religion." Most of the article is a summary of some of Eliade's position, with the conclusion that the two scholars "belong to totally opposite philosophical worlds."

F252 ———. "Mircea Eliade et la mort de Dieu." In *Mircea Eliade* D11 pp. 110-19. Translation of F253.

F253 ———. "Mircea Eliade and the Death of God." *Religion in Life* (Spring 1967) pp. 40-52. Translated as F252 which appears in D11.

Rebuttal of Altizer's *Mircea Eliade and the Dialectic of the Sacred* D3. In claiming to "use" some of Eliade's approach, Altizer has distorted or misunderstood his History of Religions. In their views of religion and transcendence, the Incarnation and essence of Christianity, Eternal Return, and other important matters, the two positions are diametrically opposed. In particular, Altizer has misunderstood Eliade's dialectic of the sacred and his use of the *coincidentia oppositorum*.

F254 ———. "In Defence of Eliade: Toward Bridging the Communications Gap between Anthropology and the History of Religions." *Religion. Journal of Religion and Religions* (1973) 3, no. 1:13-34.

Formulates a defense of Eliade by criticizing the usual total neglect of, and occasional attacks on, his History of Religions by anthropologists. Extensive critique of Leach F150. Good defense of Eliade and appeal for the merits of the History of Religions, although the author is sometimes too protective of his former teacher. For example, even an admirer of Eliade need not claim that he never ventures any answers as to his own views about reality.

F255 ———. "The Nature and Extent of Eliade's 'Jungianism.'" *Union Seminary Quarterly Review* (1970) 25:211-34.

Eliade has often been identified as, and criticized for, being a "Jungian." He shares many similarities with Jung, and some of his analysis does appear "Jungian." But this excellent article carefully examines the texts and concludes that the differences between Eliade and Jung are "even more profound than the similarities." Good formulation of the "transconscious." In F254, Ricketts arrives at a somewhat different conclusion: "those who say Eliade is a Jungian are at least partially right," and "Eliade probably is closer to Jung in his theories than he realizes."

F256 Ries, J. "Le sacrée et l'histoire des religions." In *L'Expression du sacré dans les grandes religions. I. Proche-Orient ancien et traditions bibliques*. Louvain-la-Neuve, 1978, pp. 71-100.

F257 ———. "Histoire des religions, phénoménologie, herméneutique." In *Mircea Eliade* D11 pp. 81-87.

Divides Eliade's search for a method into three processes which are presented in some sort of methodological order: first, history; second, phenomenology; finally, hermeneutics. Phenomenology is concerned with morphology and typology and refrains from the work of comparison. Hermeneutics, which involves comparative analysis and takes one beyond phenomenology, is concerned with the interpretation of meaning. For a different analysis, see D1.

F258 ———. "Mircea Eliade, Histoire des croyances et des idées religieuses." *Revue Théologie de Louvain* (1976) 7:499-504.

F259 Roman, H. "Mircea Eliade: Un coeur jeune." *Bulletin européen*, Rome (Aug.-Sept. 1967) p. 1.

F260 Romanato, G. "Il sacro e il profano in Mircea Eliade." *Il Popolo* (June 10, 1978) p. 3.

F261 "Rumanian Exile Finds U.S. Campus 'Home.'" *Washington Post* (May 12, 1961) p. A22.

F262 Saiving, V. "Androcentrism in Religious Studies." *Journal of Religion* (1976) 56:177-97.

Offers a feminist critique of androcentrism in religious studies, using *Rites and Symbols of Initiation* A83 as her case study. Contends that what Eliade "says about the *human* meaning of initiation corresponds almost exactly to what he says about *male* initiation, and that it contradicts in essential respects his understanding of *female* initiation." Once again women appear "as deviant by definition."

F263 Saliba, J.A. "Eliade's View of Primitive Man: Some Anthropological Reflections." *Religion. Journal of Religion and Religions* (1976) 6, no. 2:150-75.

There is a need for a dialogue between anthropology and the History of Religions, but Ricketts's attempt (F254) is inadequate and will not be convincing to anthropologists. Eliade's view of "primitive man" is not compatible with contemporary anthropological conceptions. The historian of religions concerned with primitive religion can adopt a method from anthropology, while anthropologists can be stimulated by some speculations in the History of Religions. This analysis is presented in expanded form in D10.

F264 Săndulescu, C.G. "Forum: Rostirea românească: Un mag al graiului universal." *Candela. Publicaţie religios-culturală a Parohiei Ortodoxe Române din Suedia* (Dec. 31, 1975) 3, no. 4:17-24.

F265 Sauesure, R. de. "Les Techniques archaïques de l'extase." *Tribune de Genève* (Aug. 25, 1963).

F266 "Scientist of Symbols." *Time* (Feb. 11, 1966) 87, no. 6: 68, 70.

F267 Sebastian, L. "Odiseia lui Mircea Iliade, sau suferinţele tânărului erotolog." *Reporter* (1937) 5, no. 19:4.

F268 Sebastian, M. "Cartea lui Mircea Eliade." *Cuvântul* (1930) 6, no. 1833:1-2.

F269 Segal, R.A. "Eliade's Theory of Millenarianism." *Religious Studies* (1978) 14:159-73.

Eliade offers a unique theory of millenarianism, which is seen not as some abnormal phenomenon but as the fulfillment of traditional values, involving the "innate desire" or "natural eschatological yearning" to abolish history and return to primordial time. His theory of millenarianism, his more general theory of eschatology, and his very general account of mythic and historical attitudes toward history are all very inadequate.

F270 Şeicaru, P. "Revista Universitară." *Cuvântul* (1926) 3, no. 434:2.

Editorial defense of Eliade's criticism of Nicolae Iorga.

F271 Simion, E. "Timpul trăirii, timpul mărturisirii." *Jurnal Parizian*, Bucharest (1977) pp. 296-301.

F272 ———. "Fantasticul la Mircea Eliade." *Luceafărul* (Jan. 17 and 24, 1976) p. 6. This is equivalent to "Mircea Eliade." In Simion, *Scriitori români de azi*. Bucharest: Editura cartea românesc, 1976, vol. 2, pp. 319-36.

F273 ———. "Demnitatea mitică a naraţiunii." *Secolul 20* (1978) 205-6:52-56.

Considers Eliade the "most important writer in the fantastic genre in modern Romanian prose...." Sees in his literature such themes as *coincidentia oppositorum*, hierophany, escape from time, and initiatory ordeals. Contrasts his works to Anglo-Saxon horror types of fantastic literature in that the fantastic emerges from the most banal characters and episodes in a very profound and complex way.

F274 Simionescu, P. "Posibile repere în opera ştiinţifică a lui Mircea Eliade." *Revista de etnografie şi folclor* (1978) 23, no. 2:231-39.

F275 Smart, N. "Beyond Eliade: The Future of Theory in Religion." *Numen* (1978) 25, no. 2:171-83.

Using Dudley's *Religion on Trial* D7, Smart suggests

his own estimate of Eliade's "place in the future of theory in religion." He expresses "much admiration both for Eliade's work and the way he has given stature to the history of religions," but concludes that "his creative hermeneutic is in the end restricted."

F276 Smith, J.Z. "The Wobbling Pivot." *Journal of Religion* (1972) 52, no. 2:134-49.

After formulating "the basic presuppositions and elements" in Eliade's analysis of sacred space and time, Smith offers some "queries and applications" regarding this analysis. He raises questions about Eliade's interpretations of "chaos," of the "Center," of mythic creations or beginnings as always paradigmatic and to be ritually repeated, and of the dichotomy between "archaic" and "modern."

F277 Şora, M. "Mircea Eliade, eseist." In Şora, *Unde şi interferenţe*. Bucharest: 1969, pp. 189-212.

Discusses Eliade's early books of essays: *Soliloquii* A10, *Oceanografie* A16, *Fragmentarium* A29, and *Insula lui Euthanasius* A36. Emphasizes author's "authenticity," his tendency to paradoxical expression, and his contemporaneity.

F278 Sorescu, M. "Dialog cu Mircea Eliade." *Luceafărul* (Aug. 17, 1978) 11, no. 33.

F279 Spaltmann, G. "Authenticity and Experience of Time: Remarks on Mircea Eliade's Literary Works." In *Myths and Symbols. Studies in Honor of Mircea Eliade* D8 pp. 365-85.

F280 Stamatu, H. "Mircea Eliade la Sorbona." *Drum. Revistă de cultură românească* (1977) 13, no. 2-4:12-14.

F281 Stancu, Z. "Generaţia în pulbere şi cu ochelari savanţi." *Floarea de foc* (1936) 3, no. 17:1, 4.

F282 ———. "Generaţia n'are ... leafă." *Floarea de foc* (1936) 3, no. 19:1, 4.

F283 ———. "Spre deplina pedepsire a pornografilor." *Reporter* (1937) 5, no. 15:1-2.

F284 Steinhardt, N. "Fantasticul lui Mircea Eliade." *Steaua* (1977) 28, no. 4:18-19.

Claims that Eliade writes literature as a form of "confession" or "salvation" that he cannot achieve when writing in the "positivistic" vein as historian of religions. Steinhardt suggests that Eliade's "fantastic literature" is more of the Oriental than of the Occidental type. The world for Eliade is a "cipher" wherein one can come to know the self and where Kantian categories dissolve.

F285 Stoica, T. "Incrucişari în actual." *Caet* (1934) 1, no. 2-3:2, 6.

F286 Strenski, I. "Mircea Eliade: Some Theoretical Problems." In *The Theory of Myth. Six Studies*. Ed. by A. Cunningham. London: Sheed and Ward, 1973, chap. 3, pp. 40-78.

An extremely powerful critique which challenges the very foundations of Eliade's History of Religions. His "methodological prescriptions are disastrous"; he is evasive, loose thinking, and anti-scientific; his "against history" approach formulates "dilemmas" that are as false as the (nonhistorical) solutions he provides; his analysis of myth cannot be justified. One could show that Eliade's method is not so totally dependent on some depth psychological, nonhistorical "intuition" or "introspection" that is "self-authenticating" and beyond verification and falsification. But these are strong criticisms, and Strenski cannot be dismissed as some "positivist" or "historicist."

F287 Stroe, V. "Magul unei generaţii." *Viaţa Literară* (1930) 5, no. 127:2.

F288 "Studenţimea ia atitudine pentru Mircea Eliade." *Vremea* (1937) 9, no. 492:9-10.

F289 Şuluţiu, O. "Romanul lui Mircea Eliade." *Cuvântul* (1931) 7, no. 1052:1.

F290 ———. "Pentru Mircea Eliade." *Vremea* (1937) 10, no. 492:8.

F291 "Le symbolisme religieux et la valorisation de l'angoisse." *Les Services publics*, Geneva (Sept. 9, 1953) no. 41. Published also in *La Suisse* (Sept. 5, 1953) 248:9; and in *La Tribune de Genève* (Sept. 6, 1953) p. 5.

F292 Taat, M. "De 'Oer-Tijd' van Mircea Eliade." *Vrij Nederland* (March 27, 1976) 37:25.

F293 Thornton, A. *People and Themes in Homer's Odyssey*. London: Methuen, in association with Dunedin, University of Otago Press, 1970, xv + 163 pp. See chap. 2.

In chapter 2, "The Wanderings of Odysseus," pp. 16-37, Thornton uses Eliade's analysis in *Shamanism* A81 "to test and fill out [Karl] Meuli's theory of shamanic elements in the Odyssean wanderings." He concludes that it is probable that "in the wanderings of Odysseus the poet used material ultimately derived from a shaman's journey into the Beyond."

F294 "Unde se vede că d. Mircea Eliade e mai puţin filozof decât vrea să pară?" *Reporter* (1937) 5, no. 14:3.

F295 "Un sfat pentru dl. Mircea Eliade." *Adevĕrul Literar şi Artistic* (1937) 864:18.

F296 Uscatescu, G. "Time and Destiny in the Novels of Mircea Eliade." In *Myths and Symbols. Studies in Honor of Mircea Eliade* D8 pp. 397-406.

F297 Vaida, M. "Mircea Eliade--romancier." *Tribuna României* (Jan. 1968) 12, nos. 2:3; and 3:3. Reprinted in Vaida, *Ospatul lui Trimalchio*. Cluj: Ed. Dacia, 1970, pp. 118-32.

F298 Vaina-Puşcă, L. "La dialettica del 'grande passaggio' nella *Ţigănci* di Mircea Eliade." *Strumenti Critici, Rivista quadrimestrale di cultura e critica letteraria* (1975) 28:393-407.

F299 Valerian, I. "Romanul lui Mircea Eliade." *Viaţa Literară* (1937) 11, no. 13:1-2.

F300 Vázquez, J.A. "Encuentro con Mircea Eliade." *La Gaceta* (June 26, 1960) p. 5.

F301 ———. "Sobre El chamanismo y las técnicas del éxtasis de Mircea Eliade." *La Gaceta* (Feb. 1964) 11, no. 114: 5, 7.

Exposition of Eliade's research on shamanism. See *Shamanism* A81.

F302 ———. "Para una biobibliografia de Mircea Eliade." *Universidad*, Sante Fé, Argentina (1964) 59:357-74.

The first bibliographical publication of Eliade's works

with a brief biographical sketch. It is extremely incomplete.

F303 Vermeulen, M. "Réception 'roumaine' à l'Académie: M. Mircea Eliade, Protée moderne, succède à la princesse Bibesco." *Le Soir* (Feb. 22, 1977).

F304 Vierne, S. "La littérature sous la lumière des mythes." In *Mircea Eliade* D11 pp. 350-54.

F305 Vignolo, R. "L'immaginazione e storia. Note all'opera di M. Eliade." *Annali delle Scuola Superiore delle Communicazioni Sociali*, Brescia (1971) 5:63-81.

F306 Voita, L. "Mircea Eliade." *Vremea* (June 27, 1943).

F307 Vollmer, U. "Zum 70 Geburtstag von Mircea Eliade." *Indo Asia* (1977) 19, no. 3:321-24.

F308 Voyta, L. "Symbolism şi magie." *Vremea* (1936) 9, no. 435:10.

F309 Vulcănescu, M. "Triptic de cărţi şi de semne: Mircea Eliade." *Azi* (1932) 1, no. 3-4:237-38.

F310 ———. "Spiritualitate. Despre M. Eliade." *Criterion* (1934) 1, no. 1:4.

F311 ———. "Generaţie." *Criterion* (1934) 1, no. 3-4:3-6.

F312 ———. "Carte pentru 'Isabel.'" *Cuvântul* (1930) 6, nos. 1951:1-2; 1959:1-2; and 1965:1-2.

F313 Wald, H. "Semnificaţia laică a religiei." *Viaţa Românească* (July 1977) 30, no. 7:32-34.

F314 Welbon, G.R. "Some Remarks on the Work of Mircea Eliade." *Acta Philosophica et Theologica* (1964) 2:465-92.

Brief introduction to Eliade's analyses of the sacred and the profane, hierophanies, symbol, myth, and ritual. The lengthiest and most controversial section is on "Being, Time, and Eliade's Image of Man."

F315 Widengren, G. "Mircea Eliade Sixty Years Old." *Numen* (1967) 14:165-66.

F316 Wikander, S. "Mircea Eliade och den moderna religionsforskningen." *Svensk Missionstidskrift* (1966) 54:217-24.

F317 Zamfir, M. "L'image de Portugal dans la littérature roumaine du XXème siècle: N. Iorga, M. Eliade, L. Blaga." *International Journal of Rumanian Studies* (1976) 1, no. 1-2:109- .

F318 Zamfirescu, G.M. "Cronica anului literar 1936." *Insemnări ieşene*, Iasi (1936) 1, no. 24:540.

F319 ———. "Anul literar 1937." *Insemnări ieşene* (1937) 3, no. 2:333.

G

CRITICAL REVIEWS

G1 *Isabel şi apele Diavolului* A9

Convorbiri Literare (1930) 63:623 by A. Bilciurescu
Cuvântul (1930) 6, no. 1893:1-2 by Perpessicus
Falca (1930) 9, no. 354:2 by L. Boz
Gândirea (1930) 10, no. 8-9:307-9 by C.D. Ionescu
România Literară (1932) 1, no. 25:3 by M. Sebastian
Viaţa Literară (1930) 5, no. 129:3 by O. Şuluţiu
Vremea (1930) 3, no. 120:5 by P. Constantinescu

G2 *Soliloquii* A10

România Literară (1932) 1, no. 17:3 by M. Sebastian
Vremea (1932) 5, no. 240:5 by P. Constantinescu

G3 *Maitreyi* A12
Das Mädchen Maitreyi A40
La Nuit Bengali A45

Bulletin Européen (Oct.-Nov. 1950) no. 15-16 by A. Pellevant-Gini
Convorbiri Literare (May 1933) pp. 487-90 by C. Gerota
Cuvântul (1933) 9, no. 2890:1-2 by Perpessicus
Cuvântul Studenţesc (1933) 8, no. 6:1 by S. Ionescu
Discobolul (1933) 9:15 by I. Şerbu
Est Eclair (Oct. 15, 1950) by J. Amsler
Insemnări ieşene (1936) 15-16:141 by D. Bădărău
Muguri Literarii (1938) 1, no. 2:33-34
Nice-Matin (April 15, 1956) by P. Rocher
România Literară (1933) 2, no. 64:3 by M. Sebastian
Russelsheimer Echo (June 23, 1975) by W. Helwig
Viaţa Literară (1933) 8, no. 144:2 by M. Ilovici
Vremea (1933) 6, no. 288:7 by P. Constantinescu

G4 *India* A13

Convorbiri Literare (1934) 67:785 by I. Dobridor
Viaţa Literară (1934) 8, no. 160:2 by E. Grozia
Vremea (1934) 7, no. 349:7 by P. Constantinescu

G5 *Intoarcerea din rai* A14

Azi (1934) 3, no. 2:1060-63 by E. Gulian
Convorbiri Literare (1934) 67:170-71 by C. Noica
Convorbiri Literare (1934) 67:369-70 by I. Cantacuzino
Familia (1934) 1, no. 1:85-89 by O. Şuluţiu
Frize (1934) 1, no. 2:9 by M. Chirnoagă
Gând Românesc (1934) 2, no. 3:155-58 by I. Chinezu
Gând Românesc (1934) 2, no. 12:3 by D. Petrasincu
Revista Fundaţiilor Regale (1934) 1, no. 4:189-95 by Ş. Cioculescu
Viaţa Literară (1934) 8, no. 155:3 by E. Grozia
Vremea (1934) 7, no. 328:7 by P. Constantinescu

G6 *Lumina ce se stinge* A15

Convorbiri Literare (1934) 67:880-83 by C. Gerota
Cuvântul (1931) 7, no. 2054:1-2 by M. Vulcănescu
Gând Românesc (1934) 2, no. 7-8:446-48 by I. Chinezu
Reporter (1934) 2, no. 34-36:3 by O. Şuluţiu
Revista Fundaţiilor Regale (1934) 1, no. 8:437-43 by M. Sebastian
Viaţa Literară (1934) 8, no. 159:2 by E. Grozia
Vremea (1934) 7, no. 346:7 by P. Constantinescu

G7 *Oceanografie* A16

Familia (1935) 1, no. 10:81-85 by O. Şuluţiu
Familia (1935) 2, no. 2:105-8 by P. Martinescu
Gândirea (1935) 14, no. 7:386-87 by O. Papadima
Viaţa Literară (1935) 9, no. 165:6 by D. Petrasincu
Vremea (1935) 8, no. 381:7 by P. Constantinescu

G8 *Revolta în deşert* C2

Reporter (1934) 2, no. 21:6

G9 *Alchimia Asiatică* A17

Familia (1935) 2, no. 4:81-83 by O. Şuluţiu

G10 *Huliganii* A18

Adevĕrul Literar şi Artistic (1935) 14, no. 784 by G. Călinescu
Familia (1936) 3, no. 2:75-78 by O. Şuluţiu

Front Literar (1936) 1, no. 1:6-7 by D. Silvaru
Gând Românesc (1936) 4, no. 8-9:490-91 by C. Stelian
Pagini Basarabene (1936) 1, no. 2:15-16 by N. Crevedia
Preocupări Literare (1936) 1, no. 2:123-24 by S. Prajbâ
Răboj (1935) 1, no. 2:4 by I. Vasiliu
Reporter (1935) 3, no. 86-88:2 by P. Martinescu
Revista Fundaţiilor Regale (1936) 3, no. 3 by Ş. Cioculescu
Viaţa Literară (1936) 10, no. 4:4 by D. Petrasincu
Viaţa Românească (1936) 28, no. 2-3:138-40 by N. Cristinoiu
Viaţa Românească (1936) 28, no. 6-8:58-60 by A. Philippide
Vremea (1936) 9, no. 420:9 by P. Constantinescu

G11 *Şantier* A19

Adevĕrul Literar şi Artistic (1935) 14, no. 767:9-10 by G. Călinescu
Azi (1935) 4, no. 2:1680-81 by P. Manoliu
Familia (1935) 2, no. 3:87-89 by O. Şuluţiu
Gândirea (1935) 14, no. 8:434-35 by O. Papadima
Revista Fundaţiilor Regale (1935) 2, no. 7 by Ş. Cioculescu
Viaţa Literară (1935) 9, no. 2:4 by D. Petrasincu
Vremea (1935) 8, no. 392:7 by P. Constantinescu

G12 *Domnişoara Christina* A20
Mademoiselle Christina A121

Adevĕrul Literar şi Artistic (1936) 15, no. 837 by G. Călinescu
Azi (1937) 6, no. 26:2432-34 by D. Trost
Familia (1937) 4, no. 1-2:95-97 by O. Şuluţiu
Gândirea (1937) 16, no. 2:89-90 by O. Papadima
Gândul Vremii (1937) 5, no. 1:19-21 by I. Gruia
Insemnări ieşene (1937) 2, no. 4:287-88 by V.I. Catarama
Le Monde (March 31, 1978) p. 18 by E. Reichmann
Pagini Basarabene (1936) 1, no. 12:8 by A.Z. Pop
Revista Fundaţiilor Regale (1937) 4, no. 2 by M. Sebastian
Vremea (1936) 9, no. 467:9 by P. Constantinescu

G13 *Yoga. Essai sur les origines de la mystique indienne* A21

Revista de Filosofie (1937) 12, no. 2:229-36 by A. Dumitriu
Viaţa Literară (1937) 11, no. 10:4 by V.G.
Vremea (1937) 10, no. 491:5

G14 *Roza Vânturilor* A22

Viaţa Literară (1937) 11, no. 12:3 by V. Damaschin

G15 *Şarpele* A24
Andronic und die Schlange A42

Gândirea (1937) 16, no. 7:362 by O. Papadima
Insemnări ieşene (1937) 2, no. 12:1116-17 by V.I. Catarama
Vremea (1937) 10, no. 490:8 by P. Constantinescu

G16 *Scrieri literare, morale şi politice* A25

Insemnări ieşene (1938) 3, no. 6:525-27 by G.M. Dragos
Preocupări Literare (1938) 3, no. 7:320 by D. Murarasu
Vremea (1937) 10, nos. 510:9; 511:5; 512:9; 513:9; 514:8; 515:5; and 516:6 by P. Constantinescu

G17 *Zalmoxis. Revue des Études Religieuses* C5

Symposion (1939) 2, no. 2-3:220-21 by G. Pavelescu

G18 *Fragmentarium* A29

Viaţa Românească (1939) 31, no. 12:117-18 by I. Frunzetti

G19 *Nuntă în Cer* A30

Adevĕrul Literar şi Artistic (1939) 19, no. 961:10 by I. Sadoveanu
Gândirea (1939) 18, no. 7:402-3 by S. Bucur
Jurnalul Literar (1939) 1, no. 25:3 by G. Lumgu
Meşterul Manole (1939) 1, no. 4:35-36 by M. Suru

G20 *Secretul Doctorului Honigberger* A31
Nächte in Serampore A50
Minuit à Serampore A56

Le Concours Médical (1956) 34:3697-98 by M. Brion
Familia (1940) 7, no. 7-8:77-79 by O. Şuluţiu

G21 *Mitul Reintegrării* A33

Zalmoxis (1940-42) 3:162-63 by J. Coman

G22 *Salazar şi revoluţia în Portugalia* A34

A Voz (Dec. 7, 1942)
Diàrio de Manha (Dec. 7, 1942)

G23 *Comentarii la legenda Meşterului Manole* A35

Revista Fundaţiilor Regale (1943) 10, no. 9:631-34 by P. Comarnescu
Saeculum (1943) 6:85-87 by G. Pavelescu

G24 *Os Romenos, Latinos do Oriente* A37

A Voz (1943) no. 17 by E. Navarro
Diàrio de Manha (April 12, 1943)
Novidades (April 25, 1943)

G25 *Techniques du Yoga* A41

Études Traditionnelles (Dec. 1948) pp. 371-72 by R. Guénon
Le Muséon (1949) 62, no. 3-4:285-86 by E. Lamotte
Paru (1948) 45:107-8 by A. Patri
Revue de l'Histoire des Religions (1949) 135:118-20 by J. Filliozat
Revue Tomiste (1948) 48:615-21 by L. Gardet

G26 *Le Mythe de l'éternel retour* A43
Der Mythos der ewigen Wiederkehr A49 (cf. A86)
The Myth of the Eternal Return A51 (cf. A64)

Arriba (Sept. 27 and Nov. 4, 1949) by E. d'Ors
Blackfriars (1955) 36:355-56 by V. White
Études (Nov. 1949) pp. 265-66 by L. Beirnaert
Études Traditionnelles (Dec. 1949) by R. Guénon
The Jewish Chronicle (Aug. 5, 1955) p. 12 by A. Altmann
Journal Asiatique (1950) 238:373-75 by J. Filliozat
Journal de Psychologie (July-Sept. 1949) pp. 366-68 by M. Dambuyant
Journal of Religion (1955) 35:263 by J.F. Hayward
The Listener (July 7, 1955) pp. 15-16 by P. Leon
Nederlands Theologisch Tijdschrift (1950) 4:114 by G. van der Leeuw
Observer (July 12, 1955) by J.M. Cohen
Paru (1949) 53:110-11 by A. Patri
La Pensée (Sept. 1951) pp. 127-30 by M. Rodinson
La Réforme (March 2, 1950) by A.M. Schmidt
Review of Religion (1956) 21:167-70 by T.H. Gaster
Revue des Sciences Religieuses (Jan.-April 1950) pp. 104-5 by A. Vincent
Revue d'Histoire et de Philosophie Religieuses (1950) 30:370-73 by R. Mehl
Social Order (1956) 6:239 by B. Chudoba
Spectator (1955) 194:399-401 by R. Graves

Les Temps Modernes (1949) 50:1139-41 by C. Ménard
Thought (1955) 30:442-43 by W.F. Lynch
Times Literary Supplement (Aug. 26, 1955)
De Zeit (1955) 1:6 by G. Bahlsen

G27 *Traité d'histoire des religions* A44
Die Religionen und das Heilige A52
Patterns in Comparative Religion A62

America (1958) 99:292-93 by C.E. Diviney
American Anthropologist (1959) 61:122-23 by W.A. Lessa
American Benedictine Review (1958) 9:251-52 by J. Gassner
The American Ecclesiastical Review (1958) 139:141-42 by J.A. Hardon
Anglican Theological Review (1958) 40:231-32 by J.M. Kitagawa
Archives de Sciences Sociales des Religions (1974) 19:209 by H. Desroche
Catholic World (1958) 187:474-75 by H.D. Noyes
Concordia Theological Monthly (1958) 29:951-52 by W.J. Danker
Downside Review (1958) 77:98-100 by B. Maitland
Erasmus (1950) 5, no. 15-16 by A.C. Bouquet
Études (June 1949) p. 421 by J. Daniélou
Foi et Vie (Nov. 1951) pp. 675-77 by A. Dumas
Hibbert Journal (1959) 57:82 by S.F. Brandon
Irish Theological Quarterly (1958) 25:391-92 by G. Mitchell
Journal Asiatique (1950) 238:373 by J. Filliozat
Journal de Psychologie (April 4, 1949) p. 6 by M. Dambuyant
Journal of Theological Studies (1959) 10:216-18 by S.H. Hooke
Man (March 1959) pp. 53-54 by Lord Raglan
Le Monde non-chrétien (1949) 10:239-41 by E. Dardel
Neues Abendland (Feb. 7, 1955) pp. 59-61 by H. Hornstein
Register (1959) 49, no. 1:2-3 by H. Smith
Review of Religion (May 1950) pp. 399-401 by A. Jeffery
Revista de filosofia (1949) 30:507-8 by G. Uscatescu
Revue de l'Histoire des Religions (July 1960) pp. 90-91 by J.M. Roux
Revue d'Histoire et de Philosophie Religieuses (1966) 46:199-200 by F. Andrieux
Stimmer (1955) 155:476-77 by H. Schade
Studi e Materiali (1950) 22:165-67 by R. Pettazzoni
Syria (1950) 27:332-35 by R. Dussaud
The Tablet (1958) 211:416 by G. Lienhardt

Les Temps Modernes (1949) 50:1139-41 by C. Ménard
Theological Studies (1958) 19:597-98 by H.J. Bihler
Thought (1959) 34:144-47 by L.V. Zabkar
Times Literary Supplement (May 23, 1958) p. 10
Tübingen Theologischen Quartalschrift (1955) pp. 231-32 by H. Fries
University of Chicago Magazine (March 1959) p. 21 by C.H. Long

G28 *Le Chamanisme* A46
Schamanismus A59
Shamanism A81

American Anthropologist (1953) 55:600-1 by E.E. Bacon
American Anthropologist (1965) 67:1305-6 by W.Z. Park
Anthropos (1953) 48:671-78 by D. Schröder
Antiquarian Bookman (1965) 36:547 by M.A. Malkin
Concordia Theological Monthly (1968) 39:205-6 by W.J. Danker
Deutsche Litteraturzeitung (1953) 74, no. 4:234-36 by W. Ruben
Erasmus (1959) 11:621-26 by M. Gusinde
International Journal of Parapsychology (1964) 6, no. 3:324-28 by M. Titiev
Journal Asiatique (1952) 240:406-7 by J. Filliozat
Journal de Psychologie (July 1952) pp. 367-69 by M. Dambuyant
Man (May 1952) pp. 74-75 by B.Z. Seligman
Le Monde non-chrétien (1952) 22:231-33 by M. Lienhardt
New York Times Book Review (July 12, 1964) pp. 24-25 by G. Sykes
Review of Religion (1952) 17:36-37 by R.A Stein
Revue des Sciences Religieuses (Jan. 1953) pp. 66-68 by A. Vincent
Revue Philosophique (1952) 142:568-70 by M. Bouteiller
The Tablet (1965) 219:40 by R. Haynes
Times Literary Supplement (March 4, 1965) p. 179
Zeitschrift für Missionswissenschaft und Religionswissenschaft (1958) 42:163-65 by J. Hasenfuss

G29 *Iphigenia* A47

Revista Fundaţiilor Regale (1941) 8, no. 2:472-75 by P. Comarnescu

G30 *Images et symboles* A48
Ewige Bilder und Sinnbilder A61
Images and Symbols A71

America (Sept. 23, 1961) by J. Boyd

Bulletin des Lettres (March 15, 1953) pp. 101-3 by V.H. Debidour
Christian Advocate (Sept. 1961) pp. 18-19 by M.L. Ricketts
Études (1955) 284:122 by L. Beirnaert
Foi et Vie (July 1953) pp. 389-90 by A. Dumas
The Heythrop Journal (1963) 4:180-82 by P. Fallon
Hibbert Journal (1961) 60:80-82 by S.F. Brandon
Life of the Spirit (1961) 16:46-47 by R. Sheed
Liturgical Arts (1961) 30:44 by G. Ellard
The Month (1962) 27:43-45 by E.I. Watkin
La Nouvelle Revue Française (May 1, 1953) pp. 900-4 by Y. Belaval
Review for Religious (1962) 21:390-91 by J. Malheikal
St. Louis Review (Jan. 9, 1961) by F. Kegel
The Sign (Dec. 1961) by T. Berry
Times Literary Supplement (Aug. 4, 1961) p. 485
Worship (1961) 35:593-94 by P. Blecker

G31 *Le Yoga. Immortalité et liberté* A53
Yoga. Immortality and Freedom A63
Yoga. Unsterblichkeit und Freiheit A70

Hibbert Journal (1959) 57:295-96 by E.J. Conze
Journal Asiatique (1955) 243:368-70 by J. Filliozat
Journal of the American Oriental Society (1962) 82, no. 2:229-31 by M. Fowler
Muséon, Louvain (1956) 69:218-21 by E. Lamotte
Orientalistische Literaturzeitung (1961) 11-12:628-32
Register (1959) 49, no. 1:2-3 by H. Smith
Revue Internationale de Philosophie (1962) 60:9-11 by K. Oedingen
San Francisco Chronicle (Nov. 16, 1958) p. 22 by C. Gentry
Studia Philosophica (1960) no. 20 by H. Kunz
Theologische Literaturzeitung (1961) 10:750-52 by F. Melzer
Theologische Zeitschrift (1962) 18:143-44 by H. van Oyen
Times Literary Supplement (March 27, 1959) p. 181.
Zeitschrift für Missionswissenschaft und Religionswissenschaft (1962) 46:317-19 by P. Hacker

G32 *Forêt interdite* A54
Noaptea de Sânziene A98
The Forbidden Forest A119

The Christian Century (Sept. 20, 1978) p. 864 by J. Cullum
Clartes (May 1956) pp. 7-12

Cuvântul Românesc (1978) 3, no. 28:11
Ethos (1973) 1:232-37 by S. Stolojan
Études (May 1956) by H. Holstein
Fapta (1956) 1, no. 2:5 by H.S.
L'Express (Apr. 27, 1956) by R. Canters
The Library Journal (May 15, 1978) by M. del Mastro
La Nouvelle Revue Française (March 1, 1956) pp. 513-14 by D. Aury
Nouvelles Littéraires (Nov. 1955) by R. Lalou
Parabola (1978) 3, no. 3:112-14 by J. Kitagawa
La Réforme (Aug. 4, 1956) by A.M. Schmidt
Religious Studies Review (1978) 4, no. 3:226 by J. Cullum
Le Soir (March 23, 1956) by V. Fosty
Sydsvenska Dagbladet Snällposten (Jan. 5, 1956) p. 4 by S. Wikander
Times Literary Supplement (Oct. 13, 1978) by V. Nemoianu
La Tour Saint-Jacques (March 1956) pp. 85-88 by R. Canters

G33 *Forgerons et alchimistes* A55
Schmiede und Alchemisten A69
The Forge and the Crucible A74

Atlantis (Nov. 1962) by K. Schier
Die Bücherkommentare (1961) no. 1 by K. Boegner
Bulletin des lettres (Feb. 15, 1957) by V.H.D.
Combat (Oct. 25, 1956) p. 7 by R. Amadou
Deutsche Zeitung (April 1961) by F. Kölling
Le Figaro Littéraire (Dec. 29, 1956) by A. Rousseaux
Frankfurter Allgemeine Zeitung (July 1961) no. 16 by W. Helwig
Gäppinger Kneisnachrichten (Feb. 1961) no. 11 by D.H.
Isis (1958) 49:451-53 by S.H. Nasr
Journal Asiatique (1956) 244:460 by J. Filliozat
Journal of Religious Thought (1964-65) 21, no. 2:162-63 by J.O. Nelson
Le Lotus bleu (Nov. 1955) pp. 197-99 by P. Mariel
Neue Deutsche Hefte (1961) 84:170-74 by G. Nebel
La Nouvelle Revue Française (Feb. 1957) pp. 329-30 by A.M. Schmidt
Le Populaire du Centre (March 21, 1957) by G. Remond
Review for Religious (1963) 22:706-7 by G. Murray
La Tour Saint-Jacques (Jan. 1957) by M.M. Davy
Zeitschrift für Ganzheitsforschung (1962) 6:188-89 by D. Mach
Zeitschrift für Volkskunde (1961) 57:146-48 by W.E. Peuckert

G34 *Das Heilige und das Profane* A57
The Sacred and the Profane A67
Le Sacré et le profane A84

American Anthropologist (1959) 61:1146-47 by W.A. Lessa
Catholic World (1959) 189:332-33 by B. Hunt
Christian Century (1959) 76:1026 by P.H. Ashby
Commentary (1959) 27:356-57 by R.E. Fitch
Dominicana (1959) 44:299-300 by R.M.D.
Good Work (1963) 26:59-64 by G. Carey
Hierós (1964) 1, no. 1:21-24 by C. Balzer
Journal of Religion (1960) 40:49 by C.H. Long
Newsletter of the Parapsychology Foundation (1959) 6, no. 4:7
Rivista di Etnografie (1965) 19:121-22 by G. Tucci
Rivista di storia e litteratura religiosa (1966) 2: 520-22 by E. Poulat
Theological Studies (1959) 20:654-55 by H.J. Bihler
Zeitschrift für Missionswissenschaft und Religionswissenschaft (1955) 39:151 by A. Antweiler

G35 *Mythes, rêves et mystères* A58
Myths, Dreams and Mysteries A68
Mythen, Träume und Mysterien A73

Anthropos (1962) 57:217-19 by A. Closs
The Beacon (May 1961) p. 96 by B.E. Hansen
Blackfriars (1960) 41:486-87 by B. Weatherhead
Chicago Tribune (March 12, 1961) by J. Randolph
The Downside Review (1961) 79:167-69 by R.F. Trevett
Encounter (1961) 17, no. 2:75-77 by P. Toynbee
Journal of Ecumenical Studies (1968) 5:395-97 by G. Vahanian
Review of Religion (1957) 22:58-63 by G.Y. Lansing
Roma (Sept. 25, 1957) p. 3 by J. Evola
The Tablet (1960) 214:1091-92 by P. Lienhardt
Theologische Revue (1963) 59:223-28 by R.J. Mohr
Theology (1961) pp. 116-17 by M.C. Perry
Times Literary Supplement (Nov. 11, 1960) p. 729
Westminster Bookman (1961) 20, no. 2:23-24 by T.J.J. Altizer
Zeitschrift für Ganzheitsforschung (1963) 7:301-6 by D. Mach
Zeitschrift für Missionswissenschaft und Religionswissenschaft (1963) 47:159-60 by A. Antweiler

G36 *Birth and Rebirth* A60 (cf. A83)
Naissances mystiques A66 (cf. A111)
Das Mysterium der Wiedergeburt A72

American Anthropologist (1959) 61:688-89 by D. Libby
Anglican Theological Review (1960) 42:61-62 by N.E. Fehl
Arbor (1961) 48, no. 183:118-22 by A. Pacios
Arts (Sept. 2 and 8, 1959) by A. Jouffroy
Christian Century (1959) 76:1281 by G. Winter
Concordia Theological Monthly (1959) 30:553 by W.J. Danker
La Flandre Liberale (May 7, 1959) by M. Fauconnier
Journal de Psychologie (July 1960) pp. 368-69 by I. Meyerson
Journal of Religion (1960) 40:131-32 by T.J.J. Altizer
Kommender (March 10, 1962) by H. Gsänger
Register (1959) 49, no. 1:1-2 by R.L. Slater
Synthèses (Sept. 1960) pp. 270-74 by F. Lancksweirt
Zeitschrift für Missionswissenschaft und Religionswissenschaft (1963) 47:158-59 by R.J. Mohr

G37 *Antaios* C28

Frankfurter Allgemeine Zeitung (July 22, 1959) by H. Demisch
Modern Language Review (1967) 62:559-60 by H. Popper

G38 *The History of Religions. Essays in Methodology* A65
Grundfragen der Religionswissenschaft A78

America (1960) 102:505-6 by J. LaFarge
Bulletin of Crozer Theological Seminary (Jan. 1961) 2:12
Canadian Journal of Theology (1961) 7:290-92 by R.M. Bennett
Christianity Today (1960) 4:424-25 by G.H. Clark
Ethics (1960) 70:343 by E.R. Goodenough
Journal of Bible and Religion (1960) 28:472-76 by D.G. Bradley
Journal of Religion (1961) 41:62 by F.S. Lusby
Journal of Theological Studies (1960) 11:449-50 by R.C. Zaehner
Nouvelle Revue Theologique (1962) 84:764-65 by J.M. Faux
Personalist (Oct. 1960) pp. 545-46 by G.A.L.
Register (April 1960) pp. 33-34 by H. Smith
Review of Religious Research (Winter 1961) pp. 138-39 by P.H. Ashby

Revue d'Histoire et de Philosophie Religieuses (1961) 41:195-96 by A. Caquot
Theologische Literaturzeitung (1965) 90:260-62 by K. Rudolph
The Westminster Bookman (1959) 43, no. 1:25-27 by E. Perry

G39 *Méphistophélès et l'Androgyne* A75
Mephistopheles and the Androgyne A82

American Anthropologist (1967) 69:262-63 by B. Saler
Anthropos (1963) 58:579-80 by A. Closs
Arcadie (Oct. 1962) pp. 559-64 by S. Talbot
Arts (Sept. 26, 1962) by J. Brosse
Commonweal (1966) 84:315-16 by W. Arnold
Études (1962) 313:420-21 by J.M. Le Blond
Journal of Ecumenical Studies (1967) 4:762-63 by G. Vahanian
La Nouvelle Revue Française (1963) 11:513-15 by H. Amer
Nouvelles Littéraires (May 17, 1962) by F. Bérence
Preuves (Feb. 1963) pp. 79-81 by A. Patri
Review for Religious (1966) 25:744-45 by W.J. Mountain
Revue de l'Histoire des Religions (1964) 166:114-15 by J.P. Roux
Revue des Deux Mondes (July 15, 1962) pp. 268-70 by P. Sérant
România (Sept.-Oct. 1962) p. 7 by V. Ierunca
Sud-Ouest (May 3, 1962) by J. Gabriel
The Tablet (1965) 219:803-4 by R. Haynes
Time (1966) 87, no. 1:41-42
Tribune de Lausanne (Dec. 2, 1962) by H. Pernet

G40 *Patañjali et le Yoga* A76
Patanjali and Yoga A94

Le Concours Médical (Sept. 22, 1962) pp. 4988-89 by M. Brion
Revue de l'Histoire des Religions (1964) 165:92-93 by A. Bareau
La Revue Nouvelle Tournai (May 15, 1962) by J. Masson

G41 *Aspects du mythe* A77
Myth and Reality A79

Arts (March 18, 1964) by J. Brosse
Cross Currents (1964) 14:372 by J. Collins
Folklore (Winter 1964) pp. 289-91 by E.O. James
Journal de Psychologie (1965) 62:123-24 by J.P. Vernant
New Blackfriars (1965) 46:378-79 by F. Radcliffe

The New Leader (1964) 47, no. 6:24-26 by H. Weisinger
New Statesman (1964) 68:578 by F. Kermode
Le Nouveau Candide (Dec. 12, 1963) by J. Monnerot
Revue de l'Histoire des Religions (1964) 165:237-39 by J.P. Roux
Times Literary Supplement (Sept. 9, 1965) p. 765
Tribune de Lausanne (July 7, 1964) by H. Pernet
Volkskunde (1966) 67, no. 2:158-61 by A.J. Bernet Kempers

G42 *Nuvele* A80

Revista Scriitorilor Români (1963) 2:154-56 by M. Niculescu

G43 *Amintiri* A85

Credinţa (1966) 16, no. 12:2 by T.M. Popescu
Roma Letterario (1966) 105, no. 289:3 by P. Gerbore
România Literară (1968) 1, no. 11 by A. Piru

G44 *From Primitives to Zen* A88 (includes A106, A107, A108, A109)

Christian Advocate (Aug. 1967) p. 19 by M.L. Ricketts
Christian Century (1968) 85:114-15 by E.J. Jurji
Lutheran Quarterly (1968) 20:87-88 by C.C. Haaland
The Month (1967) 38:148-50 by L.F. Barmann
New York Times Book Review (Aug. 11, 1974) by H. Cox
Reflection (1968) 65, no. 2:12-13 by C.D. Gunn
Religious Studies (1968) 3:561-62 by R.C. Zaehner
Revue de l'Histoire des Religions (1969) 175:241-43 by J.P. Roux
The Tablet (1967) 221:584-85 by T. Corbishley
Times Literary Supplement (June 8, 1967) p. 514
Union Seminary Quarterly Review (1968) 23:209 by G. Larson
Zeitschrift für Missionswissenschaft und Religionswissenschaft (1969) 53, no. 4:308-9 by A. Antweiler

G45 *Pe strada Mântuleasa* A90
Auf der Mântuleasastrasse A100
Le Vieil homme et l'officier A118

Ethos (1975) 2:269-74 by A. Bogdan
L'Express (March 20, 1977) pp. 60-62 by Alexandrian
Le Figaro (March 13, 1977) p. 16 by R. Kanters
Journal de Genève (March 19, 1977) by S. Stolojan
Le Monde (Feb. 4, 1977) p. 13 by E. Reichman

G46 *Maitreyi. Nuntă în Cer* A91

România Literară (March 5, 1970) by F. Manolescu

G47 *The Quest* A95
La Nostalgie des origines A99
Die Sehnsucht nach dem Ursprung A105

American Anthropologist (1971) 73:364-65 by W.A. Lessa
Archives de Sociologie des Religions (1972) 17, no. 33: 233-34 by F.A. Isambert
Atlantis (Feb. 1972) by G. Béatrice
Christian Century (1969) 86:1554 by C.A. Holbrook
Currents in Theology and Mission (1976) 3:252-53 by R. Timm
Journal de Genève (Aug. 28, 1971) by R. Christinger
Journal for the Scientific Study of Religion (1970) 9:70-72 by W.L. King
Lutheran Quarterly (1975) 27:281-82 by R. Drummond
Magazine Littéraire (June 1971) by J. Plumyène
Nederlands Theologisch Tijdschrift (1971) 25:78-80 by H.J. Drijvers
Nouvelles Littéraires (Sept. 17, 1971) p. 8 by J. Brosse
New York Times Book Review (Sept. 21, 1969) p. 20
L'Osservatore Romano (Jan. 10, 1974) p. 5 by B. Mondin
Quinzaine Littéraire (Sept. 16, 1971) by C. Baroche
Religion in Life (1970) 34:483-84 by F.J. Streng
Religious Studies (1971) 7:77-79 by N. Smart
Revue des Sciences Religieuses (1974) 48:68-69 by J.E. Menard
De Spectator (Aug. 15, 1971) by G.D.S.
The Tablet (1969) 233:951 by J. Walter
Theology Today (1970) 27:231-34 by P.H. Ashby
Times Literary Supplement (Feb. 5, 1970) p. 138

G48 *De Zalmoxis à Gengis-Khan* A97
Zalmoxis. The Vanishing God A102

Esprit (Oct. 1970) pp. 667-68 by G. Germain
The Heythrop Journal (1974) 15:244-45 by R.E.S. Tanner
Histoire et Géographie (Dec. 1970) no. 227 by A. Laronde
Journal de Genève (Aug. 28, 1971) by R. Christinger
Journal of Religious History (1975) 8:290-91 by R. Chambers
Journal for the Scientific Study of Religion (1973) 12:365-66 by T.O. Beidelman
Religion (1977) 7:105-6 by E.J. Sharpe

Revue de l'Histoire des Religions (1972) 181:187-91 by J.P. Roux
România Literară (1970) 3, no. 27:11 by D. Micu
Studies in Religion/Sciences Religieuses (1976-77) 6, no. 5:575-78 by G. Tissot
Times Literary Supplement (Oct. 23, 1970)

G49 *Fragments d'un journal* A104
No Souvenirs A117
Im Mittelpunkt A116

Banner (July 22, 1977) by T. Plantinga
Chicago Daily News (March 26, 1977) by L. McMurty
Chicago Sun-Times (March 13, 1977) by G. Forshey
Christian Scholar's Review (Spring 1978) by J.W. Cullum
Chronicle of Higher Education (March 21, 1977) p. 19 by A. Lacey
Deutsche Zeitung (Jan. 27, 1978) by G. Höhler
Ethos (1975) 2:238-45 by I. Constantin
Limitè (July 1974) no. 16 by Ş. Cristovici
Das Neue Buch (Sept. 11, 1977) p. 31 by I. Leitenberger
New Review of Books and Religion (March 1977) pp. 8-9 by G.H. Slusser
Le Nouvel Observateur (Dec. 20, 1976) pp. 54-57 by C. Roy
Parabola (1977) 2, no. 2:98-100 by M.L. Ricketts
Studies in Religion/Sciences Religieuses (1976-77) 6, no. 3:297-98 by G. Tissot

G50 *Histoire des croyances et des idées religieuses. 1* A110
A History of Religious Ideas. 1 A120
Geschichte der religiösen Ideen. 1 A125

Archives de Sciences Sociales des Religions (1976) 21: 231 by H. Desroche
Cahiers Roumains d'Études Littéraires (1977) 1:117-22 by A. Marino
Le Figaro (Aug. 15, 1976) p. 6 by R. Kanters
Le Figaro (Sept. 20, 1978) p. 28 by A. Brincourt
Itinéraires (Nov. 1977) pp. 148-50
La Libre Belgique (Sept. 1, 1976) by J.F.
Le Monde (July 17, 1976) p. 1 by G. Dumézil
Le Nouvel Observateur (Dec. 20, 1976) pp. 54-57 by C. Roy
Religious Studies Review (1976) 2, no. 4:1-4 by P. Ricoeur (trans. from *Nouvelles Littéraires*)
Revue de l'Histoire des Religions (1978) 193:226-27 by J.P. Roux

Steaua (Feb. 1977) pp. 22-25 by D. Micu
Tribuna României (1977) 6, no. 104:6 by D. Radu Popa
Universalia. Complément annuel de l'*Encyclopaedia Universalis* (1977) pp. 391-92 by J.V.

G51 *Occultism, Witchcraft, and Cultural Fashions* A113
Occultisme, sorcellerie et modes culturelles A127

Aevum (1976) 5-6:1-3 by I.P. Culianu
Aware (1976) 7, no. 1
Christian Century (1977) 94:155 by P. Green
Chronicle of Higher Education (March 21, 1977) p. 19 by A. Lacey
Horizons (1977) 4, no. 1 by J. Saliba
Humanities Association Review (1977) 28, no. 2 by L.D. Kliever
Journal for the Scientific Study of Religion (1977) 16:332-33 by R.A. Segal
Lutheran Quarterly (1977) 29:87-88 by D.C. Flatt
Parabola (1976) 1, no. 4:108-10 by C. Hyers
Religion in Life (1977) 46:122-23 by D. Bassuk
Revue de l'Histoire des Religions (1978) 194:110 by J.P. Roux
Sociological Analysis (Winter 1976) pp. 369-70 by K.M. Brown
Studies in Religion/Sciences Religieuses (1976-77) 6, no. 3:296-97 by G. Tissot
Thought (1977) 52:205 by R.H. Robbins
Zeitschrift für Religions und Geistesgeschichte (1977) 29:277-78 by U. Tworuschka

G52 *Die Pelerine* A114

Frankfurter Allgemeine (March 7, 1977) by H. Graf
World Literature Today (Summer 1977) by N. Catanoy

G53 *Mircea Eliade* A122

Le Figaro (April 9, 1978) p. 23 by J. Varenne
Le Monde (March 31, 1978) p. 18 by C. Mauriac
Ramuri (1978) 15, no. 10:16

G54 *Die drei Grazien* A123

Die Bücherkommentare (May-June 1978) by D. Middendorff
World Literature Today (Aug. 1978) p. 614 by N. Cantanoy

G55 *Phantastische Geschichten* A128

Augsburger Allgemeine (June 25, 1978) no. 24
Süddeutsche Zeitung (Sept. 2, 1978) p. 102
Die Welt (June 10, 1978) by F.A. Hoyer
Die Welt der Bücher (1978) no. 10 by H. Stamatu

Part 3
Other Works of Mircea Eliade

H

ROMANIAN NEWSPAPER ARTICLES AND OTHER OBSCURE WORKS

1921

H1 "Duşmanul viermelui de mătase" (The Enemy of the Silkworm). *Ziarul ştiinţelor populare*, Bucharest (1921) 25, no. 21: 215.

Author's first published work. Begins series of short articles reflecting his juvenile interest in entomology.

H2 "Musca albastră a cadavrelor." *Ziarul ştiinţelor populare* (1921) 25, no. 41:454-55.

H3 "Cum am găsit piatra filosofală" (How I Found the Philosopher's Stone). *Ziarul ştiinţelor populare* (1921) 25, no. 52:588-89.

Inspired by youthful fascination for chemistry and the physical sciences. In a laboratory experiment, narrator learns through a dream how to mix substances into gold. First indications of later research and scientific study of alchemy. Cf. A17.

1922

H4 "Techir-ghiolul." *Ziarul ştiinţelor populare* (1922) 26, no. 1:11.

H5 "Fauna unei locuinţe." *Ziarul ştiinţelor populare* (1922) 26, no. 2:22-23.

H6 "Subsemnatul amator naturalist." *Ziarul ştiinţelor populare* (1922) 26, no. 7:80-81.

H7 "Facultăţile fizice ale animalelor." *Ziarul ştiinţelor populare* (1922) 26, no. 11:130.

H8 "Escursii şi călătorii ştiinţifice." *Ziarul ştiinţelor populare* (1922) 26, no. 13:153-54.

H9 "Spre plaiul Ciontii." *Ziarul ştiinţelor populare* (1922) 26, no. 14:161-62.

H10 "Mijloacele de apărare ale insectelor." *Ziarul ştiinţelor populare* (1922) 26, no. 18:208-9.

H11 "Entomologie aplicată." *Ziarul ştiinţelor populare* (1922) 26, no. 18:210.

H12 "Filosoful Conta." *Ziarul ştiinţelor populare* (1922) 26, no. 21:247-48.

H13 "Industria culorilor naturale." *Ziarul ştiinţelor populare* (1922) 26, no. 25:293-94.

H14 "Ca să crească părul." *Ziarul ştiinţelor populare* (1922) 26, no. 27:317.

H15 "Facultăţile psihice ale insectelor." *Ziarul ştiinţelor populare* (1922) 26, no. 28:331-32.

H16 "Amintiri din retragere." *Ziarul ştiinţelor populare* (1922) 26, no. 31:362-63; 32:374.

H17 "Excursii şi călătorii ştiinţifice." *Ziarul ştiinţelor populare* (1922) 26, no. 32:378-79.

H18 "Din lumea animală." *Ziarul ştiinţelor populare* (1922) 26, no. 34:404-5.

H19 "Câţiva gândaci folositori." *Ziarul ştiinţelor populare* (1922) 26, no. 38:454.

H20 "Din carnetul unui cercetaş" (From the Notebook of a Boy Scout). *Ziarul ştiinţelor populare* (1922) 26, no. 43: 507-8.

Begins series of sketches of author's adventures as a Boy Scout.

H21 "Muştele." *Ziarul ştiinţelor populare* (1922) 26, no. 44: 525-26.

H22 "Secretul viepselor solitare." *Ziarul ştiinţelor populare* (1922) 26, no. 45:535-36.

H23 "Cernăuţii." *Ziarul ştiinţelor populare* (1922) 26, no. 47:556-58.

H24 "Constanţa." *Ziarul ştiinţelor populare* (1922) 26, no. 48:567.

1923

H25 "Păianjenul cu pântecele negru." *Ziarul ştiinţelor populare* (1923) 27, no. 4:36.

H26 "Păianjenii." *Ziarul ştiinţelor populare* (1923) 27, no. 5:47-48.

H27 "Păianjenul de apă." *Ziarul ştiinţelor populare* (1923) 27, no. 6:61-62.

H28 "Tabăra Sibiu." *Ziarul ştiinţelor populare* (1923) 27, no. 7:69-70.

H29 "Călugăriţa şi Urechelniţa." *Ziarul ştiinţelor populare* (1923) 27, no. 9:98-99.

H30 "Vieaţa lui Jean Jaques Rousseau." *Ziarul ştiinţelor populare* (1923) 27, no. 14:158-59.

H31 "Originea şi evoluţia insectelor." *Ziarul ştiinţelor populare* (1923) 27, no. 18:204-5.

H32 "Vieaţa în tabără." *Ziarul ştiinţelor populare* (1923) 27, nos. 19:215-17; 23:264-66.

H33 "Vieaţa şi opera lui Henrik Ibsen." *Ziarul ştiinţelor populare* (1923) 27, no. 26:299-300.

H34 "Doctorul." *Ziarul ştiinţelor populare* (1923) 27, no. 27:309-11.

H35 "O noapte furtunoasă." *Ziarul ştiinţelor populare* (1923) 27, no. 29:337-39.

1924

H36 "Din viaţa minunată a furnicilor." *Orizontul*, Bucharest (1924) 4, nos. 24:284; 25:296.

H37 "Alimentaţia, moravurile şi distracţiile furnicilor." *Orizontul* (1924) 4, no. 29:344.

H38 "Razboaiele furnicilor." *Orizontul* (1924) 4, nos. 42: 496; 49:579.

H39 "Centenarul lui Fabre." *Vlăstarul*, Bucharest (1924) 1, no. 2:7-11.

H40 "Critica contimporană." *Vlăstarul* (1924) 1, no. 4:5-6.

H41 "Cronica culturală." *Vlăstarul* (1924) 2, no. 1:9-11.

H42 "Licuriciul şi lumina rece." *Ziarul ştiinţelor populare* (1924) 28, no. 5:77-78.

H43 "Vieaţa şi opera lui Denis Diderot." *Ziarul ştiinţelor populare* (1924) 28, no. 10:155-56.

1925

H44 "Ştiinţa în cultura popoarelor." *Curentul Studenţesc*, Bucharest (1925) 1, no. 2:2.

H45 "Prietenii noştrii, carţile." *Curentul Studenţesc* (1925) 1, no. 4:2.

H46 "Naţionalismul creiator, Opera lui Hajdeu." *Curentul Studenţesc* (1925) 1, no. 5:1.

H47 "'Tinerimea română.'" *Curentul Studenţesc* (1925) 1, no. 10:1.

H48 "Panait Muşoiu." *Curentul Studenţesc* (1925) 1, no. 10:2.

H49 "Giovani Papini." *Foaia Tinerimii*, Bucharest (1925) 9, no. 8:119-21.

Papini's *Un uomo finito* served as inspiration for Eliade's *Romanul adolescentului miop* A5 and "Itinerariu spiritual" H195.

H50 "Ossendovski." *Foaia Tinerimii* (1925) 9, no. 13-14: 169-70.

H51 "Amintiri despre Anatole France." *Foaia Tinerimii* (1925) 9, no. 17-18:200-1.

H52 "Bogdan Petriceicu Hajdeu." *Foaia Tinerimii* (1925) 9, nos. 19-20:211-13; 21-22:230-31.

Hasdeu was one of Eliade's earliest spiritual idols. Cf. A25.

H53 "Intâmplare." *Foaia Tinerimii* (1925) 9, no. 19-20:228-29.

H54 "Şeref-Râmi." *Lumea*, Iasi (1925) 1, no. 24:14-15.

H55 "Bazar oriental." *Lumea* (1925) 1, no. 28:5-6.

H56 "Povestea unei regine." *Lumea* (1925) 1, no. 39:7-8.

H57 "Scrisori babiloniene" (Babylonian Letters). *Lumea* (1925) 1, no. 44:10-11.

One of several articles at the time describing ancient eastern religions in view of discovering their "secrets regarding the destiny of mankind." See H64-H76.

H58 "Limbajul furnicelor." *Orizontul*, Bucharest (1925) 5, no. 7:76.

H59 "Cum se înţeleg furnicile." *Orizontul* (1925) 5, no. 10: 110.

H60 "Inteligenţa furnicilor." *Orizontul* (1925) 5, no. 14:158.

H61 "Cum se orientează furnicile." *Orizontul* (1925) 5, no. 18:212.

H62 "Cirnitirele furnicilor." *Orizontul* (1925) 5, no. 21:248.

H63 "Paraziţii furnicelor." *Orizontul* (1925) 5, no. 31:369.

H64 "Mituri şi legende orientale, Epopeea lui Ghilgameş." *Orizontul* (1925) 5, no. 42:494.

H65 "Isprăvile lui Ghilgameş." *Orizontul* (1925) 5, no. 43:509.

H66 "In căutarea lui Utnapiştim." *Orizontul* (1925) 5, no. 44: 526.

H67 "Glose pentru Ghilgameş." *Orizontul* (1925) 5, no. 47:562.

H68 "Polemici în jurul lui Ghilgameş." *Orizontul* (1925) 5, no. 48:566.

H69 "Jensen şi Ghilgameş." *Orizontul* (1925) 5, no. 49:580.

H70 "Cosmogonia chaldeiană." *Orizontul* (1925) 5, no. 50:592.

H71 "Marduk creiază oamenii." *Orizontul* (1925) 5, no. 51:609.

H72 "Potopul chaldeian." *Orizontul* (1925) 5, no. 52:619.

H73 "Cartea morţilor." *Ştiu-tot*, Bucharest (1925) 1, no. 4: 10-11.

H74 "Isis şi Osiris." *Ştiu-tot* (1925) 1, no. 6:4-5.

H75 "Descifrarea cuneiformelor." *Ştiu-tot* (1925) 1, no. 7-8: 4-5.

H76 "Fenicienii." *Ştiu-tot* (1925) 1, no. 11:2-3.

H77 "Gândesc furnicile?" *Ştiu-tot* (1925) 1, no. 12:3-4.

H78 "453 scrisori de dragoste." *Ştiu-tot* (1925) 1, no. 12: 9-10.

A translation of a brief piece of G. Papini.

H79 "Ciudăţenii şi anecdote din viaţa lui Balzac" (Curiosities and Anecdotes from the Life of Balzac). *Ştiu-tot* (1925) 1, no. 13:3-5.

Early evidence of Eliade's lifelong passion for Balzac.

H80 "Povestea lui Satni-Khâmois." *Ştiu-tot* (1925) 1, no. 14: 1-2.

H81 "Omnia." *Vlăstarul* (1925) 2, nos. 1:i; 2:i; 3:i; 4-5:i; 6-7:i; and 8-10:i.

H82 "Epictet şi Marc Aureliu." *Vlăstarul* (1925) 2, no. 2: 10-12.

H83 "Iorga." *Vlăstarul* (1925) 2, no. 3:4-7.

H84 "Cultură şi inteligenţă." *Vlăstarul* (1925) 2, no. 4-5: 15-18.

H85 "Alchimia." *Vlăstarul* (1925) 2, no. 6-7:12-16.

H86 "Ştiinţă şi ocultism." *Vlăstarul* (1925) 2, no. 8-10: 29-39.

H87 "Scrisoare din tabără." *Vlăstarul* (1925) 2, no. 4-5:13-18. Part of A5.

H88 "Chimia în antichitate." *Ziarul ştiinţelor populare* (1925) 29, no. 31:493-95.

H89 "Originele alchimiei." *Ziarul ştiinţelor populare* (1925) 29, no. 32:516-18.

H90 "Transmisiunea technicei greco-egiptene." *Ziarul ştiinţelor populare* (1925) 29, no. 33:529-30.

1926

H91 "Ziua neînapoiată." *Adevĕrul Literar şi Artistic*, Bucharest (1926) 7, no. 291:4.

A translation of a brief piece of G. Papini.

H92 "Misterele şi iniţierea orientală." *Adevĕrul Literar şi Artistic* (1926) 7, no. 293:5-6.

H93 "Dionysos-Zagreus." *Adevĕrul Literar şi Artistic* (1926) 7, no. 295:3.

H94 "Misterele orfice." *Adevĕrul Literar şi Artistic* (1926) 7, no. 297:3.

H95 "Apologia Budismului." *Adevĕrul Literar şi Artistic* (1926) 7, no. 300:4.

H96 "Orfeu şi iniţierea orfică." *Adevĕrul Literar şi Artistic* (1926) 7, no. 303:3.

H97 "Cântarea Cântărilor." *Adevĕrul Literar şi Artistic* (1926) 7, no. 307:4.

H98 "Lămuriri pentru d. Mihail Dragomirescu şi pentru alţii" (Clarifications for Mihail Dragomirescu and Others). *Cuvântul*, Bucharest (1926) 3, no. 450:2.

In a university magazine (H142) from which he subsequently resigned, Eliade criticized the famous

Romanian historian Iorga. Here he defends his remarks and disclaims his critics.

H99 "Noi şi Nicolae Iorga" (We and Nicolae Iorga). *Cuvântul* (1926) 3, no. 604:2.

Beginning of a series of articles on Iorga, emphasizing the polygraphic and asystematic approach of his method. These were first articles to gain Eliade public recognition. Briefly, they called for a "new generation" (a catchword at the time among young Romanians) which should look to something other than history--such as the study of philosophy and religion.

H100 "Hajdeu." *Cuvântul* (1926) 3, no. 611:2.

H101 "Victor Anestin." *Cuvântul* (1926) 3, no. 612:13.

H102 "Dinamismul religios în India" (Religious Dynamism in India). *Cuvântul* (1926) 3, no. 617:1-2.

Review of C. Formichi, *Il pensiero religioso nell' India prima del Buddha*.

H103 "Experienţa religioasă" (Religious Experience). *Cuvântul* (1926) 3, no. 619:1-2.

Review of V. Macchioro, *Teoria generale della religione come esperienza*.

H104 "Brand." *Cuvântul* (1926) 3, no. 620:1-2.

H105 "Ciuang-Ţe." *Cuvântul* (1926) 3, no. 622:1-2.

H106 "Ideile lui Henry Ford." *Cuvântul* (1926) 3, no. 624:3.

H107 "Orient şi Occident." *Cuvântul* (1926) 3, no. 625:1-2.

Outlines the differences between Eastern and Western perspectives of life.

H108 "J.H. Fabre." *Cuvântul* (1926) 3, no. 628:1-2. Published also as H116.

H109 "'Sămănătorul' şi 'Falanga.'" *Cuvântul* (1926) 3, no. 630:3.

H110 "Sixtine." *Cuvântul* (1926) 3, no. 631:1-2.

H111 "Criptografia şi începuturile istoriei Românilor." *Cuvântul* (1926) 3, no. 637:1-2.

H112 "Giovanni Papini." *Cuvântul* (1926) 3, nos. 640:1-2; 643: 1-2.

H113 "'Muza'--Societate cultura-dramatica." *Cuvântul* (1926) 3, no. 646:3-4. Part of A5.

H114 "Ionel Teodoreanu: 'Drumuri.'" *Cuvântul* (1926) 3, no. 649:1-2. Published also as H140.

H115 "Magia şi Cercetările Metapsihice." *Foaia Tinerimii* (1926) 10, no. 4:59-60.

H116 "I. Henri Fabre." *Foaia Tinerimii* (1926) 10, no. 5: 68-69. Published also as H108.

H117 "O nouă istorie a ştiinţei, Cartea lui Aldo Mieli." *Foaia Tinerimii* (1926) 10, no. 6:91.

H118 "Clasicii ocultişti, Biblioteca lui Alberto Fidi." *Foaia Tinerimii* (1926) 10, no. 7-8:108-9.

H119 "Raffaele Pettazzoni." *Foaia Tinerimii* (1926) 10, no. 9:123.

Pettazzoni's work in the History of Religions served as inspiration for Eliade's own approach to this subject matter. Cf. H141 and H150.

H120 "Pagini italiene." *Foaia Tinerimii* (1926) 10, nos. 20: 247; 21:261.

H121 "Literatura celui maireligios norod de pe faţa pământului." *Lumea* (1926) 50:11-12.

H122 "Ziudsudra şi Ut-Napiştim." *Orizontul* (1926) 6, no. 1:5.

Beginning of a series of articles on flood myths.

H123 "Legenda lui Noe." *Orizontul* (1926) 6, no. 2:22.

H124 "Potopul din 'Satapatha Brâhmana.'" *Orizontul* (1926) 6, no. 4:40.

H125 "Potopul în 'Hari-Purana.'" *Orizontul* (1926) 6, no. 5:55.

H126 "Potopul în 'Mahâbharâta' şi 'Bhagavata-Purana.'" *Orizontul* (1926) 6, no. 6:62.

H127 "Deucalion." *Orizontul* (1926) 6, no. 7:82.

H128 "Ogyges şi Dardanus." *Orizontul* (1926) 6, no. 8:91.

H129 "Potopul în Asia şi arhipelagul asiatic." *Orizontul* (1926) 6, no. 9:105.

H130 "Potopul Australian şi Melanezian." *Orizontul* (1926) 6, no. 10:114.

H131 "Legendele diluviene în America." *Orizontul* (1926) 6, no. 11:124.

H132 "Potopul în Egipt?" *Orizontul* (1926) 6, no. 12:138.

H133 "Privire generală asupra Insulelor şi Arhipelagurilor Asiatice." *Orizontul* (1926) 6, no. 15:177.

H134 "Mitul lui Etana." *Orizontul* (1926) 6, no. 16:185.

H135 "Misterele orfice la Pompei." *Orizontul* (1926) 6, no. 22:258.

H136 "Taoismul." *Orizontul* (1926) 6, no. 43:506.

H137 "Adolfo Bonilla y San Martin." *Orizontul* (1926) 6, no. 49:582.

H138 "Pe marginea unor cărţi metapsihice." *Revista Universitară*, Bucharest (1926) 1, no. 1:15-17.

H139 "Criptografia şi istoria românească." *Revista Universitară* (1926) 1, no. 1:21-28.

H140 "Ionel Teodoreanu." *Revista Universitară* (1926) 1, no. 2:50-53. Published also as H114.

H141 "I Misteri." *Revista Universitară* (1926) 1, no. 2:67-70.

Review of R. Pettazzoni's book of the same title.

H142 "Sinteza istorică a d-lui Iorga" (Iorga's Historical Synthesis). *Revista Universitară* (1926) 1, no. 3: 85-90.

Points out some deficiencies in the work of the famous Romanian historian Nicolae Iorga. Cf. H98.

H143 "La Scuole Ionica." *Revista Universitară* (1926) 1, no. 3:107-8.

H144 "Din literatura indiană." *Ştiu-tot* (1926) 2, no. 15-16: 4-5.

H145 "Turnul lui Babel." *Ştiu-tot* (1926) 2, no. 17:2-3.

H146 "Idilă." *Universul Literar*, Bucharest (1926) 42, no. 27:10-11.

H147 "Eva." *Universul Literar* (1926) 42, no. 51:10-11.

1927

H148 "Misticismul orfic al lui Heraclit." *Adevĕrul Literar şi Artistic* (1927) 7, no. 320:5-6.

H149 "Lao-Ţe." *Adevĕrul Literar şi Artistic* (1927) 7, no. 329:7.

H150 "O carte despre Dumnezeu" (A Book about God). *Adevĕrul Literar şi Artistic* (1927) 8, no. 348:7.

Criticizes Tylor's evolutionist theory of religion as too rationalistic and mechanistic. Favors the work of R. Pettazzoni.

H151 "Dedicaţie (Schiţa)." *Cuvântul* (1927) 3, no. 651:5.

H152 "Medelenii şi 'medelenismul.'" *Cuvântul* (1927) 3, no. 652:1-2.

H153 "Poezia Alexandrină." *Cuvântul* (1927) 3, no. 654:1-2.

H154 "Mitul Arghezian." *Cuvântul* (1927) 3, no. 657:1-2.

H155 "Mistica lui Papini." *Cuvântul* (1927) 3, no. 661:1-2.

H156 "Domnul care mă admiră" (A Man who Admires Me). *Cuvântul* (1927) 3, no. 662:1-2.

On a trip to Italy, Eliade visited Giovanni Papini, whose works he greatly admired. Cf. H49.

H157 "Spătarul Milescu." *Cuvântul* (1927) 3, no. 663:1-2.

H158 "Jérôme Coignard." *Cuvântul* (1927) 3, no. 667:1-2.

H159 "Ernesto Buonaiuti." *Cuvântul* (1927) 3, no. 670:1-2.

Product of a conversation with Buonaiuti in Italy.

Eliade gained respect for this scholar's ideas and later collaborated with him in the periodical *Ricerche Religiose* B5 and B8.

H160 "Criticul." *Cuvântul* (1927) 3, no. 678:1-2.

H161 "Asvaghoşa." *Cuvântul* (1927) 3, nos. 693:1-2; 696:1-2.

H162 "Emanoil Bucuţa." *Cuvântul* (1927) 3, no. 699:1-2.

H163 "Dela Hermes Trismegist la Nicolae Iorga." *Cuvântul* (1927) 3, no. 701:1-2.

H164 "Impulsul poligrafic." *Cuvântul* (1927) 3, no. 704:1-2.

H165 "Religiile misterice." *Cuvântul* (1927) 3, no. 708:1-2.

H166 "Intre Apollo şi Isus." *Cuvântul* (1927) 3, no. 712:1-2.

H167 "Romanul lui Dem. Cantemir." *Cuvântul* (1927) 3, no. 717: 1-2.

H168 "Gib. I. Mihăiescu." *Cuvântul* (1927) 3, no. 720:1-2.

H169 "Alfredo Panzini." *Cuvântul* (1927) 3, no. 722:1-2.

H170 "Lecturile." *Cuvântul* (1927) 3, no. 724:1-2.

H171 "'Jean' Minulescu." *Cuvântul* (1927) 3, no. 730:1-2.

H172 "Rudolf Steiner." *Cuvântul* (1927) 3, no. 734:1-2.

Criticism of Steiner's publications for the Anthroposophic Society.

H173 "Cronica literară." *Cuvântul* (1927) 3, nos. 738:1; 740:1.

H174 "Venezia." *Cuvântul* (1927) 3, nos. 746:1; 748:1; and 750:1-2.

H175 "Jurnal Florentin" (Florentine Journal). *Cuvântul* (1927) 3, no. 754:1-2.

One of several "travel impressions" of author's trip to Italy in which he collected material for his master's thesis.

H176 "Pentru o bibliotecă." *Cuvântul* (1927) 3, no. 761:1.

H177 "Roma lui Panzini." *Cuvântul* (1927) 3, no. 762:1-2.

H178 "Propaganda d-lui Porn." *Cuvântul* (1927) 3, no. 763:1.

H179 "Studenţii 'români' la Pisa." *Cuvântul* (1927) 3, no. 764:1.

H180 "Cezar Petrescu: 'Intunecare.'" *Cuvântul* (1927) 3, no. 768:1-2.

H181 "Giovanni Vailati." *Cuvântul* (1927) 3, no. 773:1-2.

H182 "Adrian Maniu: 'Meşterul.'" *Cuvântul* (1927) 3, no. 775: 1-2.

H183 "Eugen Relgis: Glasuri în surdină." *Cuvântul* (1927) 3, no. 776:1.

H184 "Napoli." *Cuvântul* (1927) 3, no. 778:1-2.

H185 "Vezuviu-Pompeiu." *Cuvântul* (1927) 3, no. 782:1.

H186 "Magie şi metapsihică" (Magic and Metaphysics). *Cuvântul* (1927) 3, no. 786:1-2.

Contagious magic is not the result of a prelogical mentality; it is a consequence of repeated observations --a forebearer to the notion of scientific causality.

H187 "Poezia lui Tudor Arghezi." *Cuvântul* (1927) 3, no. 788: 1-2.

H188 "Remy de Gourmont. Note." *Cuvântul* (1927) 3, no. 790:1-2.

H189 "Milarepa." *Cuvântul* (1927) 3, nos. 822:1-2; 824:1-2.

H190 "Metodele gourmontiene. Note." *Cuvântul* (1927) 3, no. 829:1-2.

Truth is derived not only from a series of causes but also from a direct contemplation of facts and their correspondences.

H191 "Reflecţii imprudente în jurul unei comemorări (Hajdeu)." *Cuvântul* (1927) 3, nos. 832:1-2; 835:1-2.

H192 "Abbazzia." *Cuvântul* (1927) 3, no. 837:1-2.

H193 "In Prater, după revoluţie." *Cuvântul* (1927) 3, no. 842:1-2.

H194 "Geneva. Le Foyer des étudiants." *Cuvântul* (1927) 3, no. 850:1-2.

H195 "Itinerariu spiritual, I. Linii de orientare" (Spiritual Itinerary, I. Lines of Orientation). *Cuvântul* (1927) 3, no. 857:1-2.

Initiates a series of 12 articles that are the most significant of Eliade's youthful publications. Concerns the subject of his own spiritual development as well as that of his generation of young Romanians. Focuses on the notion of "method"--a prospectus for achieving a creative expression of metaphysical truth from a multitude of experiences. Argues that positive science and the study of religion are not mutually exclusive. Perceives the study of history as a philosophy of history. Hence "a historian is also a metaphysician." Experiences and intuition are critical to the experimental method. The spirit is an organic hierarchy of "planes" corresponding or "sympathizing" with reality. This correspondence or equilibrium within diversity functions as a "soteriology" for the human spirit and the quest for knowledge.

H196 "Itinerariu spiritual, II. Critica diletantismului." *Cuvântul* (1927) 3, no. 860:1-2.

H197 "Itinerariu spiritual, III. Către un nou diletantism." *Cuvântul* (1927) 3, no. 862:1-2.

H198 "Itinerariu spiritual, IV. Intre catedra şi laborator." *Cuvântul* (1927) 3, no. 867:1-2.

H199 "Itinerariu spiritual, V. Experienţele." *Cuvântul* (1927) 3, no. 874:1-2.

H200 "Amiel. Note." *Cuvântul* (1927) 3, nos. 876:1-2; 879:1-2.

H201 "Henri Massis: 'Apărarea Occidentului.'" *Cuvântul* (1927) 3, no. 883:1.

H202 "Itinerariu spiritual, VI. Cultura." *Cuvântal* (1927) 3, no. 885:1-2.

H203 "Itinerariu spiritual, VII. Insuficienţa literaturii." *Cuvântul* (1927) 3, no. 889:1-2.

H204 "'Conspiraţia tăcerii.'" *Cuvântul* (1927) 3, no. 893: 1-2.

H205 "'Glorie' şi 'Tăcere.'" *Cuvântul* (1927) 3, no. 900:1-2.

H206 "Itinerariu spiritual, VIII. Teozofie?" *Cuvântul* (1927) 3, no. 903:1-2.

H207 "'Studi Rumeni.'" *Cuvântul* (1927) 3, no. 907:1-2.

H208 "Itinerariu spiritual, IX. Misticismul." *Cuvântul* (1927) 3, no. 911:1-2.

H209 "D. Dekobra la Ateneu." *Cuvântul* (1927) 3, no. 911:2.

H210 "Religiozitatea în filosofia rusă." *Cuvântul* (1927) 3, no. 914:2.

H211 "Itinerariu spiritual, X. Intre Luter şi Ignatiu de Loyola." *Cuvântul* (1927) 3, no. 915:1-2.

H212 "Psichologia foiletonului." *Cuvântul* (1927) 3, no. 918: 1-2.

H213 "Paul Zarifopol." *Cuvântul* (1927) 3, no. 921:1.

H214 "Itinerariu spiritual, XI. Ortodoxie." *Cuvântul* (1927) 3, no. 924:1-2.

H215 "Clasicism şi reliqie." *Cuvântul* (1927) 3, no. 925:2.

H216 "Itinerariu spiritual, XII. Final." *Cuvântul* (1927) 3, no. 928:1-2.

H217 "Ovid Densuşianu." *Cuvântul* (1927) 3, no. 931:1-2.

H218 "Ce-a priceput ..." *Cuvântul* (1927) 3, no. 935:1-2.

H219 "Cronică italiană." *Cuvântul* (1927) 3, no. 939:1.

H220 "Ocultismul în cultura contemporană." *Cuvântul* (1927) 3, no. 943:1-2.

H221 "Archeion." *Cuvântul* (1927) 3, no. 943:2.

H222 "Vasile Pârvan." *Cuvântul* (1927) 3, no. 945:1-2.

H223 "Pastilă argheziană." *Cuvântul* (1927) 3, no. 949:1-2.

H224 "Intelectualii de rasă." *Cuvântul* (1927) 3, no. 956:1-2.

H225 "Elogiul compromiterii." *Cuvântul* (1927) 3, no. 960: 1-2.

H226 "Itinerirea d'lui Branişte." *Cuvântul* (1927) 3, no. 961:2.

H227 "Despre confesiuni." *Cuvântul* (1927) 3, no. 964:1.

H228 "Cu Moş-Ajunul." *Cuvântul* (1927) 3, no. 967:6-7. Part of A5.

H229 "Gbur-Ama." *Cuvântul* (1927) 3, 969:1-2.

H230 "O generaţie." *Cuvântul Studenţesc*, Bucharest (1927) 4, no. 2:1.

H231 "Treizeci şi unu Decembrie." *Est Vest*, Bucharest (1927) 1, no. 1:11-14.

H232 "Religia în viaţa spiritului." *Est Vest* (1927) 1, no. 1:28.

H233 "Răsărit, pe mare." *Est Vest* (1927) 1, no. 2:18-21.

H234 "Theòs eghenou ex antropu." *Gândirea*, Bucharest (1927) 7, no. 12:355-57.

There are basically two dimensions of the human spirit: one complex and polyvalent; the other irrational and transcendent.

H235 "Dionysos-Christ." *Orizontul* (1927) 7, no. 5:52.

H236 "India şi Budismul." *Orizontul* (1927) 7, no. 9:98.

H237 "Iubirea prietenului meu." *Sinteza*, Bucharest (1927) 5-6:7-8.

H238 "Cel care trebue ascultat." *Universul Literar* (1927) 43, no. 14:215.

H239 "Martin Eden." *Universul Literar* (1927) 43, no. 16:252.

H240 "De vorbă cu Giovanni Papini." *Universul Literar* (1927) 43, no. 19:291-92.

H241 "In întunerec." *Universul Literar* (1927) 43, no. 21: 326-27.

H242 "Arturo Farinelli sau 'De Erudiţia.'" *Universul Literar* (1927) 43, no. 25:394-95.

H243 "Corigenţă." *Universul Literar* (1927) 43, no. 27:422-23. Part of A5.

H244 "Luni 8-9, Germana." *Universul Literar* (1927) 43, no. 31:491-92. Part of A5.

H245 "Intre Don-Juani." *Universul Literar* (1927) 43, no. 34: 536-37. Part of A5.

H246 "Gânduri pentru pomenirea lui Hajdeu." *Universul Literar* (1927) 43, no. 35:549.

H247 "Novembrie." *Universul Literar* (1927) 43, no. 36:565-66. Part of A5.

H248 "Omul care a voit să tacă, Lui Haig Acterian." *Universul Literar* (1927) 43, no. 37:583-84, 586.

H249 "Eu, Sfântul Diavol şi cele şaisprezece păpusi." *Universul Literar* (1927) 43, no. 41:650-51.

H250 "Papini, eu şi lumea." *Viaţa Literară*, Bucharest (1927) 2, no. 65:1-2. Part of A5.

H251 "Scrisoare din universitate." *Vlăstarul* (1927) 4, no. 1-2:7-8.

H252 "Post-scriptum." *Vlăstarul* (1927) 4, no. 4:4.

1928

H253 "Anno Domini." *Cuvântul* (1928) 4, no. 973:3.

Imagines 1928 as the final time left before the destruction of the world. An attempt to defeat time by accomplishing in one year what would normally take a lifetime. Expresses his generation's disregard for time and his own terror of time.

H254 "Farinelli hispanizant." *Cuvântul* (1928) 4, no. 974: 1-2.

H255 "Tragicul masculin." *Cuvântul* (1928) 4, no. 982:1.

H256 "Diletantism în jurul lui Iisus." *Cuvântul* (1928) 4, no. 988:2.

H257 "Suflete moarte." *Cuvântul* (1928) 4, no. 995:3.

H258 "Pastile polemice." *Cuvântul* (1928) 4, no. 997:2.

H259 "'Fiul lui Satan.'" *Cuvântul* (1928) 4, no. 1002:2.

H260 "Diletantism în jurul misticismului." *Cuvântul* (1928) 4, no. 1004:3-4.

H261 "Marcelin Berthelot şi Alchimia." *Cuvântul* (1928) 4, no. 1016:1-2.

H262 "Impotriva Moldovei" (Against Moldavia). *Cuvântul* (1928) 4, no. 1021:1-2.

Author's emotional polemic against his Moldavian ancestors from whom he believed he had inherited the moods of melancholia and nostalgia.

H263 "Sensul nebuniei." *Cuvântul* (1928) 4, no. 1027:3.

H264 "Sören Kierkegaard. Logodnic, pamfletar şi eremith." *Cuvântal* (1928) 4, no. 1035:1-2.

H265 "La moartea lui Blasco Ibanez." *Cuvântul* (1928) 4, no. 1036:2.

H266 "Ura oamenilor şi a eroilor." *Cuvântul* (1928) 4, no. 1042:1-2.

H267 "Osândirea clericilor." *Cuvântul* (1928) 4, no. 1051: 3-4.

H268 "Fragmente." *Cuvântul* (1928) 4, nos. 1057:1; 1186:1; and 1282:1.

H269 "Wien bei Nacht ..." *Cuvântul* (1928) 4, no. 1066:1-2.

H270 "Pe via Garibaldi ..." *Cuvântul* (1928) 4, no. 1068:1-2.

H271 "Menéndez y Pelayo." *Cuvântul* (1928) 4, no. 1078:1-2.

H272 "Tarvisio-Venezia." *Cuvântul* (1928) 4, no. 1082:1-2.

H273 "Propagandă şi traduceri." *Cuvântul* (1928) 4, no. 1084:2.

H274 "Ştiri despre noi în India." *Cuvântul* (1928) 4, no. 1084:2.

H275 "La Tivoli, cu eruditţii ..." *Cuvântul* (1928) 4, no. 1091:1.

H276 "Linii şi culori romane." *Cuvântul* (1928) 4, nos. 1092: 1; 1095:1.

H277 "Contribuţiile românilor la congresul de studii romane." *Cuvântul* (1928) 4, no. 1098:2.

H278 "De vorbă cu Giovanni Gentile ..." *Cuvântul* (1928) 4, no. 1100:1-2.

H279 "Leonardo." *Cuvântul* (1928) 4, no. 1105:1-2.

H280 "La Ernesto Buonaiuti." *Cuvântul* (1928) 4, no. 1112:1.

H281 "Archeion." *Cuvântul* (1928) 4, no. 1119:2.

H282 "Despre cuvinte şi despre cutezanţă." *Cuvântul* (1928) 4, no. 1123:1-2.

H283 "Un nedreptatit: D. Mihail ..." *Cuvântul* (1928) 4, no. 1128:1-2.

H284 "Victor Eftimiu." *Cuvântul* (1928) 4, no. 1131:1-2.

H285 "Precizări pentru o discuţie." *Cuvântul* (1928) 4, no. 1133:1.

H286 "Un institut 'Nicolae Iorga.'" *Cuvântul* (1928) 4, no. 1137:1.

H287 "Tot despre 'Noua Generaţie.'" *Cuvântul* (1928) 4, no. 1141:1-2.

H288 "Voluptatea promovată." *Cuvântul* (1928) 4, no. 1145:1-2.

H289 "... şi Camil Petrescu." *Cuvântul* (1928) 4, no. 1148:1.

H290 "Răspunsul domnului Profesor." *Cuvântul* (1928) 4, no. 1152:1-2.

H291 "Varnamâlă sau 'Ghirlanda literelor.'" *Cuvântul* (1928) 4, no. 1155:1-2.

Review of Sir John Woodroffe, *The Garland of Letters*.

H292 "Final de polemică." *Cuvântul* (1928) 4, no. 1162:1-2.

H293 "Don Juan." *Cuvântul* (1928) 4, no. 1168:1-2.

H294 "Istoria ştiinţelor în România" (History of Science in Romania). *Cuvântul* (1928) 4, no. 1174:1-2.

Delineates the general benefits of a study of the history of European science.

H295 "Recunoştinţă futurismului." *Cuvântul* (1928) 4, no. 1182:1-2.

H296 "Confuzia metodelor" (Confusion of Methods). *Cuvântul* (1928) 4, no. 1190:1-2.

Highly critical of positivistic methods in the science of religion that disregard religious experiences within history.

H297 "Trecutul ..." *Cuvântul* (1928) 4, no. 1192:1-2.

H298 "Francisco Sánchez." *Cuvântul* (1928) 4, no. 1213:1-2.

H299 "Adam, Cain şi Eva." *Cuvântul* (1928) 4, no. 1217:1-2.

The tragedy of human existence is that one desires to live in the Absolute but lives instead isolated in the Cosmos.

H300 "Incompetenţa." *Cuvântul* (1928) 4, no. 1222:1.

H301 "Prodigioasa existenţă a lui Antonio Magliabecchi." *Cuvântul* (1928) 4, no. 1225:1-2.

H302 "'Cărţi reprezentative în viaţa omenirii.'" *Cuvântul* (1928) 4, no. 1229:1-2.

H303 "Filozofia în Universitate." *Cuvântul* (1928) 4, no. 1234:1-2.

H304 "Fragment monden." *Cuvântul* (1928) 4, no. 1237:1-2.

H305 "Confesiuni şi semnificaţii." *Cuvântul* (1928) 4, no. 1242:1-2.

H306 "Virilitate şi asceză" (Virility and Asceticism). *Cuvântul* (1928) 4, nos. 1247:1-2; 1253:1.

Virility is to live in the Absolute both in flesh and in spirit.

H307 "Institutul de Istoria Medicinei." *Cuvântul* (1928) 4, no. 1267:1-2.

H308 "Aventura" (Adventure). *Cuvântul* (1928) 4, no. 1271:1-2.

Existence has two points of disclosure, two sources: adventure and the Absolute.

H309 "Sarton şi istoria ştiinţelor" (Sarton and the History of Science). *Cuvântul* (1928) 4, no. 1278:1-2.

Endorsement of George Sarton's *Introduction to the History of Science* in which the different scientific methods evidenced through history are brought together and evaluated for a new humanism. Cf. H509.

H310 "Crize nominaliste" (Outbreaks of Nominalism). *Cuvântul* (1928) 4, no. 1280:1-2.

Rejects nominalism. Advocates realism which consists of planes of experiences--mysticism being the ultimate and irreducible plane.

H311 "Fals Jurnal de bord." *Cuvântul* (1928) 4, no. 1305:1-2.

H312 "Alexandria." *Cuvântul* (1928) 4, no. 1308:1-2.

H313 "Cairo." *Cuvântul* (1928) 4, no. 1313:1-2.

H314 "Beatrice şi Don Chuichotte." *Gândirea* (1928) 8, no. 1:31-32.

H315 "Tâlcuri noui lui Martin Luther." *Gândirea* (1928) 8, no. 4:182-84.

H316 "Cuvinte despre o filozofie." *Gândirea* (1928) 8, no. 6-7:299-300.

H317 "Apologia virilităţii" (Defense of Virility). *Gândirea* (1928) 8, no. 8-9:352-59.

Borrows notion of virility from Giovanni Papini's *Maschilito*--a mode of being in the world as an instrument of knowledge. Virility is a "dynamic phenomenology" of attitudes and experiences in the context of life. By preserving the dynamism of vying powers of the flesh and the spirit, the virile person can achieve points of synthesis to that of an ultimate spiritual unity or "superlife." Mixture of sensuality and metaphysical exuberance.

H318 "Soliloquiu." *Gândirea* (1928) 8, no. 11:458-59.

H319 "Toamnă veneţiană." *Sinteza* (1928) 10-11:5.

H320 "Feminitate." *Sinteza* (1928) 10-11:8-9.

H321 "Furtună la schit." *Viaţa Literară* (1928) 3, no. 79:3. Part of A7.

H322 "Celalt." *Viaţa Literară* (1928) 3, no. 83:3.

H323 "Sensul 'Itinerariului spiritual.'" *Viaţa Literară* (1928) 3, no. 87:1-2.

H324 "Kreutzer-Sonate." *Viaţa Literară* (1928) 3, no. 90:2.

H325 "Maddalena." *Viaţa Literară* (1928) 3, no. 92:2.

H326 "Spiritualitate şi Ortodoxie" (Spirituality and Orthodoxy). *Viaţa Literară* (1928) 3, no. 93:1-2.

Accepts Rudolf Otto's irrational "numinous" as an identification of the absolute plane of the spirit and Kierkegaard's "qualitative leap" as a designation of the difference in planes of the spirit.

H327 "Tatăl." *Viaţa Literară* (1928) 3, no. 95:2.

1929

H328 "Port-Said." *Cuvântul* (1929) 5, no. 1337:1-2.

Begins series of reports or "travel impressions" of trip to India, 1929 to 1931. A number of these are reproduced in A13.

H329 "Canalul de Suez." *Cuvântul* (1929) 5, no. 1341:1-2.

H330 "Pe Marea Roşie cu japonezii ..." *Cuvântul* (1929) 5, no. 1342:1-2.

H331 "Pe Oceanul Indian." *Cuvântul* (1929) 5, no. 1344:1-2.

H332 "Curikşâ în Colombo ..." and "Kandy şi Anuradhapura." *Cuvântul* (1929) 5, nos. 1349:1-2; 1355:1-2. Reprinted as H552 and in A13 pp. 13-21.

H333 "Pelerinagiu la Rameshwaram ..." *Cuvântul* (1929) 5, no. 1357:1-2. Reprinted in A13 pp. 22-26.

H334 "Găzduire în Madura ..." *Cuvântul* (1929) 5, no. 1358: 1-2. Reprinted in A13 pp. 27-39.

H335 "Adyar." *Cuvântul* (1929) 5, no. 1366:1-2.

H336 "Craciunul la Poonamallee ..." *Cuvântul* (1929) 5, no. 1370:1-2.

H337 "Fragmente." *Cuvântul* (1929) 5, no. 1373:1-2.

H338 "Biblioteca Maharadjhahului." *Cuvântul* (1929) 5, no. 1385:1-2.

H339 "Calcutta." *Cuvântul* (1929) 5, no. 1390:1-2.

H340 "India şi Occidentul." *Cuvântul* (1929) 5, no. 1393:1-2.

Unlike Europe, India perceives no hiatus between doctrine and life.

H341 "Primavara ..." *Cuvântul* (1929) 5, no. 1399:1-2.

H342 "Schiţă pentru un îndreptar." *Cuvântul* (1929) 5, no. 1406:1-2.

H343 "Nihil novus?" *Cuvântul* (1929) 5, no. 1412:1-2.

Rejects forms of reason and argumentation which try to explain things by isolating them from their particular context.

H344 "Intelectualism şi Intelectualişti." *Cuvântul* (1929) 5, no. 1414:1-2.

H345 "Cel dintai Yogin ..." *Cuvântul* (1929) 5, no. 1423:1-2.

H346 "Cosma de Körös." *Cuvântul* (1929) 5, nos. 1431:1; 1432:1.

H347 "Gandhi, după Ramazan şi Holi." *Cuvântul* (1929) 5, no. 1438:1-2.

H348 "Moartea unui mag." *Cuvântul* (1929) 5, no. 1441:1, 2, 5.

H349 "Hafiz Lisanu'l-Ghaib sau 'Glasul Nevăzutului.'" *Cuvântul* (1929) 5, nos. 1442:1-2; 1444:1-2.

H350 "Hafiz Tarjumanu'l-Asrar sau 'Tâlcuitorul Misterelor.'" *Cuvântul* (1929) 5, no. 1449:1-2.

H351 "Hafiz din Shiraz." *Cuvântul* (1929) 5, no. 1452:1-2.

H352 "110° Fahrenheit, Ciclon direcţie S.V." *Cuvântul* (1929) 5, no. 1471:1-2. Reprinted in A13 pp. 40-47.

H353 "Jurnal himalayan." *Cuvântul* (1929) 5, no. 1483:1-2. Reprinted in A13 pp. 112-18.

H354 "Vilegiatură la Darjeeling." *Cuvântul* (1929) 5, no. 1490:1-2. Reprinted in A13 pp. 119-26.

H355 "Funerarii la Lebong." *Cuvântul* (1929) 5, no. 1496:1-2. Reprinted in A13 pp. 134-40.

H356 "Pe 'Colina Tigrului.'" *Cuvântul* (1929) 5, no. 1499: 1-2. Reprinted in A13 pp. 127-33.

H357 "La mânăstirea Zok-chen-pa." *Cuvântul* (1929) 5, no. 1501:1-2. Reprinted in A13 pp. 141-47.

H358 "Când vine monsoonul." *Cuvântul* (1929) 5, no. 1505: 1-2. Reprinted in A13 pp. 148-56.

H359 "Filologie şi cultură" (Philology and Culture). *Gândirea* (1929) 9, no. 3:103-5.

Philology, as a limited science, confuses facts with the cultural and spiritual significance of those facts. History is a continual creation of the spirit as an expression of the spirit's self-affirmation.

H360 "Carnaval." *Viaţa Literară* (1929) 4, no. 108:2.

H361 "La Şantiniketan." *Viaţa Literară* (1929) 4, no. 122:3. Reprinted in A13 pp. 236-46.

H362 "Tinereţe fără bătrâneţe." *Vremea* (1929) 2, no. 94:5. Part of A9.

1930

H363 "Durga-Puja." *Cuvântul* (1930) 6, no. 1688:3. Reprinted in A13 pp. 262-69.

H364 "Isabel sau apele diavolului. Unul printre zece mii." *Cuvântul* (1930) 6, no. 1795:3-4.

H365 "Spre Hardwar." *Cuvântul* (1930) 6, no. 2041:3. Reprinted in A13 pp. 157-64.

H366 "Umanismul Indian" (Indian Humanism). *Gândirea* (1930) 10, no. 1-2:34-41.

Decries prejudicial and proselytistic attitudes of the West. India's humanism, supported by long-suffering and a wealth of spiritual traditions, nourishes an integral life that reaches toward transcendence. In this wisdom, facts are apprehended as symbols.

1931

H367 "Hardwar." *Cuvântul* (1931) 7, no. 2047:3-4. Reprinted in A11. Revised in A13 pp. 165-74.

H368 "Rishikesh." *Cuvântul* (1931) 7, no. 2049:1-2. Reprinted in A11. Revised in A13 pp. 175-82.

H369 "Swarga-Ashram." *Cuvântul* (1931) 7, no. 2051:1-2. Reprinted in A11; and in A13 pp. 183-90.

H370 "Viaţa ermiţilor în Swarga-Ashram." *Cuvântul* (1931) 7, no. 2053:1-2. Reprinted in A11; and in A13 pp. 191-98.

H371 "Cobra neagră." *Cuvântul* (1931) 7, no. 2055:1-2. Reprinted in A13 pp. 207-13.

H372 "Lumina ce se stinge." *Cuvântul* (1931) 7, nos. 2057:3 through 2123:3, except for nos. 2072 and 2118. Reprinted in A15 part 1.

H373 "Peşterile din Brahmapuri." *Cuvântul* (1931) 7, no. 2068:1-2. Reprinted in A13 pp. 199-206.

H374 "Leproşii." *Cuvântul* (1931) 7, no. 2074:1-2. Reprinted in A11; and in A13 pp. 214-19.

H375 "Vorbeşte Rabindranath Tagore" (Rabindranath Tagore Speaks). *Cuvântul* (1931) 7, no. 2401:3, 6. Reprinted in A13 pp. 247-56.

Report of a conversation with Tagore. Eliade was extremely impressed by the thought and lifestyle of this charismatic poet-scholar.

H376 "Nirbhay." *Cuvântul* (1931) 7, no. 2401:3. Translation of part of S. Dasgupta's *Mahuja*.

H377 "Solitudine." *Viaţa Literară* (1931) 6, no. 134:2.

1932

H378 "Crepuscul." *Azi*, Bucharest (1932) 1, no. 1:1-8. Reprinted in A10.

H379 "Nou şi mai nou." *Azi* (1932) 1, no. 1:82-83.

H380 "Modernul Aldous Huxley." *Azi* (1932) 1, no. 1:85-87.

H381 "Spiritualitate şi mister femenin." *Azi* (1932) 1, no. 2:202-5.

H382 "Şantier." *Azi* (1932) 1, no. 3-4:242-57. Reprinted in A19 pp. 185-217.

H383 "Victorii." *Azi* (1932) 1, no. 5:375-85. Reprinted in A14 part 1, chap. 6.

H384 "Papini şi 'Gog.'" *Cuvântul* (1932) 8, no. 2407:1-2.

H385 "Plantele lui Jagadish Bose." *Cuvântul* (1932) 8, no. 2425:1-2. Reprinted in A29 pp. 68-73.

H386 "Colonelul Lawrence." *Cuvântul* (1932) 8, no. 2430:1-2.

H387 "Snobismul ignoranţei lui Petru Comarnescu." *Cuvântul* (1932) 8, no. 2447:1-2.

H388 "Jad." *Cuvântul* (1932) 8, no. 2461:1-2. Reprinted in A29 pp. 60-65. French translation in A122 pp. 63-64.

H389 "Mudra." *Cuvântul* (1932) 8, nos. 2475:1-2; 2479:1-2.

H390 "Encheiresis Naturae." *Cuvântul* (1932) 8, no. 2486:3.

H391 "Mâini şi Icoane." *Cuvântul* (1932) 8, no. 2493:1-2.

H392 "Barbellion." *Cuvântul* (1932) 8, no. 2500:1-2. Reprinted in A36 pp. 341-46.

H393 "Porumbiţe din apocalips." *Cuvântul* (1932) 8, no. 2504:3-4. Part of A14.

H394 "Institute de cultură." *Cuvântul* (1932) 8, no. 2511:3.

H395 "Vasile Conta." *Cuvântul* (1932) 8, no. 2516:1.

H396 "Vulgaritate şi literatură." *Cuvântul* (1932) 8, no. 2521:1-2.

H397 "Dacă aş fi în America." *Cuvântul* (1932) 8, no. 2523:1.

H398 "Vorbeşte Srimati Devi." *Cuvântul* (1932) 8, no. 2524:3. Reprinted in A13 pp. 257-61.

H399 "Gioacchino da Fiore." *Cuvântul* (1932) 8, nos. 2527:1-2; 2528:1-2. Reprinted in A36 pp. 356-64.

H400 "Jurnalul d-nei Sei Shonagon." *Cuvântul* (1932) 8, no. 2532:1-2. Reprinted in A36 pp. 352-55.

H401 "Istoria medicinii la Cluj." *Cuvântul* (1932) 8, no. 2539:1-2. Revised and enlarged as B18; and in A36 pp. 162-69.

H402 "O carte a morţilor." *Cuvântul* (1932) 8, no. 2542:1-2.

H403 "Om sau legenda." *Cuvântul* (1932) 8, no. 2543:3.

H404 "Literatură şi sport." *Cuvântul* (1932) 8, no. 2557:3.

H405 "Agonia şi trecerea." *Cuvântul* (1932) 8, no. 2560:1-2.

H406 "Raiul şi ladul." *Cuvântul* (1932) 8, no. 2569:1.

H407 "Lauda lui Krishna." *Cuvântul* (1932) 8, no. 2570:3. Translation from Sanskrit of *Śrimad-Bhagavad-Gita* chap. 11.

H408 "Bluze albastre." *Cuvântul* (1932) 8, no. 2585:1.

H409 "Glosse pentru scriitorii tineri." *Cuvântul* (1932) 8, no. 2592:1-2.

H410 "Ephemeris Dacoromana." *Cuvântul* (1932) 8, no. 2598:3.

H411 "Folclor şi literatură" (Folklore and Literature). *Cuvântul* (1932) 8, no. 2599:1-2. Revised in A36 pp. 370-74.

Folklore is a collective expression of the fantastic, numinous qualities of life.

H412 "Ţara lenuţei cocoş." *Cuvântul* (1932) 8, no. 2608:1.

H413 "Literatură şi gazetărie." *Cuvântul* (1932) 8, no. 2609:1-2.

H414 "Moda bărbătească." *Cuvântul* (1932) 8, no. 2610:1-2. Reprinted in A16 pp. 118-21.

H415 "Apologie pentru decor." *Cuvântul* (1932) 8, no. 2613: 1-2. Reprinted in A16 pp. 122-27.

H416 "Sugestii pentru problema cărţii." *Cuvântul* (1932) 8, no. 2620:1-2.

H417 "Despre Aldous Huxley." *Cuvântul* (1932) 8, nos. 2625: 1-2; 2634:1-2; 2641:1-2; and 2648:1-2. Reprinted in A36 pp. 232-50.

H418 "Vacanţă culturală." *Cuvântul* (1932) 8, no. 2626:1.

H419 "N. Söderblom şi G.F. Moore." *Cuvântul* (1932) 8, no. 2627:3.

H420 "România şi eroii neamulul." *Cuvântul* (1932) 8, no. 2629:1.

H421 "Război civil." *Cuvântul* (1932) 8, no. 2631:1.

H422 "Scriş pe nisip." *Cuvântul* (1932) 8, no. 2636:1.

H423 "Pro-Nudism." *Cuvântul* (1932) 8, no. 2637:1.

H424 "Războiul din fotolui." *Cuvântul* (1932) 8, no. 2638:1.

H425 "După comemorarea lui Hajdeu." *Cuvântul* (1932) 8, no. 2641:3.

H426 "Vilegiatură în vecini." *Cuvântul* (1932) 8, no. 2645:1.

H427 "Bhagavad-Gita în româneşte." *Cuvântul* (1932) 8, no. 2655:1-2.

H428 "Ispitire." *Cuvântul* (1932) 8, no. 2661:3-4.

H429 "Gandhi ante-mortem." *Cuvântul* (1932) 8, no. 2662:1-2.

H430 "Recunoştinţă pedagogiei." *Cuvântul* (1932) 8, no. 2669:1-2.

H431 "Per oposicion." *Cuvântul* (1932) 8, no. 2676:1-2. Reprinted in A36 pp. 320-24.

H432 "Note despre arta indiană." *Cuvântul* (1932) 8, no. 2685: 1-2. Reprinted in A36 pp. 309-14.

H433 "Tinerii la lucru." *Cuvântul* (1932) 8, no. 2687:1.

H434 "Note de iconografie indiană." *Cuvântul* (1932) 8, no. 2693:1-2. Reprinted in A36 pp. 315-19.

H435 "Unamuno după revoluţie." *Cuvântul* (1932) 8, no. 2700:1.

H436 "Edmund Gosse." *Cuvântul* (1932) 8, no. 2702:1-2.

H437 "Despre moarte şi istorie literară." *Cuvântul* (1932) 8, no. 2703:3. Reprinted in A16 pp. 109-12.

H438 "Ceasul tinerilor?" *Cuvântul* (1932) 8, no. 2708:1-2. Reprinted in A16 pp. 207-12.

H439 "Un debut: Fântâneru." *Cuvântul* (1932) 8, no. 2710:3.

H440 "Solomon Reinach." *Cuvântul* (1932) 8, no. 2716:1.

H441 "Cu d. profesor Rădulescu-Motru, despre destinele culturii româneşti." *Cuvântul* (1932) 8, no. 2717:3.

H442 "'Criterion.'" *Cuvântul* (1932) 8, no. 2729:1.

Polemic against anti-Criterionists. Cf. H586.

H443 "Despre oameni şi roman." *Cuvântul* (1932) 8, no. 2748:3. Reprinted in A16 pp. 104-8.

H444 "Exultavit." *Cuvântul* (1932) 8, no. 2759:1.

H445 "Confesiunile unui tânăr al secolului." *Cuvântul* (1932) 8, no. 2759:3, 6.

H446 "Să închidem Universitaţile." *Viaţa Literară* (1932) 7, no. 137:1.

H447 "Benares." *Vremea*, Bucharest (1932) 5, no. 225:5. Reprinted in A13 pp. 48-57.

H448 "Amritsar şi tempul de aur." *Vremea* (1932) 5, no. 226:5. Reprinted in A13 pp. 69-79.

H449 "Intr'o mânăstire din Himalaya." *Vremea* (1932) 5, no. 227:7. Part of A11; revised in A13.

H450 "4.000.000 la Kumbh-Mela." *Vremea* (1932) 5, no. 228:5. Reprinted in A13 pp. 58-68.

H451 "De vorbă cu un naţionalist Indian." *Vremea* (1932) 5, no. 229:4. Reprinted in A13 pp. 270-79.

H452 "Jaipur." *Vremea* (1932) 5, no. 230:5. Reprinted in A13 pp. 80-92.

H453 "Itinerariu Rajput." *Vremea* (1932) 5, no. 231:5. Reprinted in A13 pp. 93-102.

H454 "Crocodili." *Vremea* (1932) 5, no. 232:5. Reprinted in A13 pp. 103-11.

H455 "Kipling a minţit." *Vremea* (1932) 5, no. 233:5.

H456 "Upanishade." *Vremea* (1932) 5, no. 234:5.

H457 "Primăvara în Bengal." *Vremea* (1932) 5, no. 235:14.

H458 "Erotica mistică în Bengal." *Vremea* (1932) 5, no. 241:6.

H459 "Rituale erotice." *Vremea* (1932) 5, no. 242:6.

H460 "Femeia şi dragostea." *Vremea* (1932) 5, no. 243:6.

H461 "Limbagiul secret al misticei Indiene." *Vremea* (1932) 5, no. 244:7.

H462 "Literatura mistic-erotică." *Vremea* (1932) 5, no. 245:6.

H463 "Magie şi erotică." *Vremea* (1932) 5, no. 247:7.

H464 "Impresii." *Vremea* (1932) 5, no. 250:6.

H465 "Romanul poliţist." *Vremea* (1932) 5, no. 251:7. Reprinted in A16 pp. 134-39.

H466 "Despre anumiţi celibatari." *Vremea* (1932) 5, no. 252:7. Reprinted in A16 pp. 140-44.

H467 "Haşdeu şi cultura românească." *Vremea* (1932) 5, no. 253:7.

H468 "Puncte de vedere." *Vremea* (1932) 5, no. 254:4. Reprinted in A16 pp. 113-17.

H469 "Despre un nou umanism" (Concerning a New Humanism). *Vremea* (1932) 5, no. 255:4.

Eliade was very preoccupied now and for many years afterward with the notion of the "New Man," a dynamic being who would synthesize all contraries not only within himself but also within the history of science in general. Cf. H309 and H509.

H470 "Literatură şi document intim." *Vremea* (1932) 5, no. 256:4.

H471 "Cooperaţie şi gaşcă." *Vremea* (1932) 5, no. 257:6.

H472 "Mohenjo-Daro." *Vremea* (1932) 5, no. 258:5.

H473 "Pseudo-Indika." *Vremea* (1932) 5, no. 260:7.

H474 "Voga jurnalului intim." *Vremea* (1932) 5, no. 261:6.

H475 "Jurnale de pictori: Alaska şi Marquesas." *Vremea* (1932) 5, no. 262:7. Reprinted in A36 pp. 347-51.

H476 "Despre un aspect al eternităţii." *Vremea* (1932) 5, no. 263:6. Reprinted in A16 pp. 40-44.

H477 "Despre femeile superioare." *Vremea* (1932) 5, no. 264:6. Reprinted in A16 pp. 145-49.

H478 "Despre adevărurile găsite la întâmplare." *Vremea* (1932) 5, no. 265:6. Reprinted in A16 pp. 35-39.

H479 "Sex." *Vremea* (1932) 5, no. 266:6. Reprinted in A16 pp. 128-33.

H480 "Invitaţie la ridicul." *Vremea* (1932) 5, no. 267:5. Reprinted in A16 pp. 23-28.

H481 "Tendinţele tinerei generaţii." *Vremea* (1932) 5, no. 268:4.

1933

H482 "A nu mai fi român!" *Axa*, Bucharest (1933) 1, no. 18:1. Published also as H573. Reprinted in A16 pp. 193-200.

H483 "Studenţii români cer revizuirea tratatelor." *Axa* (1933) 1, no. 18:5. Published also as H524.

H484 "Intâmplări de vară." *Azi* (1933) 2, no. 1:486-503. Reprinted in A19 pp. 217-53.

H485 "Traduceri Alexandru Marcu." *Azi* (1933) 2, no. 2:768-73.

H486 "Literatura românească în Italia." *Azi* (1933) 2, no. 4: 857-59.

H487 "Spiritualitate 1932" (Spirituality, 1932). *Cuvântul* (1933) 9, no. 2766:1.

Having returned to Romania from India, Eliade assures his generation of his dedication to continue to inspire them in spiritual matters.

H488 "De ce faci filozofie?" *Cuvântul* (1933) 9, no. 2774:1-2. Reprinted in A16 pp. 213-19.

H489 "Homo Americanus." *Cuvântul* (1933) 9, no. 2781:1-2.

H490 "Problema tineretului în Italia." *Cuvântul* (1933) 9, no. 2782:3.

H491 "Simple presupuneri." *Cuvântul* (1933) 9, no. 2802:1-2. Reprinted in A16 pp. 220-25.

H492 "Despre scris şi scriitori." *Cuvântul* (1933) 9, no. 2803:3.

H493 "Note şi extrase despre alchimia asiatica." *Cuvântul* (1933) 9, nos. 2809:1-2; 2816:1-2; and 2830:1-2. Notes for A17.

H494 "La Grande România." *Cuvântul* (1933) 9, no. 2814:1.

H495 "Gramatică." *Cuvântul* (1933) 9, no. 2817:1.

H496 "O carte cu femei." *Cuvântul* (1933) 9, no. 2823:1-2.

H497 "Metafizica Upanishadelor." *Cuvântul* (1933) 9, nos. 2837:1-2; 2844:1-2; 2851:1-2; and 2865:1-2.

H498 "Cultura în provincie." *Cuvântul* (1933) 9, no. 2841:1.

H499 "Bernard Shaw şi fecioara neagră." *Cuvântul* (1933) 9, no. 2860:1. Reprinted in A36 pp. 333-35.

H500 "Romanul şi esseul, genuri preferate." *Cuvântul* (1933) 9, no. 2870:3.

H501 "Maidanul cu dragoste." *Cuvântul* (1933) 9, no. 2883:3.

H502 "Moment nespiritual." *Cuvântul* (1933) 9, no. 2910:1-2. Reprinted in A16 pp. 226-30.

H503 "Scriitorii." *Cuvântul* (1933) 9, no. 2922:1.

H504 "Opere complecte." *Cuvântul* (1933) 9, no. 2932:1.

H505 "Dante vivo." *Cuvântul* (1933) 9, no. 2938:1-2.

H506 "Puţină inteligenţa." *Cuvântul* (1933) 9, no. 2971:1.

H507 "Institutul de cultură comparată dela Oslo." *Cuvântul* (1933) 9, no. 2973:1-2. Revised and enlarged as B10.

H508 "Sociologie românească." *Cuvântul* (1933) 9, no. 2978:1.

H509 "Istoria ştiinţelor şi noul umanism." *Cuvântul* (1933) 9, no. 2980:1-2. Cf. H309 and H469.

H510 "'Luminile' secolului al XVIII-lea." *Cuvântul* (1933) 9, no. 2981:1. Reprinted in A36 pp. 329-32.

H511 "Renaştere." *Cuvântul* (1933) 9, no. 2985:1-2.

H512 "Reviste de rendez-vous." *Cuvântul* (1933) 9, no. 2987:1.

H513 "In Spania şi la noi." *Cuvântul* (1933) 9, no. 2989:1. Reprinted in A36 pp. 325-28.

H514 "Români care nu pot fi români." *Cuvântul* (1933) 9, no. 2991:1.

H515 "Mi-e foame!" *Cuvântul* (1933) 9, no. 2992:1.

H516 "Congresul licenţiaţilor." *Cuvântul* (1933) 9, no. 2993:1.

H517 "Creaţie etnică şi gândire politică." *Cuvântul* (1933) 9, no. 2994:1.

H518 "Să învăţăm turceşte." *Cuvântul* (1933) 9, no. 2996:1-2.

H519 "Traduceri din autorii români." *Cuvântul* (1933) 9, no. 2998:1.

H520 "Se tipăresc esseuri!" *Cuvântul* (1933) 9, no. 2999:1.

H521 "Un Shakespeare viu." *Cuvântul* (1933) 9, no. 3000:1.

H522 "Gandhi şi Pax Britanica." *Cuvântul* (1933) 9, no. 3001: 1-2.

H523 "Rasism în cinematograf." *Cuvântul* (1933) 9, no. 3006:1.

H524 "Studenţii Români cer revizuirea tratalelor." *Cuvântul* (1933) 9, no. 3015:1. Published also as H483.

H525 "O convertire la românism." *Cuvântul* (1933) 9, no. 3021:1.

H526 "Tragism 1933." *Cuvântul* (1933) 9, no. 3023:1.

H527 "Annie Besant." *Cuvântul* (1933) 9, no. 3026:1.

H528 "Moltke Moe." *Cuvântul* (1933) 9, no. 3029:1-2.

H529 "Caritate pentru poezie." *Cuvântul* (1933) 9, no. 3035:1.

H530 "Cum concepe folclorul Moltke Moe." *Cuvântul* (1933) 9, no. 3036:1.

H531 "Nu ne trebuie intelectuali." *Cuvântul* (1933) 9, no. 3037:1.

H532 "Epoca pre-revoluţionară." *Cuvântul* (1933) 9, no. 3040:1.

H533 "Ferme şi temple din vechea Norvegie." *Cuvântul* (1933) 9, no. 3043:1-2.

H534 "Ediţia lui Eminescu." *Cuvântul* (1933) 9, no. 3057:1-2.

H535 "Un institut de studii iraniene." *Cuvântul* (1933) 9, no. 3064:1-2.

H536 "Afghanistan." *Cuvântul* (1933) 9, no. 3065:18. Reprinted in A13 pp. 220-35.

H537 "Mătrăguna." *Cuvântul* (1933) 9, no. 3077:1-2.

H538 "Legenda mătrăgunei." *Cuvântul* (1933) 9, no. 3084:1-2.

H539 "Hasdai Ben Abraham Crescas." *Cuvântul* (1933) 9, no. 3091:1-2.

H540 "A face." *Cuvântul* (1933) 9, no. 3098:1-2. Reprinted in A16 pp. 231-35.

H541 "Cultură." *Cuvântul* (1933) 9, no. 3105:1-2.

H542 "Intre cultură şi alfabet." *Cuvântul* (1933) 9, no. 3112: 1-2.

H543 "Originalitate şi autenticitate." *Discobolul*, Bucharest (1933) 7-8:4. Reprinted in A16 pp. 174-78.

H544 "Un nou clasicism." *Discobolul* (1933) 9:4.

H545 "Pasoptism şi umanism." *Floarea de foc*, Bucharest (1933) 2, no. 1:2.

H546 "Justificarea bucuriei." *Floarea de foc* (1933) 2, no. 3:1-2. Reprinted in A16 pp. 179-86.

H547 "Maitreyi." *România Literară*, Bucharest (1933) 2, nos. 57:3; 62:3. Part of A12.

H548 "Floria Capsali şi Gabriel Negri." *România Literară* (1933) 2, no. 64:1-2.

H549 "Autorul şi cărţile sale." *România Literară* (1933) 2, no. 68:1-2.

H550 "Fragment despre moarte" (Fragment on Death). *România Literară* (1933) 2, no. 84:1. Reprinted in A16 pp. 267-72.

Death of the individual is a transitory and superficial event; a ritual of death in folklore is a lasting and global intuition of reality.

H551 "Divagaţie." *România Literară* (1933) 2, no. 88:1.

H552 "Ceylan." *Vremea* (1933) 6, no. 269:5. Reprint of H332. Cf. A13 pp. 13-21.

H553 "Despre entuziasm şi altceva." *Vremea* (1933) 6, no. 271: 6. Reprinted in A16 pp. 72-77.

H554 "Despre destinul înţelegerii." *Vremea* (1933) 6, no. 272: 6. Reprinted in A16 pp. 29-34.

H555 "Despre o anumită experienţă." *Vremea* (1933) 6, no. 274: 7. Reprinted in A16 pp. 67-71.

H556 "Despre numai zece oameni." *Vremea* (1933) 6, no. 275:7. Reprinted in A16 pp. 62-66.

H557 "Despre tinereţe şi bătrânete." *Vremea* (1933) 6, no. 276:7. Reprinted in A16 pp. 162-67.

H558 "Despre sinceritate şi prietenie." *Vremea* (1933) 6, no. 277:7. Reprinted in A16 pp. 156-61.

H559 "Oceanografie." *Vremea* (1933) 6, no. 278:11. Enlarged in A16 pp. 5-21.

H560 "Cetind pe Axel Munthe." *Vremea* (1933) 6, no. 279:7.

H561 "Despre bărbaţii superiori." *Vremea* (1933) 6, no. 280:6. Reprinted in A16 pp. 150-55.

H562 "Maitreyi." *Vremea* (1933) 6, no. 281:6. Part of A12.

H563 "Pierdeţi-vă timpul." *Vremea* (1933) 6, no. 282:7. Reprinted in A16 pp. 50-55.

H564 "Renaştere religioasă." *Vremea* (1933) 6, no. 283:4.

H565 "Viaţa neverosimilă şi foarte utilă a Maharajahului de Kassimbazar." *Vremea* (1933) 6, no. 283:11.

H566 "Motive religioase în Upanishade." *Vremea* (1933) 6, no. 284:7.

H567 "Itinerarii şi reportagii." *Vremea* (1933) 6, no. 285:7.

H568 "Despre stimulare." *Vremea* (1933) 6, no. 286:6. Reprinted in A16 pp. 44-49.

H569 "Isis." *Vremea* (1933) 6, no. 287:6.

Comments on *Isis*, a periodical of the history of science and philosophy of culture edited by George Sarton.

H570 "Fragmente nefilozofice." *Vremea* (1933) 6, nos. 289:6; 290:6; 291:6; 293:6; 294:7; 299:7; 302:7; 306:9; and 310:5. Revised in A16 pp. 243-62, 268-85, 289-92.

H571 "Despre speciile gândirii." *Vremea* (1933) 6, no. 292:7. Reprinted in A16 pp. 78-83.

H572 "Despre un anumit sentiment al morţii." *Vremea* (1933) 6, no. 303:7. Reprinted in A16 pp. 90-94.

H573 "A nu mai fi român!" *Vremea* (1933) 6, no. 304:6. See H482. Reprinted in A16 pp. 193-206.

H574 "Superstiţia gazetăriei." *Vremea* (1933) 6, no. 305:7.

H575 "Invitaţie la bărbăţie." *Vremea* (1933) 6, no. 307:1. Reprinted in A16 pp. 297-301.

H576 "La vida es sueño!" *Vremea* (1933) 6, no. 309:6. Reprinted in A16 pp. 56-61.

H577 "Despre fericirea concretă." *Vremea* (1933) 6, no. 311:6. Reprinted in A16 pp. 84-89.

H578 "Cum se scrie." *Vremea* (1933) 6, no. 312:6-7.

H579 "Jurnal." *Vremea* (1933) 6, no. 314:6-7.

H580 "Exerciţii spirituale." *Vremea* (1933) 6, no. 316:5. Reprinted in A16 pp. 187-92.

H581 "Bărbăţia păcii." *Vremea* (1933) 6, no. 318:3.

1934

H582 "Căile spiritului." *Azi* (1934) 3, no. 4:1183-85.

H583 "Şantier." *Convorbiri Literare*, Bucharest (1934) 67, no. 1:3-7. Reprinted in A19 pp. 92-102.

H584 "In jurul lui Gobineau." *Convorbiri Literare* (1934) 67, no. 2:144-46. Reprinted in A36 pp. 336-40.

H585 "Glosse pentru omul nou." *Convorbiri Literare* (1934) 67, no. 4:302-5. Reprinted in A16 pp. 201-6.

H586 "Poimâine" (The Day after Tomorrow). *Criterion*, Bucharest (1934) 1, no. 1:5.

Voice of group "Criterion": a series of public lecture-symposia sponsored by Eliade and other young writers at the time. Eventually banned by government, which labeled it a "pro-Communist" organization.

H587 "De ce sunt intelectualii laşi?" *Criterion* (1934) 1, no. 2:2.

H588 "Două cărţi italieneşti." *Criterion* (1934) 1, no. 3-4:7.

H589 "Despre prof. N. Iorga." *Criterion* (1934) 1, no. 3-4:8.

H590 "Să ne închipuim că." *Criterion* (1934) 1, no. 5:2.

H591 "Lupta se îndreaptă spre mare." *Cuvântul* (1934) 10, no. 3114:4. A translation; reprinted in C2.

H592 "Cultură viscerală." *Cuvântul* (1934) 10, no. 3119:3.

H593 "Pentru cultura şi contra politicii culturale." *Familia. Revista Lunara de Cultura*, Bucharest (1934) 1, no. 3:1-3.

H594 "Revolta în deşert." *Reporter*, Bucharest (1934) 2, nos. 18:4; 19:4. A translation; reprinted in C2.

H595 "Români deştepţi şi nemulţumiţi." *Viaţa Literară* (1934) 9, no. 165:1.

H596 "Intoarcerea din rai." *Vremea* (1934) 7, no. 321:6. Reprinted in A14 part 3.

H597 "Tucci." *Vremea* (1934) 7, no. 322:6.

H598 "Mentalitatea francmasonică." *Vremea* (1934) 7, no. 323:7. Reprinted in A16 pp. 168-73.

H599 "Marginalia." *Vremea* (1934) 7, no. 325:7. Reprinted in A16 pp. 285-89.

H600 "Compromiterea românismului." *Vremea* (1934) 7, no. 329:3.

H601 "Colonelul Lawrence intră în acţiune." *Vremea* (1934) 7, no. 332:8-9.

H602 "Un institut de cultură." *Vremea* (1934) 7, no. 335:2.

H603 "Câteva cuvinte mari." *Vremea* (1934) 7, no. 341:3.

H604 "Despre miracol şi întâmplare." *Vremea* (1934) 7, no. 342:7. Reprinted in A16 pp. 95-98.

H605 "Fragmente filozofice." *Vremea* (1934) 7, no. 343:7. Reprinted in A16 pp. 262-64.

H606 "Haig Acterian sau păcatul de a nu fi lichea." *Vremea* (1934) 7, no. 344:4.

H607 "Un volum de cercetări literare." *Vremea* (1934) 7, no. 345:7.

H608 "Tot despre 'Cercetări Literare.'" *Vremea* (1934) 7, no. 346:7.

H609 "Judaism şi Antisemitism." *Vremea* (1934) 7, no. 347:5.

Discussion of "anti-semitic" remarks of Nae Ionescu.

H610 "Creştinătatea faţă de Judaism." *Vremea* (1934) 7, no. 349:3.

H611 "O ultimă lămurire." *Vremea* (1934) 7, no. 352:3.

H612 "Consideraţii oarecum actuale." *Vremea* (1934) 7, no. 352:7. Revised in A16 pp. 266-68, 292-95.

H613 "O nouă viaţă a lui 'Gianfalco.'" *Vremea* (1934) 7, no. 353:8. Reprinted in A36 pp. 375-79.

H614 "Fericitul scriitor român." *Vremea* (1934) 7, no. 354:7.

H615 "Nu rezistă celula?" *Vremea* (1934) 7, no. 360:6.

H616 "O ruşine naţională." *Vremea* (1934) 7, no. 362:3.

H617 "De ce imortalitate?" *Vremea* (1934) 7, no. 363:2.

H618 "Unde ne e omenia?" *Vremea* (1934) 7, no. 364:3.

H619 "Ieremia Petrescu a rămas singur." *Vremea* (1934) 7, no. 366:2.

H620 "Gabriel Negry şi problemele dansului folcloric." *Vremea* (1934) 7, no. 367:6.

H621 "Fragmente de jurnal 1931." *Vremea* (1934) 7, no. 368:22. Revised in A19 pp. 252-68.

1935

H622 "Reabilitarea Spiritualităţii" (The Rehabilitation of Spirituality). *Criterion* (1935) 2, no. 6-7:1.

Rejects the ideology of Marxism and calls for a return to spiritual values.

H623 "Despre cartile româneşti traduse în străinătate." *Criterion* (1935) 2, no. 6-7:1.

H624 "Despre revistele din Ardeal." *Criterion* (1935) 2, no. 6-7:1.

H625 "Technica şi educaţia culturii spiritului." *Familia* (1935) 2, no. 4:3-7. Revised in A29 pp. 77-80.

H626 "Reverie şi automatism mental." *Familia* (1935) 2, no. 5-6:27-31.

H627 "Contemplaţia" (Contemplation). *Familia* (1935) 2, no. 7-8:62-65.

Contemplation not only restores spiritual equilibrium and gives a sense of existence beyond sensations, but also encourages one to experiment with reality in a social context.

H628 "Meditaţia." *Familia* (1935) 2, no. 9-10:29-33.

H629 "Câţi din D-voastră?" *Răboj*, Bucharest (1935) 2, no. 2:1.

H630 "Traduceri." *Viaţa Literară* (1935) 10, no. 1:1.

H631 "Scriitorul şi publicul său." *Viaţa Literară* (1935) 10, no. 2:1.

H632 "Momentul Eminescu." *Viaţa Literară* (1935) 10, no. 3:1.

H633 "Cultura scriitorului." *Viaţa Literară* (1935) 10, no. 4:1.

H634 "'Debutanţi' şi cetitori." *Viaţa Literară* (1935) 10, no. 6:1.

H635 "O sută de milioane pentru cărămizi." *Vremea* (1935) 8, no. 370:3.

H636 "Sus inima, scriitori români." *Vremea* (1935) 8, no. 371:3.

H637 "Viitorul inteligenţii?" *Vremea* (1935) 8, no. 372:9.

H638 "Noul barbar." *Vremea* (1935) 8, no. 373:3.

H639 "Cum se consolidează Statul Cultural." *Vremea* (1935) 8, no. 374:3.

H640 "Criza românismului?" *Vremea* (1935) 8, no. 375:3.

H641 "Alchimia asiatică." *Vremea* (1935) 8, nos. 376:4; 379:10; and 381:10. Published also as A17.

H642 "Cultură sau politică?" *Vremea* (1935) 8, no. 377:3.

H643 "Cum încep revoluţiile." *Vremea* (1935) 8, no. 380:3.

H644 "Intelectualii e fascişti!" *Vremea* (1935) 8, no. 381:6.

H645 "'Turnul de fildeş.'" *Vremea* (1935) 8, no. 382:3.

H646 "Scriitorii şi preşedintele lor." *Vremea* (1935) 8, no. 383:7.

H647 "Renaştere românească." *Vremea* (1935) 8, no. 385:7.

H648 "Românismul, complexele de inferioritate." *Vremea* (1935) 8, no. 386:3.

H649 "Bucureşti, centru viril." *Vremea* (1935) 8, no. 387:10.

H650 "Simplu comentariu." *Vremea* (1935) 8, no. 388:6.

H651 "Lawrence, intelectualul." *Vremea* (1935) 8, no. 389:6.

H652 "Roumain, Rumanian, Rumäne, Rumeno ..." *Vremea* (1935) 8, no. 390:3.

H653 "Cuvântul masselor ..." *Vremea* (1935) 8, no. 391:6.

H654 "Realităţi româneşti." *Vremea* (1935) 8, no. 392:6.

H655 "Simplu intermezzo." *Vremea* (1935) 8, no. 394:3.

H656 "In jurul unei polemici." *Vremea* (1935) 8, no. 394:6.

H657 "Românismul d-lui Rădulescu-Motru." *Vremea* (1935) 8, no. 395:6.

H658 "Carducci." *Vremea* (1935) 8, no. 397:11.

H659 "Navigare necesse est." *Vremea* (1935) 8, no. 398:7. Reprinted as H905 and in A29 pp. 73-77.

H660 "Mitul generaţiei tinere." *Vremea* (1935) 8, no. 399:3.

H661 "Sechestru şi literatura." *Vremea* (1935) 8, no. 401:3.

H662 "Fragmente." *Vremea* (1935) 8, no. 401:9. Reprinted in A29 pp. 110-13, 123-24.

H663 "Destinul lui Panait Istrati." *Vremea* (1935) 8, no. 402:10.

H664 "Restaurarea demnităţii româneşti" (The Restoration of Romanian Dignity). *Vremea* (1935) 8, no. 403:3.

Examines two great resources of Romanian culture: the intellectuals and the peasants.

H665 "Moartea doctorului Laufer." *Vremea* (1935) 8, no. 404:11.

H666 "D'Annunzio şi 'Cartea Secretă.'" *Vremea* (1935) 8, no. 405:9.

H667 "Dela recenzie la critică." *Vremea* (1935) 8, no. 406:6.

H668 "Români peste hotare." *Vremea* (1935) 8, no. 407:6.

H669 "Despre critică şi monografii." *Vremea* (1935) 8, no. 408:6.

H670 "România în eternitate" (Romania in Eternity). *Vremea* (1935) 8, no. 409:3.

Romania has a "historic mission" to retain her original and creative identity amidst the pressures and dangers of history.

H671 "1918-1921." *Vremea* (1935) 8, no. 411:3.

H672 "Demagogie pre-revoluţionară." *Vremea* (1935) 8, no. 413:3.

H673 "Documente, Arhiva de Folclor." *Vremea* (1935) 8, no. 414:2.

H674 "Fragmente şi texte." *Vremea* (1935) 8, no. 415:4. Reprinted in A29 pp. 109-10, 124-26, 129-31.

H675 "Popor fără misiune?" *Vremea* (1935) 8, no. 416:3.

H676 "Paradoxele primatului politic, O partidă de şah în tranşee." *Vremea* (1935) 8, no. 417:3.

H677 "Renaştere şi prerenaştere." *Vremea* (1935) 8, no. 418:6.

1936

H678 "Cultură şi Creaţie" (Culture and Creation). *Cuvântul Studenţesc* (1936) 11, no. 2:3-4.

Expresses an attempt to "make culture" by rejecting sterility in life and generating a current "meaning of existence," so imitating God's creation.

H679 "Destinele culturii româneşti." *Da şi nu. Revistă de critică*, Bucharest (1936) 1, no. 1:1-2.

H680 "Despre destinele romanului românesc." *Da şi nu* (1936) 1, no. 4:4-5. Reprinted in A29 pp. 82-86.

H681 "Maica Domnului." *Familia* (1936) 3, no. 6:33-38.

H682 "Studentul de ieri, studentul de azi." *Luceafărul Literar şi Critic*, Bucharest (1936) 10, no. 1:14.

H683 "Pentru durerea Basarabiei." *Pagini Basarabene*, Bucharest (1936) 1, no. 2:3.

H684 "Despre romanul său 'Huliganii.'" *Preocupări Literare*, Bucharest (1936) 2, no. 2:123-24.

H685 "Incă un fel de trădare." *Vremea* (1936) 9, no. 422:11.

H686 "Marele scriitor Kipling." *Vremea* (1936) 9, no. 423:10.

H687 "Dramaturgie românească." *Vremea* (1936) 9, no. 424:11.

H688 "Sensul libertăţii." *Vremea* (1936) 9, no. 425:2.

H689 "Fragment despre dispreţ." *Vremea* (1936) 9, no. 426:11. Reprinted in A29 pp. 136-39.

H690 "Hajdeu ziarist." *Vremea* (1936) 9, no. 427:10.

H691 "Hajdeu 'esseist' romantic." *Vremea* (1936) 9, no. 428:4.

H692 "Destinuri româneşti" (Romanian Destinies). *Vremea* (1936) 9, no. 430:3.

Romania has preserved and exhibited a unity of people, language, and religious life.

H693 "Psihologie şi creaţie populară." *Vremea* (1936) 9, no. 431:8.

H694 "Mântuire, Istorie, Politică." *Vremea* (1936) 9, no. 434:3.

H695 "O seară de poezie." *Vremea* (1936) 9, no. 435:11.

H696 "10 Mai s'au revoluţia permanentă." *Vremea* (1936) 9, no. 436:3.

H697 "Fragmente." *Vremea* (1936) 9, nos. 437:4; 460:9; and 466:4. Reprinted in A29 pp. 113-15, 148-52.

H698 "Generaţia în pulbere." *Vremea* (1936) 9, no. 438:3.

H699 "'Diurnele' generaţiei tinere." *Vremea* (1936) 9, no. 440:2.

H700 "Scrisoare deschisă d-lui Corpus Barga." *Vremea* (1936) 9, no. 441:3.

H701 "Doctor Gaster." *Vremea* (1936) 9, no. 442:9.

H702 "G.K. Chesterton." *Vremea* (1936) 9, no. 443:9. Reprinted in A36 pp. 251-56.

H703 "Mai multe feluri de naţionalişti." *Vremea* (1936) 9, no. 444:3.

H704 "Miracole din România Mare." *Vremea* (1936) 9, no. 455:3.

H705 "Spania lui Unamuno." *Vremea* (1936) 9, no. 456:3. Reprinted in A36 pp. 365-69.

H706 "Cele două Românii." *Vremea* (1936) 9, no. 457:9.

H707 "Specula cărţilor didactice." *Vremea* (1936) 9, no. 458:3.

H708 "Soarta scriitorului tânăr." *Vremea* (1936) 9, no. 459:3.

H709 "Arbitrul Masaryk." *Vremea* (1936) 9, no. 461:4.

H710 "Cenzura cărţilor." *Vremea* (1936) 9, no. 461:10.

H711 "Ungaria şi Yolanda Foldes." *Vremea* (1936) 9, no. 462:8.

H712 "Textele filmelor." *Vremea* (1936) 9, no. 462:11.

H713 "Profesorul Nae Ionescu." *Vremea* (1936) 9, no. 463:7, 9. Part of afterword of A22.

H714 "Giubbe Rosse." *Vremea* (1936) 9, no. 464:8.

H715 "Elogiu Transilvaniei." *Vremea* (1936) 9, no. 465:2.

H716 "... et altera pars." *Vremea* (1936) 9, no. 467:8. Reprinted in A29 pp. 86-89, 115-18.

H717 "Democraţie şi problema României." *Vremea* (1936) 9, no. 468:5.

1937

H718 "Teme folclorice şi creaţie artistică." *Rampa*, Bucharest (1937) 20, no. 5693:1. Reprinted in A36 pp. 370-74.

H719 "Literatura veche românească." *Viaţa Literară* (1937) 11, no. 10:1.

H720 "Scriitorul de mâine." *Viaţa Literară* (1937) 11, no. 11:1.

H721 "Lucian Blaga la Academie." *Viaţa Literară* (1937) 11, no. 12:1.

H722 "Nedumeriri." *Vremea* (1937) 10, no. 469:13. Reprinted in A29 pp. 139-43.

H723 "Ungurii la Bucureşti." *Vremea* (1937) 10, no. 470:3.

H724 "Unamuno şi mitul Spaniol." *Vremea* (1937) 10, no. 471:9. Reprinted in A36 pp. 257-64.

H725 "Ion Moţa şi Vasile Marin." *Vremea* (1937) 10, no. 472:3.

H726 "Fragmente." *Vremea* (1937) 10, nos. 473:4; 491:11; and 515:5. Reprinted in A29 pp. 98-100, 130-34, 144-47.

H727 "Meditaţie asupra arderii catedralelor." *Vremea* (1937) 10, no. 474:3.

H728 "Coincidenţe." *Vremea* (1937) 10, no. 475:8. Reprinted in A29 pp. 118-20, 134-35.

H729 "Comentarii la un jurământ." *Vremea* (1937) 10, no. 476:2.

H730 "De unde începe misiunea României?" (Where Does Romania's Mission Begin?). *Vremea* (1937) 10, no. 477:3.

Romania's mission is not political. It is ontological: to create a "new man" with a valued sense of existence.

H731 "Cosmos şi magie în Mesopotamia." *Vremea* (1937) 10, nos. 478:11; 479:10.

H732 "Metale, plante, sex şi magie." *Vremea* (1937) 10, no. 480:10. Revised in A23.

H733 "'Dictatura' şi 'Personalitatea.'" *Vremea* (1937) 10, no. 481:3.

H734 "Alchimia babiloniană." *Vremea* (1937) 10, no. 484:10. Revised in A23.

H735 "Naţionalismul." *Vremea* (1937) 10, no. 486:3.

H736 "Criteriile operei de artă." *Vremea* (1937) 10, no. 487:4.

H737 "Glosse." *Vremea* (1937) 10, no. 488:10.

H738 "Controverse." *Vremea* (1937) 10, no. 490:9. Reprinted in A29 pp. 89-90, 103-5.

H739 "Câteva semne." *Vremea* (1937) 10, no. 493:8. Reprinted in A29 pp. 90-92, 96-98.

H740 "Pentru clasicism." *Vremea* (1937) 10, no. 494:8.

H741 "Notă despre patriotism." *Vremea* (1937) 10, no. 495:2. Reprinted in A29 pp. 23-27.

H742 "Carnet de vacanţă" (Vacation Notebook). *Vremea* (1937) 10, nos. 500:5; 504:4.

Human beings have an ontological thirst to unify the cosmos, to reunite the sacred-profane, micro-macro dimensions of reality.

H743 "Convorbiri cu Lucian Blaga" (Conversations with Lucian Blaga). *Vremea* (1937) 10, no. 501:10-11.

In a context of unending suffering, the Romanian people desire to return to their glorious past. They will not fulfill themselves through specializations or party factions, but only through cosmocentric and polytechnical approaches to reality.

H744 "Piloţii orbi." *Vremea* (1937) 10, no. 505:3.

H745 "In jurul poeziilor lui Haşdeu." *Vremea* (1937) 10, nos. 507:3; 509:8.

H746 "Heidelberg." *Vremea* (1937) 10, no. 508:5, 10.

H747 "Protoistorie sau Ev Mediu." *Vremea* (1937) 10, no. 509:9. Reprinted in A29 pp. 34-40.

H748 "Note despre conversaţie." *Vremea* (1937) 10, no. 510:9. Reprinted in A29 pp. 31-34.

H749 "Notă despre geniu." *Vremea* (1937) 10, no. 511:4. Reprinted in A29 pp. 11-14.

H750 "Despre misterele degradate." *Vremea* (1937) 10, no. 512:8. Reprinted in A29 pp. 19-23.

H751 "Despre un anumit 'sacrificiu.'" *Vremea* (1937) 10, no. 513:9. Reprinted in A29 pp. 7-10.

H752 "Notă despre 'bolnavi.'" *Vremea* (1937) 10, no. 514:9. Reprinted in A29 pp. 14-18.

H753 "'Sa veniţi odată în Maramureş.'" *Vremea* (1937) 10, no. 516:2.

H754 "Valorificări ale Evului Mediu." *Vremea* (1937) 10, no. 517:5. Reprinted in A29 pp. 44-48.

1938

H755 "Strigoii." *Cuvântul* (1938) 15, no. 3120:2.

H756 "Cât e de greu." *Cuvântul* (1938) 15, no. 3121:2.

H757 "Scriitori români peste hotare." *Cuvântul* (1938) 15, no. 3122:2.

H758 "Poezie populară în limba franceză." *Cuvântul* (1938) 15, no. 3123:2.

H759 "Nu piere" (Not Lost). *Cuvântul* (1938) 15, no. 3127: 2.

Romania has preserved an identifiable "mental structure" through more than 2,000 years of history because she has not lost the metaphysical values associated with her folkloric traditions.

H760 "Filozofia la Fontenay-aux-Roses." *Cuvântul* (1938) 15, no. 3129:2.

H761 "Speologie." *Cuvântul* (1938) 15, no. 3130:2. Reprinted in A29 pp. 56-58.

H762 "Istorie, folklor, speologie." *Cuvântul* (1938) 15, no. 3133:2. Reprinted in A29 pp. 58-60.

H763 "Un institut de studii latine." *Cuvântul* (1938) 15, no. 3134:2.

H764 "Operă provincială." *Cuvântul* (1938) 15, no. 3136:2.

H765 "Este 'cultura' dăunătoare scriitorului?" *Cuvântul* (1938) 15, no. 3139:2.

H766 "Folklor românesc." *Cuvântul* (1938) 15, no. 3140:3.

H767 "Hokusai Bunka Shinkokai." *Cuvântul* (1938) 15, no. 3141:2.

H768 "Un institut oriental." *Cuvântul* (1938) 15, no. 3144:2.

H769 "'Tradiţie şi actualitate românească.'" *Cuvântul* (1938) 15, no. 3146:2.

H770 "Organizarea culturii." *Cuvântul* (1938) 15, no. 3147:3.

H771 "'La Femme et la Courtisane.'" *Cuvântul* (1938) 15, no. 3148:2.

H772 "Amintirile unui 'sămănătorist.'" *Cuvântul* (1938) 15, no. 3149:2.

H773 "Martorii sfintelor patimi." *Cuvântul* (1938) 15, no. 3151:2.

H774 "Un administrator model." *Cuvântul* (1938) 15, no. 3153:2.

H775 "'Jos Farsa.'" *Cuvântul* (1938) 15, nos. 3155:3; 3161:3.

H776 "Dante profet." *Cuvântul* (1938) 15, no. 3156:2.

H777 "Gânditorul politic." *Cuvântul* (1938) 15, no. 3158:2.

H778 "Mărturisire." *Cuvântul* (1938) 15, no. 3162:2.

H779 "Un ciclu Balzac." *Cuvântul* (1938) 15, no. 3163:2.

H780 "Gabriele condottiere." *Cuvântul* (1938) 15, no. 3165:2.

H781 "'Vânători de microbi.'" *Cuvântul* (1938) 15, no. 3167:2.

H782 "Bibliotecile publice." *Cuvântul* (1938) 15, no. 3168:3.

H783 "Romana." *Cuvântul* (1938) 15, no. 3169:2.

H784 "Epica Renaşterii." *Cuvântul* (1938) 15, no. 3170:2.

H785 "Bătrâneţe creiatoare." *Cuvântul* (1938) 15, no. 3172:2.

H786 "Locotenentul Gironde." *Cuvântul* (1938) 15, no. 3174:2.

H787 "O bibliotecă centrală." *Cuvântul* (1938) 15, no. 3175:3.

H788 "'Izvoarele istoriei Românilor.'" *Cuvântul* (1938) 15, no. 3176:2.

H789 "Amintiri despre Léon Bloy." *Cuvântul* (1938) 15, no. 3177:2.

H790 "'Oameni mari.'" *Cuvântul* (1938) 15, no. 3179:2.

H791 "Muncă." *Cuvântul* (1938) 15, no. 3181:2.

H792 "Urme istorice în folklorul balcanic." *Cuvântul* (1938) 15, no. 3182:3.

H793 "Folklor şi istorie" (Folklore and History). *Cuvântul* (1938) 15, no. 3183:2.

Individual facts and persons eventually lose their particular characteristics through time and become impersonal types as evidenced, for example, in folklore. These impersonal terms basically constitute a metaphysics.

H794 "O editură." *Cuvântul* (1938) 15, no. 3186:2.

H795 "Anunţul percepţiei de verde." *Cuvântul* (1938) 15, no. 3188:2.

H796 "Când savanţii au 80 de ani." *Cuvântul* (1938) 15, no. 3189:3.

H797 "Creştinătate." *Cuvântul* (1938) 15, no. 3193:2.

H798 "Un fel de iubire." *Cuvântul* (1938) 15, no. 3198:2.

H799 "Franţa şi Italia." *Cuvântul* (1938) 15, no. 3200:2.

H800 "'Pasiune'--sau 'specialitate'?" *Cuvântul* (1938) 15, no. 3202:2.

H801 "Orientul viu." *Cuvântul* (1938) 15, no. 3203:3.

H802 "Echos d'Orient." *Cuvântul* (1938) 15, no. 3205:2.

H803 "Teama de necunoscut." *Vremea* (1938) 11, no. 520:5. Reprinted in A29 pp. 40-44.

H804 "Fragmente." *Vremea* (1938) 11, no. 521:5. Part reprinted in A29 pp. 28-31.

H805 "Noua aristocraţie legionară." *Vremea* (1938) 11, no. 522:2.

H806 "'Sfat celui care merge la războiu.'" *Vremea* (1938) 11, no. 523:8. Reprinted in A29 pp. 65-68.

H807 "Provincia 'ratează'?" *Vremea* (1938) 11, no. 524:8.

H808 "Provincia şi legionarismul." *Vremea* (1938) 11, no. 525:8.

H809 "Cronica săptămânală." *Vremea* (1938) 11, nos. 526:9; 527:8.

H810 "Un savant trist." *Vremea* (1938) 11, no. 528:8.

H811 "Lecturi şi cultură." *Vremea* (1938) 11, no. 529:9.

H812 "D'Annunzio, Papini şi războiul." *Vremea* (1938) 11, no. 530:8.

H813 "Când Asia devine asiatică." *Vremea* (1938) 11, no. 531:9.

H814 "Două Congrese." *Vremea* (1938) 11, no. 532:8.

International Congress of Religious Problems, Calcutta, 1936.

H815 "Note şi fragmente." *Vremea* (1938) 11, no. 535:8. Part reprinted in A29 pp. 153-55.

H816 "Un catolic excomunicat." *Vremea* (1938) 11, no. 536:8.

H817 "Cine va stăpâni Asia?" *Vremea* (1938) 11, no. 539:7.

H818 "Japonia, China, America." *Vremea* (1938) 11, no. 541:5.

H819 "Japonia şi Rusia Sovietică." *Vremea* (1938) 11, no. 542:12.

H820 "Mongolia, mărul discordiei." *Vremea* (1938) 11, no. 543:12.

H821 "Dela Genghiz Khan la Stalin." *Vremea* (1938) 11, no. 544:12.

H822 "China se pregăteşte de război." *Vremea* (1938) 11, no. 545:12.

H823 "Iulie 1937." *Vremea* (1938) 11, no. 546:12.

H824 "Pagini regăsite." *Vremea* (1938) 11, no. 566:9.

H825 "Nuntă în Cer." *Vremea* (1938) 11, no. 568:53-56. Part of A30.

1939

H826 "Intâlnirea în ianuarie, fragment din 'Nuntă în Cer.'" *Universul Literar* (1939) 48, no. 11:3, 5. Part of A30.

H827 "Vocaţia lui Mefistofelis." *Universul Literar* (1939) 48, no. 12:1-2. Reprinted in A33 pp. 9-16.

H828 "Magna mater." *Universul Literar* (1939) 48, no. 13:1-2. Reprinted in A33 pp. 16-22.

H829 "Pământul şi zeiţele lui." *Universul Literar* (1939) 48, no. 14:1, 12. Reprinted in A33 pp. 23-30.

H830 "Firul vieţii." *Universul Literar* (1939) 48, no. 15:1, 7. Reprinted in A33 pp. 30-35.

H831 "Pantheon indic." *Universul Literar* (1939) 48, no. 16:1, 5. Reprinted in A33 pp. 35-41.

H832 "Şarpele, fratele soarelui." *Universul Literar* (1939) 48, no. 17:1, 8. Reprinted in A33 pp. 41-47.

H833 "Intuneric şi lumină." *Universul Literar* (1939) 48, no. 18:1, 8. Reprinted in A33 pp. 47-53.

H834 "Când fiinţă nu era, nici nefiinţă." *Universul Literar* (1939) 48, no. 21:1, 8. Reprinted in A33 pp. 60-67.

H835 "Ignoranţă şi libertate." *Universul Literar* (1939) 48, nos. 22:1, 7; 24:3, 6.

H836 "Asta e o teorie care-i greu de înţeles." *Universul Literar* (1939) 48, no. 23:1, 8.

H837 "Scriitorul N.M. Condiescu." *Universul Literar* (1939) 48, no. 25:1, 5.

H838 "Mătrăguna în România." *Universul Literar* (1939) 48, no. 26:1, 8.

H839 "Cultul mătrăgunei." *Universul Literar* (1939) 48, no. 27:1, 8.

H840 "Culegerea mătrăgunei." *Universul Literar* (1939) 48, no. 28:1, 7.

H841 "Mătrăguna, Doamna bună." *Universul Literar* (1939) 48, no. 29:1, 3.

H842 "Valea Rhinului (Carnet de vacanţă, 1937)." *Universul Literar* (1939) 48, no. 30:1, 3.

H843 "Rhinul, memoria ..." *Universul Literar* (1939) 48, no. 34:3.

H844 "Clujul, centru de cultură." *Universul Literar* (1939) 48, no. 38:3.

H845 "Séraphita." *Universul Literar* (1939) 48, no. 50:1, 8. Reprinted in A33 pp. 71-79.

H846 "Iphigenia, dramă." *Universul Literar* (1939) 48, no. 51:3, 8. See H1009 and A47.

1940

H847 "Mitul generalului Cantacuzino." *Luceafărul* (1940) 4, no. 27:1.

H848 "In căutarea lui Adam." *Universul Literar* (1940) 49, no. 3:1.

H849 "Adam şi Eva." *Universul Literar* (1940) 49, no. 5:1, 8. Reprinted in A33 pp. 89-99.

H850 "Despre cultura dirijată." *Universul Literar* (1940) 49, no. 6:1, 7.

H851 "Operă postumă a lui D. Russo." *Universul Literar* (1940) 49, no. 7:1.

H852 "Cărţi fundamentale." *Universul Literar* (1940) 49, no. 9:1.

H853 "Sincopa literaturii româneşti." *Universul Literar* (1940) 49, no. 10:1.

H854 "Pentru cunoaşterea Orientului." *Universul Literar* (1940) 49, no. 11:1.

H855 "Relaţii culturale italo-române." *Universul Literar* (1940) 49, no. 12:1.

H856 "Profesorul Nae Ionescu." *Universul Literar* (1940) 49, no. 13:1, 8.

H857 "Divinităţi androgine." *Universul Literar* (1940) 49, no. 14:1, 8. Reprinted in A33 pp. 99-108.

1941

H858 "Funcţiunea socratică a lui Nae Ionescu." *Pan* (1941) 1, no. 3:4.

1942

H859 "Latina Ginta e Regina." *Acção*, Lisbon (Feb. 5, 1942).

H860 "Camões e Eminescu." *Acção* (Sept. 3, 1942) 72:3. Also as "Camöens y Eminescu." *El Español*, Madrid (Nov. 7,

1942) p. 6.

The works of the great Romanian poet, Mihail Eminescu, reveal a "latin genius" which stems from a nostalgia for "reintegration into the Cosmos."

H861 "Eminescu--Poeta da Raça Romena." *Acção* (Oct. 1, 1942).

H862 "Dor--a saudade romena." *Acção* (Dec. 31, 1942) 89:3. Also as "'Dor,' nostalgia rumana." *El Español* (May 1, 1943) p. 6.

H863 "Canções romenas do Natal." *A Voz*, Lisbon (Dec. 25, 1942).

1943

H864 "A lenda de Mestre Manolé." *Acção* (April 29, 1943) 106:3, 6.

H865 "Liviu Rebreanu." *Acção* (Aug. 26, 1943) 123:1, 4.

H866 "Estado Salazarista." *Acção* (Sept. 30, 1943) 128:1, 4. Translated part of A34.

H867 "Cultura Latina--Alguns lusofilos romenos." *A Voz* (Feb. 6, 1943).

H868 "Panorama intelectual da Roménia." *Diario de Lisboa* (Sept. 2, 1943).

H869 "La valoración de la cultura latina." *El Español* (Aug. 21, 1943) p. 4.

1944

H870 "Nicolau Iorga." *Acção* (Feb. 24, 1944).

H871 "Um mito romeno da morte." *Acção* (Sept. 9, 1944) 178:3.

H872 "A literatura romena contemporânea." *Bazar* literary supplement to *A Voz* (April 15, 1944).

H873 "A sociologia, instrumento de reforma social?" (Sociology, an Instrument of Social Reform?). *Vida Mundial*

Ilustrada, Lisbon (June 22, 1944).

Brief description of the efforts of D. Gusti, professor of sociology at the University of Bucharest and director of Instituto Social Romeno.

1948

H874 "Cuvânt de început." *Luceafărul. Revista Scriitorilor Români în Exil*, Paris (1948) 1, no. 1:3-4.

H875 "Două tradiţii spirituale româneşti." *Luceafărul* (1948) 1, no. 1:21-29. Translations: Spanish B114. English B195.

H876 "Un om mare." *Luceafărul* (1948) 1, no. 1:66-68. Short story. Reprinted as H984 and in A80 and A92. English translation in A93.

H877 "Sextil Puşcariu." *Uniunea Română*, Paris (1948) no. 5.

H878 "Nicolaie Iorga." *Uniunea Română* (1948) no. 5.

1949

H879 "Scrisul şi misiunea literaturii" (The Writer and the Mission of Literature). *Luceafărul* (1949) 2:129-35.

Examines various forms of literature and contends that an artist's goal should be ultimately metaphysical: that is, to live and write within the determinations of Time (e.g., the historic moment) but finally to become free, or to act as a model of freedom, from Time.

H880 "Fratele risipitor." *Luceafărul* (1949) 2:162-70.

H881 "La mission des intellectuels roumains." *L'Union Roumaine*, Paris (1949) no. 6-7.

H882 "Révolution sur commande." *L'Union Roumaine* (1949) no. 9-10.

H883 "Destinul culturii româneşti." *Uniunea Română* (1949) no. 6.

H884 "Revoluţionari cu normativ." *Uniunea Română* (1949) no. 6.

H885 "Dragoş Protopopescu." *Uniunea Română* (1949) no. 6.

H886 "Ora 25." *Uniunea Română* (1949) no. 7.

H887 "Păstori nevrednici." *Uniunea Română* (1949) no. 8.

H888 "Rusificare." *Uniunea Română* (1949) no. 9-11.

H889 "Sangele martirilor." *Uniunea Română* (1949) no. 12.

H890 "Eminescu." *Uniunea Română* (1949) no. 13-14.

1950

H891 "Glossarium." *Contemporains* (Dec. 1950) pp. 203-15.

H892 "Glossarium: Fii sufleteşti." *Indreptar. Foaie pentru gând şi fapte crestineasca*, Munich (Dec. 1950) 1, no. 1:2.

H893 "Originile şi difuzarea civilizatiei." *Orizonturi* (1950) 7-9:33-40. French publication B77.

H894 "Impotriva desnădejdii." *Uniunea Română* (1950) no. 15-16.

H895 "Unitate spirituală." *Uniunea Română* (1950) no. 17-18.

1951

H896 "Glossarium." *Caete de Dor*, Paris (1951) 2:1-5.

Discusses Kierkegaard and his contemporaries.

H897 "'1241.'" *Caete de Dor* (1951) 4:4-10. First act of a play never completed.

H898 "Glossarium: Imutabilitatea formelor." *Indreptar* (1951) 1, no. 2:2.

H899 "Glossarium: Când omul era creator." *Indreptar* (1951) 1, no. 4:2.

H900 "Probleme de cultură românească" (Problems of Romanian Culture). *Indreptar* (1951) 1, no. 6:2-3.

Romania is caught between several extremes: traditionalism and modernism; the East and the West; rich folkloric traditions and positivism.

H901 "I'a mâncat capul politica." *Indreptar* (1951) 1, no. 9:1, 3.

H902 "Glossarium: Istorism şi interiorizare." *Indreptar* (1951) 1, no. 10-11:2.

H903 "Cum se face o cultură." *Indreptar* (1951) 1, no. 12:1, 3.

H904 "Glossarium." *Inşir'te mărgărite*, Rio de Janeiro (1951) 1, no. 4:1-2.

H905 "Navigare necesse est ..." *România*, Buenoş Aires (1951) 3:3. Reprint of H659.

H906 "Cultura şi propaganda culturală." *Românul*, Munich (1951) 1:4.

H907 "Literatura românească în exil." *Românul* (1951) 8:4.

1952

H908 "'Opiumul Boborului.'" *Buciumul*, Paris (1952) 2:3-5.

H909 "Jurnal din Cordoba." *Caete de Dor* (1952) 5:1-16. Part of A8.

H910 "In jurul unui simbol eminescian." *Cahiers Sextil Puscariu* (1952) 1, no. 1:49-56.

H911 "Catastrofa şi mesianism. Note pentru o Teologie a Istoriei." *Destin. Revistă de cultură românească*, Madrid (1952) 3:41-47.

H912 "'Descubrimientos espirituales.'" *Indreptar* (1952) 2, no. 4:1-2.

H913 "Zeu solar et Cnia." *Indreptar* (1952) 2, no. 5:2.

H914 "Intre Tomis şi Ravenna." *Indreptar* (1952) 2, no. 8: 1, 3.

H915 "Infelix culpa." *Indreptar* (1952) 2, no. 10.

H916 "Căderea în istorie" (The Fall into History). *Indreptar* (1952) 2, nos. 11:1, 3; 12:1, 5; and 3, no. 1:1, 3.

Romania's history is one of successive tragedies. Now her mission is to "sabotage history," which is not unchristian.

H917 "Glossarium: Teme iniţiatice şi teme literare." *Inşir'te mărgărite* (1952) 2, no. 5:25-28.

H918 "14.000 capete de vită." *Inşir'te mărgărite* (1952). Short story. Reprinted as H991, H1010 and in A80 and A92. English translation in A93.

H919 "Glossarium: Aspecte ale Barocului." *Orizonturi* (1952) 4, no. 2:25-27.

H920 "Examen Leprosorum." *Preuves*, Paris (April 1952) pp. 26-29.

H921 "Préambule." *La Revue de Culture Européenne* (1952) 2, no. 4:315-17.

H922 "Europa şi Cortina de Fier." *Tribuna*, London (1952) 1, no. 3-4:14-23.

1953

H923 "Creştinismul românesc." *Buciumul* (1953) 8:8-9.

H924 "Fragment autobiographic." *Caete de Dor* (1953) 7:1-13.

Discusses the tension he felt between his literary and scientific publications from 1934 to 1938, including his popularity as a novelist, his fear of dilettantism, and his wanting to be recognized as a scholarly writer. Directs attention to his works on alchemy and folklore (see A17 and A23) in which he discovered "metaphysical" values, quite the contrary to the "scientific," "personal," and particular "cultural" or "provincial" interpretations of the day. Also recalls the "fantastic" and pseudo-autobiographical qualities of his earliest writings, and relates his experiences in writing *Şarpele* A24.

H925 "Destinul culurii româneşti." *Destin* (1953) 6-7:19-32.

H926 "Satul arde şi ..." *Indreptar* (1953) 3:3.

H927 "Goodbye, Mr. Chip!" *Indreptar* (1953) no. 8.

H928 "A Florence chez Papini." *Nouvelles Littéraires* (March 5, 1953). An interview.

H929 "Adventure." *Revue générale Belge* (1953) 89:691-707. French translation of "Aventură" in A24.

1954

H930 "Fragmente de Jurnal." *Caete de Dor* (1954) 8:16-29. Part of A8 from 1941 to 1944. Cf. 1945 to 1969 in French in A104.

H931 "Cultural Murder in Eastern Europe." *Eastern Europe's Tribune* (1954) 1, no. 1:3-6.

H932 "Dintr'un jurnal balzacian." *Exil*, Rio de Janeiro (1954) 2:10-12. Part of A8.

1955

H933 "Fata Căpitanului." *Anotimpuri*, Paris (1955) 1:3-15. Short story. Reprinted as H999 and in A80 and A92.

H934 "Jurnalul 'Nopţii de Sânziene.'" *Caete de Dor* (1955) 9:6-31. Contains parts of A8 from 1949 to 1954 concerning A98 [which has French and English trans.]. Part translated into French in A104 pp. 108-221.

1956

H935 "Calatoria din urma." *Destin* (1956) 10:69-92. Part of novel A98.

H936 "Minuit à Serampore." *Lectures pour tous* (1956) 6:42-49. Part of A56.

H937 "Amintiri despre Papini." *Perspective crestine* (1956) 2, no. 1:10.

H938 "Pastori, haiduci, pribegi." *România*, New York (1956) p. 3.

1957

H939 "Elogiul lui Grigore Gafencu." *Românul* (Feb.-July 1957) p. 6.

1958

H940 "Domniţă Ileana; Meditaţii asupra Crezului." *România* (March 1958) p. 6.

1959

H941 "'Lupii' şi 'Lupoaica.'" *România* (Feb. 1959). See French B165.

H942 "Tradiţii universaliste în cultura românească." *România* (1959) 4:38-39.

1960

H943 "Carnet de vară." *Caete de Dor* (1960) 13:19-33. Part of A8 in 1957. Translations: French in A104 pp. 231-55. English in A117 pp. 1-25.

1961

H944 "Amintiri despre Alexandru Busuioceanu." *România* (1961) 6, no. 57:7-8.

H945 "In memoriam ..." *Românul* (1961) 12, no. 2-3:3.

1962

H946 "Tăcerile lui Lucian Blaga." *Cuvântul în Exil*, Munich (1962) 1:1, 4.

H947 "Moduri de a fi în lume." *Cuvântul în Exil* (1962) 2:2.

H948 "A vedea Lumea ca în clipa dintâi a Creiatiei." *Cuvântul în Exil* (1962) 3:1, 3.

H949 "In amfiteatrul Titu Maiorescu." *Cuvântul în Exil* (1962) 4:1, 3.

H950 "O Revistă Universitară." *Cuvântul în Exil* (1962) 6:1, 4.

H951 "Glossarium." *Cuvântul în Exil* (1962) 7:2.

H952 "La Ţigănci." *Destin* (1962) 12:13-49. Short story. Reprinted as H965, H990, and in A80 and A92. See A80 for references to French, English, and German translations.

H953 "Fragmente de Jurnal." *Revista Scriitorilor Români*, Munich (1962) 1:7-29. Part of A8 in 1959. Translations: French in A104 pp. 273-98. English in A117 pp. 41-54.

1963

H954 "Glossarium." *Cuvântul în Exil* (1963) 7:2; 8:2; 9:2; 10:2; 12:2; 13:2.

H955 "Destinul lui Haşdeu." *Cuvântul în Exil* (1963) 11:1-2.

H956 "Ultimele zile ale lui Jung." *Cuvântul în Exil* (1963) 13:2.

H957 "Drumul către real." *Cuvântul în Exil* (1963) 14:3. Fragment of afterword to A22.

H958 "Dela Mioriţa--la 'destinul Mioritic.'" *Cuvântul în Exil* (1963) 16:1, 4; 17:1, 4.

H959 "Eminescu--sau despre Absolut." *Cuvântul în Exil* (1963) 19:1, 3.

H960 "Dintr'o carte de amintiri." *Fiinţa Românească*, Paris (1963) 1:23-40. Reprinted in A85 chap. 5.

H961 "Şanţurile." *Revista Scriitorilor Români* (1963) 2:50-70. Short story. Reprinted in A115.

1964

H962 "Glossarium." *Cuvântul în Exil* (1964) 20:2.

H963 "Papini văzut de un român." *Cuvântul în Exil* (1964) 22:1, 3; 23-24:1, 4.

H964 "L'importance du 'mythe vivant.'" *Cuvântul în Exil* (1964) no. 25.

H965 "La Ţigănci." *Cuvântul în Exil* (1964) 28-30:4, 6. Reprint of H952, which has additional references.

H966 "Intr'o cazarmă." *Destin* (1964) 13-14:84-92. Short story.

H967 "India la douăzeci de ani" (India at Twenty Years). *Fiinţa Românească* (1964) 2:27-46. A sequel (Part II, chap. 1) to A85. French translation in A122 pp. 34-46.

Autobiography of Eliade's studies and personal experiences in India, 1929 through 1931.

H968 "Războiul la şcoala primară." *Revista Scriitorilor Români* (1964) 3:55-70. Reprinted in A85.

1965

H969 "Fragment dintr'o carte de amintire" (Fragment from a Book of Memories). *Cuvântul în Exil* (1965) 31-32: 2, 5. Sequel (fragment of Part III, chap. 1) to A85.

Mainly a report on seeing again, after his return from India in 1932, his Bucharest friends and acquaintances: Rădulescu-Motru, Mircea Vulcănescu, Nae Ionescu, Constantin Noica, Emil Cioran, Petru Comarnescu. Also discusses work on his doctoral dissertation, on *Soliloquii* A10, and for review *Azi*.

H970 "Primul examen cu Nae Ionescu." *Cuvântul în Exil* (1965) no. 33-34. Part of A85 chap. 6.

H971 "O scrisoare a lui Mircea Eliade." *Cuvântul în Exil* (1965) no. 33-34:4.

H972 "Stâncile de la Matsushima." *Cuvântul în Exil* (1965) nos. 35-36 and 37-39. Part of A8 in 1958. Translations: French in A104 pp. 259-72. English in A117 pp. 27-40.

H973 "Italia lui Papini, Buonaiuti, Macchioro ..." *Cuvântul în Exil* (1965) no. 37-39. Part of A85 chap. 7.

H974 "Itinerariu spiritual. 'Tânăra Generaţie.'" *Cuvântul în Exil* (1965) 40-41:1, 4. Part of A85 chap. 7.

H975 "Adio!" *Revista Scriitorilor Români* (1965) 4:7-25. Short story. Reprinted as H1000 and in A92.

1966

H976 "Scriitor la Bucureşti" (Writer in Bucharest). *Cuvântul în Exil* (1966) 48-50: 1, 5. Sequel (fragment of Part III, chap. 3) to A85.

Discusses preparation of several volumes: *Alchimia Asiatică* A17, *Cosmologie şi alchimie babiloniană* A23, Hasdeu edition A25, *Şantier* A19, and his doctoral dissertation *Yoga* A21. Gives ideas he had for several more novels and scientific works. Confesses his passion at the time to write a literary *opus*, in effect to "make Romanian culture" and thus to "save" his other, less outstanding, publications.

H977 "Popas la cincisprezece ani." *Destin* (1966) 15:13-14.

H978 "Amintiri din liceu." *Destin* (1966) 15:23-44. Part of A85.

H979 "Nopţi de iarna la Clinceni. Dintr'o carte de amintiri." *Drum* (1966) 2, no. 2:23-27. Part of A85.

H980 "Podul." *Fiinţa Românească* (1966) 4:71-94. Short story. Reprinted as H993 and in A92.

H981 "La moartea lui Matila Ghyka." *Fiinţa Românească* (1966) 4:153-56.

H982 "'Om uitător, ireversibil ...'" *Revista Scriitorilor Români* (1966) 5:82-113. Part of A8 in 1963. Translations: French in A104 pp. 416-54. English in A117 pp. 181-215.

H983 "Anton şi Liza Zigmund-Cerbu." *Revista Scriitorilor Români* (1966) 5:139-42.

1967

H984 "Un om mare." *Cronica*, Iasi (1967) 2, no. 49. Reprint of H876. Cf. A80.

H985 "Când cel din urmă pleacă dintre noi ..." *Cuvântul în Exil* (1967) 58-59:8.

H986 "Bucureşti, 1937." *Fiinţa Românească* (1967) 5:47-66. Sequel (Part III, chap. 4) to A85.

Gives reasons why *Yoga* A21, published in 1936, although well accepted by noted Indianists abroad, was not very well received at home. Relates his need at the time to be taken seriously as a "man of science," indicating that what he had published in scientific works from 1933 to 1939 contained the basic ideas which were elaborated in French publications after 1946. Recalls work on Ionescu's *Roza Vânturilor* A22, *Domnişoara Christina* A20, Hasdeu edition A25, *Şarpele* A24, and articles in *Revista Fundaţiilor Regale* (see section B). Briefly tells of a trip in 1936 to Berlin for research and to London to observe the Oxford Group Movement. Also discusses accusations of pornography directed against him in 1936 and 1937.

H987 "Fragment pentru Dan Botta." *Prodromos*, Paris (1967) 7:19-21.

H988 "La moartea lui George Racoveanu." *Revista Scriitorilor Români* (1967) 6:135-36.

H989 "Aspecte ale mitului." *Secolul 20*, Bucharest (1967) 9:6-21. Reprinted as H992. Translation of A77, chap. 7 and part of chap. 9.

H990 "La Ţigănci." *Secolul 20* (1967) 9:25-55. Reprint of H952, which has additional references.

H991 "Douăsprezece mii de capete de vită." *Tribuna*, Cluj (1967) 11, no. 49. Reprint of H918. Cf. A80.

1968

H992 "Aspecte ale mitului." *Ateneu* (1968) 5, no. 11:13. Reprint of H989.

H993 "Podul." *Cronica* (1968) 3, no. 27-28. Reprint of H980. Cf. A92.

H994 "Craciun 1944." *Destin* (1968) 16:35-45. Part of A98 [which has French and Eng. trans.].

H995 "Ivan." *Destin* (1968) 17-18:23-40, 19-20:56-77. Short story. Reprinted in A115.

H996 "Trepte pentru Mircea Vulcănescu." *Prodromos* (1968) 8-9:15-16.

H997 "In curte la dionis ..." *Revista Scriitorilor Români* (1968) 7:5-47. Short story. Reprinted in A115.

H998 "Haşdeu, basarabeanul." *România* (1968) 13, no. 98.

H999 "Fata Căpitanului." *Tribuna*, Sibiu (Jan. 25, 1968). Reprint of H933. Cf. A80.

H1000 "Adio!" *Viaţa Românească* (1968) 21, no. 6:5-19. Reprint of H975. Cf. A92.

1969

H1001 "Cele dintâi întâlniri cu Jung." *Revista Scriitorilor Români* (1969) 8:12-28. Part of A8 from 1950 to 1952. Translated into French in A104 pp. 127-88.

1970

H1002 "Pagini de Jurnal." *Limite*, Paris (July 1970) 4:6-7. Part of A8 in 1970-1971.

H1003 "Profesorul Nae Ionescu, 30 ani dela moarte." *Prodromos* (1970) 10:1-2.

H1004 "Coloana nesfârşită." *Revista Scriitorilor Români* (1970) 9:3-49. A play. Reprinted as H1016.

Eliade's imaginative presentation of the creation of the "Endless Column" by the famous Romanian sculptor, Constantin Brâncuşi.

1971

H1005 "Martin Heidegger." *Destin* (1971) 21-23:9.

H1006 "Iarnă în Mexic." *Destin* (1971) 21-23:94-116. Part of A8 in 1965. Translations: French in A104 pp. 475-98. English in A117 pp. 237-59.

1972

H1007 "Jurnal Parizian." *Destin* (1972) 24-25:66-88. Part of A8 in 1945-1946. French translation in A104 pp. 7-34.

1973

H1008 "Istoria religiilor din 1912 până în zilele noastre." *Revista de Filozofie* (1973) 20, no. 11:1275-93. Cf. English in A95 chap. 2.

H1009 "Caiet." *Revista Scriitorilor Români* (1973) 12:29-34. Part of A8.

1974

H1010 "Douăsprezece mii de capete de vită." In *Cu bilet de voie. O ontologie (posibila) a schiţei româneşti.* Ed. by M. Zaciu. Cluj: 1974, pp. 240-52. Reprint of H918.

H1011 "Caiet de Toamnă." *Limite* (March 1974) 15:8-10. Part of A8 in 1973.

H1012 "Ifigenia." *Manuscriptum*, Bucharest (1974) 5, no. 14: 27-57. A play. Reprint of A47. Cf. H846.

1975

H1013 "Eminescu." *America* (June 23, 1975). Reprint of H890.

H1014 "Roma nu va mai fi aceeasi ..." *Limite* (1975) 20:6.

H1015 "Jurnal în Scandinavia." *Revista Scriitorilor Români* (1975) 13:12-33. Part of A8 in 1970.

1976

H1016 "Coloana nesfârşită." *Secolul 20* (1976) 189-91:175-210. Reprint of H1004.

1977

H1017 "Scrisoare către Nicolaie Cârja." *Actiunea Românească* (1977) 6, no. 23:8.

H1018 "Balada Meşterului Manole. Variante balcanice." In *Frumosul românesc şi viziunea poporului.* Bucharest: Editura Eminescu, 1977, pp. 195-200. Part of A35.

H1019 "Fişier." *Revista Scriitorilor Români* (1977) 14:34-44. Part of A8 in 1973.

1978

H1020 "Dragoş-vodă şi 'vînătoarea rituală.'" *Luceafărul* (April 15, 1978) pp. 7-8. Cf. French B255, which has additional references.

H1021 "Mircea Eliade la 70 de ani" (Recepţia la Academia Regală Belgiană). Discursul său despre Martha Bibescu. *Limite* (1978) 26-27:12-14. Translation of B298, with preface by I.P. Culianu.

I

INTERNATIONAL TRANSLATIONS OF ELIADE'S WORKS

1. Books in Spanish

* *Los Rumanos. Breviario Historico.* Madrid: Editorial Stylos, Instituto Rumano de Cultura, 1943, 95 pp. A37.

I1 *La Noche Bengali.* Translation of A45 by M. Peyrou. Colección "Grandes Novelistas." Buenos Aires: Emecé Editores, 1951, 194 pp. New ed., 1962. See A12 and A91.

I2 *El Mito del Eterno Retorno.* Translation of A43 by R. Anaya. Colección "Grandes Ensayistas." Buenos Aires: Emecé Editores, 1952, 188 pp. New ed. Colección Piragua, 1962. See A51 and A64.

I3 *Tratado de Historia de las Religiones.* Translation of A44 by A. Medinaveitia. Madrid: Biblioteca de Cuestiones Actuales, Instituto de Estudios Politicos, 1954, 453 pp. New trans. Madrid: Ediciones Cristiandad, 1974, 2 vols. New trans. by T. Segovia. México: Ediciones Era, 1972, 462 pp. See A62.

I4 *Imágenes y Simbolos.* Translation of A48 by C. Castro. Ensayistas de hoy, 1. Madrid: Ediciones Taurus, 1955, 196 pp. See A71.

I5 *Yoga. Immortalidad y libertad.* Translation of A53 by S. de Aldecoa. Buenos Aires: Ediciones Leviatan, 1957, 439 pp. See A63.

I6 *Herreros y Alquimistas.* Translation of A55 by the publisher. Ser y tiempo, 6. Madrid: Ediciones Taurus, 1959, 211 pp. See A74.

I7 *El Chamanismo y las técnicas arcaicas del éxtasis*. Translation of A46 by E. de Campourcin and revised by L. Zavala. Mexico City and Buenos Aires: Fondo de Cultura Economica, 1960, 454 pp. New enl. ed., 1976, 486 pp. See A81.

I8 *Mitos. Sueños y Misterios*. Translation of A58 by L.Z.D. Galtier. Buenos Aires: Compañia General Fabril Editora, 1961, 277 pp. See A68.

I9 *Tecnicas del Yoga*. Translation of A41 by O. Andrieu. Buenos Aires: Compañia General Fabril Editora, 1961, 232 pp. See A41.

I10 *Lo Sagrado y lo Profano*. Translation of A84 by L. Gil. Madrid: Ediciones Guadarama, 1967, 231 pp. See A67.

I11 *Mito y Realidad*. Translation of A77 by L. Gil. Colección Punto omega, 25. Madrid: Ediciones Guadarama, 1968, 239 pp. 2nd ed., 1973. See A79.

I12 *Mefistópheles y el Andrógino*. Translation of A75 by F. Garcia-Prieto. Colección Punto omega, 79. Madrid: Ediciones Guadarama, 1969, 276 pp. See A82.

I13 *La Busqueda*. Translation of A95 by D.S. de Plou and M.T. La Valle. Buenos Aires: Ediciones Megápolis, 1971, 206 pp. See A95.

I14 *Iniciaciones místicas*. Translation of A66 by J.M. Diaz. Madrid: Ediciones Taurus, 1975, 225 pp. See A60 and A83.

I15 *Introducción a las religiones de Australia*. Translation of A101 by I. Pardal. Buenos Aires: Amorrositu Editores, 1975, 181 pp. See A103.

I16 *Ocultismo, brujeria y modas culturales*. Translation of A113 by E. Butelman. Buenos Aires: Marymar, 1977, 216 pp. See A113.

I17 *De los Primitivos al Zen*. Translation of A88 by E.J. Míguez and D.R. de Vignolo. Buenos Aires: Ediciones Megápolis, 1977, 4 vols. See A88.

2. Books in Italian

I18 *Passione a Calcutta*. Translation of A12 by G. Caroncini. Rome: Casa Editrice "La Caravella," 1945, 221 pp. See A12 and A91.

I19 *Tecniche dello Yoga*. Translation of A41 by A. Macchioro de Martino. Turin: Edizioni Einaudi, 1952, 232 pp. 2nd ed. Turin: Boringhieri, 1972. See A41.

I20 *Lo Sciamanismo e le tecniche dell'estasi*. Translation of A46 by C. d'Altavilla. Rome and Milan: Fratelli Bocca Editori, 1953, 378 pp. Rev. trans. of the 2nd French ed. by F. Pintore. Rome: Edizioni Mediterranee, 1974, 547 pp. See A81.

I21 *Trattato di Storia delle Religioni*. Translation of A44 by V. Vacca. Turin: Edizioni Einaudi, 1954, 538 pp. 2nd ed. Turin: Boringhieri, 1972, 556 pp. See A62.

I22 *Mito e Realtà*. Translation of A77 by G. Cantoni. Turin: Borla Editore, 1966, 252 pp. New ed. Milan: Rusconi Editore, 236 pp. See A79.

I23 *Il Sacro e il Profano*. Translation of A84 by E. Fadini. Turin: Boringhieri, 1967, 171 pp. 2nd ed., 1973. See A67.

I24 *Il Mito dell'Alchimia*. Translation of A55 by F. Garlato. Rome: Avanzini e Torraca Editori, 1968, 232 pp. See A74.

I25 *Il Mito dell'eterno ritorno*. Translation of A43 by G. Cantoni. Turin: Borla Editore, 1968, 205 pp. New ed. Milan: Rusconi Editore, 1975, 170 pp. See A51 and A64.

I26 *Mefistofele e l'Androgine*. Translation of A75 by E. Pinto. Rome: Edizione Mediterranee, 1971, 200 pp. See A82.

I27 *La Nostalgia delle Origini. Storia e significato nella religione*. Translation of A99 by A.C. Bortolini. Brescia: Morcelliana, 1972, 213 pp. See A95.

I28 *Lo Yoga. Immortalità e libertà*. Translation of A53 by G. Pagliaro. Milan: Rizzoli Editore, 1973, 430 pp. See A63.

I29 *La Nascita mistica. Riti e simboli d'iniziazione*. Translation of A66 by A. Rizzi. Brescia: Morcelliana, 1974, 224 pp. See A60 and A83.

I30 *Da Zalmoxis a Gengis-Khan*. Translation of A97 by A. Sobrero. Rome: Ubaldini Editore, 1975, 225 pp. See A102.

I31 *Giornale*. Translation of A104 by L. Aurigemma. Turin: Boringhieri, 1976, 443 pp. See A117.

I32 *Miti, Sogni e Misteri*. Translation of A58 by G. Cantoni. Milan: Rusconi, 1976, 272 pp. See A68.

3. Books in Portuguese

* *Os Romenos, Latinos do Oriente*. Translated from the original French manuscript by E. Navarro. Collecção Gládio, 12. Lisbon: Livraria Classica Editora, 1943, 95 pp. A37.

I33 *Noite Bengali*. Translation of A12 by M.L. Buesco. Lisbon: Editora Ulisseia, 1961, 230 pp. See A12 and A91.

I34 *O Sagrado e o Profano. A Essencia das Religiões*. Translation of A84 by R. Fernandes. Lisbon: Livros do Brasil, 1962, 174 pp. See A67.

I35 *Bosque proibido*. Translation of A54 by M.L. Buesco. Clássicos do romance contemporâneo, 6. Lisbon: Editora Ulisseia, 1963, 621 pp. See A119.

I36 *Mito e realidade*. Translation of A79 by P. Civelli. Sao Paulo: Editora Perspectiva, 1972, 179 pp. See A79.

I37 *Tratado de Historia das Religiões*. Translation of A44 by N. Nunes and F. Tomaz. Lisbon: Edições Cosmos, 1977, 552 pp. See A62.

I38 *O Mito do eterno retorno*. Translation of A43 by M. Torres. Perspectivas do Homem, 5. Lisbon: Edições 70, 1978, 175 pp. See A51 and A64.

I39 *Rua Mântuleasa*. Translation of A90 by R. Alberty. Clássicos do romance contemporâneo, 36. Lisbon: Editora Ulisseia, 1978, 160 pp. See A90.

4. Books in Dutch

I40 *Het gewijde en het profane. Een studie over de religieuze essentie*. Translation of A84 by H. Andreus. Hilversum: C. de Boer Jr./Paul Brand, 1962, 133 pp. New ed. as *Het heilige en het profane*. Translation of A84 by H. Andreus. Amsterdam: Meulenhoff, 1977, 162 pp. See A67.

I41 *Beelden en symbolen. Opstellen over symboliek in magie en godsdienst*. Translation of A48 by A. Monshouwer. Hilversum: C. de Boer Jr./Paul Brand, 1963, 173 pp. See A71.

I42 *De Mythe van de eeuwige terugkeer*. Translation of A43 by A. Monshouwer. Hilversum: C. de Boer Jr./Paul Brand, 1964, 165 pp. See A51 and A64.

I43 *De Mântuleasa-straat*. Translation of A90 by L.Z. des Plantes. Amsterdam: Ed. Meulenhoff, 1975, 159 pp. See A90.

5. Books in Danish

I44 *Helligt og Profant*. Translation of A84 by G. Lipowsky and C. Nielsen. Copenhagen: Biilmann and Eriksen, 1965, 152 pp. See A67.

I45 *Myten om den evige tilbagekomst*. Translation of A43 by V. Duekilde. Munksgaardserien, 19. Copenhagen: Munksgaard, 1966, 177 pp. See A51 and A64.

6. Books in Swedish

I46 *Heligt och profant*. Translation of A84 by A. Ahlberg. Stockholm: A.B. Verbum, 1968, 205 pp. See A67.

7. Books in Norwegian

I47 *Det hellige og det profane*. Translation of A84 by T.B. Eriksen. Oslo: Gyldendal Norsk orlag, 126 pp. See A67.

8. Books in Greek

I48 *Kosmos kai Istoria. O mythos tes aenaoy epanalepsieos.* Translation of A43 by T.T. Lazakis. Athens: 1966, 160 pp. See A51 and A64.

9. Books in Serbo-Croatian

I49 *Mit i zbilja*. Translation of A79 by M. Cvitan and L. Mifka. Zagreb: Edition Matica Hrvatska, 1970, 187 pp. See A79.

10. Books in Polish

I50 *Traktat o historii religii*. Translation of A44 by J. Wierusz-Kowalski, with an Introduction by L. Kolakowski. Warsaw: Ksiazka i Wiedza, 1966, 556 pp. See A62.

I51 *Sacrum-Mit-Historia*. Translation of fragments from A43, A48, A58, A75, and A84 by M. Czerwiński. Warsaw: Panstwowy Instyţut Wydawniczy, 1974, 299 pp. See A51, A67, A68, A71, and A82.

I52 *Wesele w Niebie*. Translation of A30 by R. Florans. Warsaw: Czytelnik, 1977, 190 pp. See A30 and A91.

11. Books in Hungarian

I53 *Különös Kalandok*. Translation of "La Ţigănci" in A92 and three other short stories by B. György, K. Béla, and Z. Péter. Budapest: Kozmosz Könyvek, 1976, 302 pp. See A92 and A80.

12. Books in Korean

I54 *Uji wa Yukksa*. Translation of A64 by C. Chung. Seoul: Ed. Hyon-dae Sa-san Sa, 1977, 322 pp. See A51 and A64.

13. Books in Japanese

I55 *Shūkyōgaku-nyūmon*. Translation of A65 by H. Kishimoto *et al*. Tokyo: Tokyo-daigaku-shuppankai, 1962, 234 pp. See A65.

I56 *Ei-en kaiki no Shinwa*. Translation of A43 by I. Hori. Tokyo: Miraisha, 1963, 236 pp. See A51 and A64.

I57 *Daichi, Nōkō, Josei*. Translation of A62 Foreword and chaps. 1, 7-9 by I. Hori. Tokyo: Miraisha, 1968, 314 pp. See A62.

I58 *Sei to Zoku*. Translation of A57 by T. Kazama. Tokyo: Hosei-daigaku-shuppankyoku, 1969, 282 pp. See A67.

I59 *Sei to Saisei*. Translation of A60 by I. Hori. Tokyo: Tokyo-daigaku-shuppankai, 1971, 288 pp. See A60 and A83.

I60 *Shinwa to Musō to Higi*. Translation of A58 by S. Oka. Tokyo: Kokubunsha, 1972, 320 pp. See A68.

I61 *Shamanizumu*. Translation of A46 by I. Hori. Tokyo: Tokyo-daigaku-shuppankai, 1974, 792 pp. See A81.

I62 *Munturyassa-dōri de*. Translation of A100 by A. Naono. Tokyo: Hosei-daigaku-shuppankyoku, 1977, 174 pp. See A90.

I63 *Eliāde Chosakushū* (Works of Eliade). A collection of volumes, 163a-163m, translated under the direction of I. Hori. Tokyo: Serika-shobō, 1972 to 1977.

I63a *Taiyō to Tenkūshin*. Translation of A44 Part I by H. Kume. 1974, 286 pp. See A62.

I63b *Hōjō to Saisei*. Translation of A44 Part II by H. Kume. 1974, 306 pp. See A62.

I63c *Seinaru Kūkan to Jikan*. Translation of A44 Part III by H. Kume. 1974, 244 pp. See A62.

I63d *Imēji to Simbolu*. Translation of A48 by K. Maeda. 1974, 272 pp. See A71.

I63e *Kajishi to Renkinjutsushi*. Translation of A55 by M. Ōmuro. 1973, 262 pp. See A74.

I63f *Akuma to Ryōseiguyū*. Translation of A75 by A. Miyaji. 1973, 302 pp. See A82.

I63g *Shinwa to Genjitsu*. Translation of A79 by K. Nakamura. 1973, 242 pp. See A79.

I63h *Shūkyō no Rekishi to Imi*. Translation of A95 by K. Maeda. 1975, 310 pp. See A95.

I63i *Yōga. 1*. Translation of A63 Part I by M. Tachikawa. 1975, 323 pp. See A63.

I63j *Yōga. 2*. Translation of A63 Part II by M. Tachikawa. 1975, 286 pp. See A63.

I63k *Zarmoxis kara Jingis Kan he. 1*. Translation of A97 Part I by S. Saitō. 1976, 306 pp. See A102.

I63l *Zarmoxis kara Jingis Kan he. 2*. Translation of A97 Part II by S. Saitō and T. Hayashi. 1977, 278 pp. See A102.

I63m *Shūkyōgaku to Geijutsu* (History of Religions and Art). Translated by K. Nakamura. 1977, 318 pp. Selection of pieces by Eliade.

14. Articles in Various Languages

* "Il male e la liberazione nella filosofia Sâmkhya-Yoga." *Ricerche Religiose* (1930) 6:200-21. B5.

* "Il Rituale Hindu e la vita interiore." *Ricerche Religiose* (1932) 8:486-504. B8.

* "Lo Yoga e la spiritualità indiana." *Asiatica* (1937) 3: 229-40. B23.

* "La concezione della libertà nel pensiero indiano." *Asiatica* (1938) 4:345-54. B38.

* "Eminescu, o poeta da raça romena." In M. Eminescu's *Poesias*. Translated by V. Buescu. Lisbon: Fernandes, 1950, pp. 21-32. B89.

* "Dos tradiciones culturales y la situacion actual de la cultura rumana." *Revista Oriente* (1953) 3:213-18. B114.

I64 "La nostalgia del Paradiso nelle tradizioni primitive." *Diogène* (1953) 3:279-91. See B108.

I65 "La nostalgia del paraiso en las tradiciones primitives." *Diogène* (1953) 3:33-46. See B108.

I66 "Los mitos en el mundo moderno." *La Torre* (1954) 2:69-85. See B113.

I67 "Sub osigno de Zalmoxis." *Cetatea Luminii* (1954) 1:1, 12. See A102 chap. 2.

I68 "El Mito del buen salvaje o los prestigios del origen." *La Torre* (1955) 3:49-66. See B136.

I69 "La funcion creadora del mito." *La Gaceta* (July 1957). See B149.

I70 "Prestigios del mito cosmogonico." *Diógenes* (1958) 6: 3-17. See B158.

* "Religione dei Turco-Mongoli." *Le Civiltà dell'Oriente* (1958) 3:849-68. B156.

I71 "Scienza, idealismo e fenomeni paranormali." In E. de Martino, *Il Mondo magico*. 2nd ed. Turin: Einaudi, 1958, pp. 305-11. See B75.

I72 "Simbolos y culturas." *Revista de Educación* (1959) 4: 645-48. See A71 part of chap. 5.

I73 "Divinità." In *Enciclopedia Universale dell'Arte*. Rome: Istituto per la Collaborazione Culturale, 1960, vol. 4, cols. 361-66. See B181.

I74 "Un Nuevo humanismo." *La Gaceta* (April 1961) 6, no. 80: 1, 6. See B183.

I75 "Symbolika Środka. Studium religioznawcze." *Znak* (1961) 10, no. 88:1379-1403. See B162.

I76 "Imágenes divinas y creación artística." *Philosophia. Revista del Instituto de Filosofia* (1962) 25:24-35. See B181.

I77 "Repetizione della cosmogonia." In *Magia e Civiltà*. Ed. by E. de Martino. Milan: Garzanti, 1962, pp. 168-82. See A51 part of chap. 1.

I78 "Maschera." In *Enciclopedia Universale dell'Arte*. Rome: Istituto per la Collaborazione Culturale, 1963, vol. 8, cols. 877-82. See B210.

I79 "L'orizzonte mitico della ballata di Mastro Manole." *Annali del Museo Pitrè* (1964) 14-15:80-94. See B152.

* "Rosa del Conte: *Mihail Eminescu o dell'Assoluto*." *Belfagor. Rassegna di varia umanità* (1964) 19:367-71. B208.

I80 "Los sueños y las visiones de iniciacion entre los Shamanes de Siberia." In *Los Sueños y las Sociedades Humanas*. Ed. by G.E. von Grunebaum. Buenos Aires: Sudamericana, 1964, pp. 417-30. See B225.

I81 "Mity a 'mass-media.'" *Współczesność* (1965) 8:16-17. See A79 part of chap. 9.

I82 "Mitologias de la memoria y el olvido." *Estudios Orientales* (1966) 1, no. 2:3-23. See B196.

I83 "W poszukiwaniu 'poczatków' religii." *Znak* (1966) 18, no. 145-46:899-913. See B213.

I84 "E structura y función del mito cosmogonico." *Universidad de Buenos Aires, Facultad de Filosofia y Letras*. Departemento de Filosofia, 1969, p. 23. See B163.

I85 "Bunka-riron no Ryūkō to Shūkyōgaku." In J.M. Kitagawa, ed. *Gendai no Shūkyōgaku* (The History of Religions in the Present Age). Translated by I. Hori *et al*, 1970, pp. 21-41. See B241.

I86 "Dioses Superiores Sudamericanos I." *Humanidades* (1970-71) 4:69-89. See B254.

* "Mitologiás de la muerte: una introducción." *Dialogos* (1974) 58:4-10. B281. See A113 chap. 3, and B302.

I87 "Myternas storhet och fall." *Jakobs Stege* (1977) 3:4-14. See A79.

I88 "Shāman no Yume to Genkaku." *Epistéme* (July 1978) pp. 36-47. See B225.

Indexes

TITLE INDEX

Books

Books in English

Books in French

Books in Romanian

Books in German

Books in Portuguese (original publications)

Books in Spanish (original publications)

Articles

Articles in English

Articles in French

Articles in Romanian

Articles in German

Articles in Italian (original publications)

Articles in Spanish (original publications)

Articles in Portuguese (original publications)

AUTHOR INDEX